Flat Race Jockeys:
THE GREAT ONES

By the same author

STEEPLECHASE JOCKEYS: THE GREAT ONES

Flat Race Jockeys:
THE GREAT ONES

TIM FITZGEORGE-PARKER

With a Foreword by
The Rt. Hon. Lord Wigg

PELHAM BOOKS

First published in Great Britain by PELHAM BOOKS LTD
52 Bedford Square, London, W.C.1
JUNE 1973
SECOND IMPRESSION SEPTEMBER 1973

ISBN 0 7207 0502 9

Printed in Great Britain by
Hollen Street Press Ltd at Slough
and bound by James Burn at Esher, Surrey

Acknowledgement

I wish to acknowledge with thanks the permission of Messrs Hodder and Stoughton to quote from Sir Gordon Richard's *My Story* and of Messrs Hutchinsons to quote from Eph Smith's *Riding to Win*.
I also wish to thank the Rt. Hon. Lord Wigg for his introduction, the jockeys, in particular Lester Piggott, who helped me in the compilation of this book, and *The Sun* and *The Daily Mail,* without whose employment I would have been unable to gather so much of the material.

T. FITZGEORGE-PARKER

Contents

Illustrations

Acknowledgement

The author's thanks are due to the following, whose pictures are reproduced in this book:

Sports & General: 1, 2, 4, 5, 7, 12, 13.
Central Press: 3, 8, 10, 11.
Syndication International: 6.
Rex Coleman of Baron Studios: 9.

Foreword

by

THE RT. HON. LORD WIGG

The author of this book loves racing and his qualifications to write on the subject stand in need of no recommendation from me. Thus he has produced a book which is full of interest. He draws upon a fund of behind-the-scenes information – not only about jockeys and great horses but also incidents and people.

Besides being very big business, racing is essentially a spectacular and absorbing sport, for the sight of horses in a blanket finish ridden by top class jockeys, all masters of their trade, is an unforgettable and stimulating experience. On the other hand, a view of unskilled or undisciplined riders in action can be something of an anti-climax, even when you have backed the winner!

At one time the quality of British race-riding was second to none, but today in my opinion, despite Tim's view to the contrary, that is no longer true. We have fallen far behind in the training of apprentices. Indeed, the apprentice system which should have been either abolished or reformed years ago is today in too many stables used only as a method of obtaining cheap labour. I believe we can learn a lot from Australia, for their jockeys possess sensitivity and apply sound theory to considerable practical advantage. This is exemplified by their copybook seat, quiet style, sense of balance, judgment of pace and discreet application of the whip as an aid to propulsion. Australians ride with a sensible length of stirrup leathers for, to them, jockeyship is an art. They use their heads and practise a covert understanding of the thoroughbred and its idiosyncracies that, with the exception of a dwindling handful of British jockeys, is becoming increasingly rare.

My admiration of the Australian system of producing and training young jockeys does not extend to the ultra bobbing style practised by Scobie Breasley, but that outrage to my aesthetic sense apart, the Australians produce good jockeys because they train them. The French have an Apprentice Training School at Chantilly which has to be seen to be believed. The French method is to leave the training of the apprentice to the employing trainer. Their Training School exists to educate the young men and give them a chance to grow up into understanding and civilised citizens. We have made a beginning in Great Britain but it is only a start. We are still miles behind other countries and I am afraid we shall remain so for as long as the Jockey Club countenances the continuance of the present apprentice system. But Nemesis is just round the corner.

With increasing affluence lads, who will not weigh much more than 8 stone at maturity, will become a rarity and, before long, we shall run into a dearth of the human material from which at present we draw apprentices. Moreover, with the passing of the years the availability of stable 'lads' will also dry up. Which leads me to express amazement at the fact that owners who must either have inherited or acquired great wealth, who will pay thousands for a yearling, will then, without a thought, entrust it to an untrained child who, through sheer ignorance, can ruin the equine baby beyond the possibility of reform. And still no-one will put their hands in their pockets or their shoulders to the wheel to produce an effective system of training for the lads who fail to make the grade of jockeys and who are condemned to do their four as long as they remain in a racing stable.

When Tim first asked me to write this introduction I had no idea that I would appear in part of the book as one of the central figures and so I shall say nothing about his story as it affects myself.

As I write, I am about to conclude fifteen years of active service to racing, first with the Racecourse Betting Control Board, then the Horserace Totalisator Board and the last five years with the Horserace Betting Levy Board. My task has been made easier by the existence of brave men like Tim Fitzgeorge-Parker who have served racing by speaking their minds. He will remember the occasion at Ascot when one of the Establishment's staunch supporters referred to him as my Aide de Camp. The gentleman in question went on to say he did not know what my terms of reference were but he was sure the spending of the Levy should be left to the Jockey Club. This has been the bone of contention during the period of my Chairmanship of the Levy Board, as, indeed, it was of my predecessor. The truth is that the levy is taxation, for it is money taken from the punters' pockets by the bookmakers and passed on to the Levy Board, to be spent in accordance with activities and schemes approved by the Home Secretary. Tim Fitzgeorge-Parker knows this and, knowing it, he has become a critic of those who think otherwise. He is right and they are wrong.

There is much that Tim writes with which I do not agree. There is one thing of which I am sure; he understands racing and loves it sufficiently to tell the truth as he sees it. The future of racing – indeed, the British way of life itself – rests in the hands of men who do just that. For me Tim Fitzgeorge-Parker must be read, if only to find out the extent to which his enthusiasm has led him from the path of accuracy, but I would sooner have one Fitzgeorge-Parker than several of the tedious bores who churn out interminably their everlasting praise of the Establishment.

Preface

The last ten years have been the most important in the history of British racing. They have seen a complete revolution, thanks to the tactful administration of Major-General Sir Randle Feilden, the Chairman of the Turf Board and the vision, tenacity and drive of Lord Wigg as Chairman of the Levy Board.

During this period one jockey has dominated the scene, the brilliant controversial Lester Piggott. With the help of his contemporary riders I have tried to paint the picture of the painful years that have produced the industry of today. On such a wide canvas there have inevitably been omissions. For example, great jockeys like Charlie Elliott, Charlie Smirke and Harry Wragg were contemporaries of Sir Gordon Richards. But in the build-up to the present only one man of that era was needed and Gordon had to represent them all, followed by the Smith brothers who bridged the gap.

Similarly, outstanding young jockeys like Pat Eddery, who are leading a wonderful resurgence of British youth are not included because they are still on their way into the hall of fame, which they will undoubtedly grace in the near future.

Undoubtedly the turning point in the history of the industry came with the appointment of Lord Wigg as Chairman of the Levy Board at the end of 1967 after the retirement of Lord Harding. Even then he was persuaded by his own former Cabinet colleague to take over the thankless £6,000 a year job only after a Tory, Viscount Head, had turned it down. 'No one else wanted the job,' he says.

Many of the Tory Establishment have never forgiven him for his part in the Profumo affair. Their dislike of him has scarcely been concealed and he has had to fight obstruction to nearly all his reforms. Nevertheless he has preserved and carried them through, gaining the confidence of the bookmakers and earning, if not always getting, the gratitude of every section of the racing industry. He has nearly trebled the levy. He has ridden the betting tax, fought for and won a reduction in the on-course tax. He has ensured the future of three great race-courses, Epsom, Sandown and Kempton.

He has, in accordance with his terms of reference, distributed money with scrupulous fairness for the benefit of the public, of all branches of the industry and for the betterment of the breed. Race-course amenities, National Stud, prize-money, apprentice training, technical services, including patrol camera, starting stalls and racecourse commentaries, transport of horses, veterinary research projects, a racing industry benefit scheme, overnight declarations, point-to-points, suppression of doping and overall security. All these and many other things have been organised with amazing grasp of essentials and a wonderful sense of priorities. One of his greatest contributions has been the exposure and removal of the vested interest in many different branches of the racing industry.

Even when his salary was revised to £7,000 he was obviously grossly underpaid for a job at which he has worked tirelessly all day seven days a week. By the time this book is published there will be a new Levy Board Chairman, Stanley Raymond.

'It doesn't matter if I go now,' says George. 'Everything has been set in train.'

I think it does matter, very much.

The Old Guard of the Jockey Club finally met their Waterloo with the setting up of the new Jockey Club, uniting the Jockey Club and the National Hunt Committee, streamlining all administrations under the direction of Sir Randle Feilden.

One of the most important reforms was the right to appeal against sentences imposed by the Jockey Club. In all inquiries the accused may now be represented by lawyers and, although not yet open to the Press as they undoubtedly should be, these tribunals are not the Star Chambers that they were a few years ago. The results of racecourse inquiries are at least promulgated, although, unhappily, the standard of some local stewards leaves something to be desired. The need for at least one professional steward in the hierarchy at every meeting, is still, I consider, essential.

Still, the fact that so much has been done, in face of considerable opposition, to provide an efficient working body in the executive stewards of the Jockey Club to organise and administrate this sport of ours, is a credit to the Boss, Gerry Feilden, who is now retiring. Let us hope that his successor, Lord Leverhulme, will carry on the good work. There is still a lot to be done.

1: Sir Gordon Richards

That Monday in 1953 was the most glorious first of June ever.

It was the eve of the Coronation and the entire country was *en fête*. After a lovely fresh, hazy start, the sun was already blazing down when we returned from first lot on the Lambourn downs to breakfast and the newspapers. There we read that our sport had been honoured at last. Gordon Richards, champion of champion jockeys, had received a knighthood in the Coronation Honours List. The very same Gordon, who was riding our little filly Mirabelle in the second race at Leicester that afternoon.

A week earlier, ridden by my apprentice, she had finished second at Warwick. Now she was tipped by all the papers to win the Billesdon Plate for the new knight. He had four other fancied rides, but it was still quite a responsibility for a small trainer, particularly since this beautiful tiny little brown model two-year-old was one of my bargains. I had paid only a hundred guineas for the daughter of Mirza II at Ballsbridge in September.

We drove fast to get to 'the Oadby track', as the more fanciful journalists called it, in good time. We needn't have worried. As always, the little champion was complete master of the situation. Any excitement he may have felt was quite hidden behind the big, twinkling eyes and the charming self-deprecating smile as he received the congratulations which were showered on him from all sides. In fact during all the years I have known him I have never known Gordon to change in any way.

He finished fourth in the first race and, when I put him up, he admitted that he would dearly love to ride at least one winner on that memorable day.

It is hard to explain the extraordinary sense of confidence a trainer felt when he put Gordon on a horse. When the animal belonged to someone else, you knew that your owner was extremely happy, that you had done your best and that, if you did not win, it would be because the horse was just not good enough.

Lord Rosebery said that of all the jockeys in his long and wide experience Gordon was the one who lost the fewest races that he should have won. So, when he strutted into the paddock with that characteristic walk, square-shouldered, upright, neat and crisp, you felt a curious satisfaction and pride, knowing that your rivals were jealous of your jockey. Instead of fretting and worrying as you went back to the stand, you walked away from the paddock serenely happy and at peace with the world. It was unique.

When it was your own horse, as on this occasion, the feeling was, of course, intensified. I was lucky enough to have had Gordon riding for me quite a lot during the three years that remained to him from the time I started training and I look back to each experience with warm, heartfelt gratitude. It was that sort of experience.

I have a splendid picture of Gordon, when he had just got on Mirabelle, adjusting his 'jerk' – the length of his stirrup leathers – and it is fascinating to see how long he actually rode. It is almost a good hunting length. In the paddock we had not talked of the race – just about the Coronation next day, to which we were all going. Gordon had received special seats from St James's Palace.

Our little filly and her jockey were admirably suited. Starting at 5/2 on, she flew out of the gate, made all the running and won by eight lengths to tremendous cheers.

It was the new knight's only winner that day and, when I thanked him, he typically thanked me more, as he did the following year when I gave him the only winner on his fiftieth birthday, Mabledon in the Rose Stakes at Sandown.

On both occasions people said: 'That's a memory for life. No-one can ever take that away from you.' How right they were!

We saw the papers early the next morning in London while we waited for that wonderful Coronation ceremony. Despite the approach of the Derby, space was naturally short for racing and most of it was devoted to that little race at Leicester. My favourite headline read: 'ALL SIR GORDON!'

And that, I suppose, just about sums up the racing scene from the start of 1925 – when, in his first year as a fully-fledged jockey, Gordon Richards took over the championship from Steve Donoghue – to 1954, when he retired. Thirty years in which the Jockey Club's autocratic rule was somehow compensated for the public by the phenomenal, unprecedented success of the Shropshire miner's son who was to earn his spurs in one of the toughest and most demanding professions, as well as any Knight at King Arthur's Round Table.

He was one of eight children – twelve, if you count the others that died. Thinking as a journalist, it is all too easy to romanticise and so to exaggerate the rags-to-riches angle. By the time Gordon was born in 1904 his father Nathan and uncle Matthew Richards were both mining contractors, doing well, employing labour and earning good money with a great pride in their work, which they instilled into their men and into their own children.

See a picture of Nathan in middle-age. The same big, intelligent head with jutting brows over eyes set well apart and that ultra-strong determined chin – features that were to become so well-known and so beloved in his son.

Nevertheless it was Gordon's mother, a highly intelligent woman with a strong business sense, who kept the family going in troubled times by buying land, building and renting a few houses, erecting stables and hiring out ponies and traps, which her children looked after and drove.

Moreover she kept Gordon out of the mines and sent him, when he left school at thirteen, as a junior clerk in a warehouse near home.

Although strict Primitive Methodists, whose children went to church four times every Sunday, his parents did not object when Gordon applied for a job and was accepted as a racing apprentice by Martin Hartigan, who was then training for the financier Jimmy White way out on the Wiltshire downs at famous Foxhill. The stable jockey was the champion, lovable, carefree, brilliant Steven Donoghue when Gordon joined the many apprentices and – typically, despite his age and junior status – quickly raised a football team.

Foxhill was so unique among the mighty training establishments which still held sway in those days that it should not be forgotten. Gordon describes the fabulous scene.

'When Mr White went round stables at night, he would ask me how my football team was coming along, and he always stopped and had a chat with me in the box. Foxhill has left a deep impression on my mind. There was something unreal about it. It seems a fairy story to me now. No expense was ever spared in anything. Think of the staff: Martin Hartigan the trainer, Jack Fallon the head lad, Lang Ward the travelling head lad, Steven Donoghue the stable jockey! Every one of them right at the top of his profession.

'And the famous people who used to come down for Mr White's fantastic parties! Those week-end parties were really something, especially to me who had come so recently from a miner's family and had never even imagined such parties before. Mr Jimmy White had lots of friends in the sporting and theatrical worlds, and there was always a large number of them down every week-end, as his guests. Mr White was always thorough and things were done really properly.

'The programme started on Saturday evening, when Mr White brought his guests round stables. Everything was wonderfully done. We all wore spotless white jackets, not a speck to be seen anywhere, very smart. Fresh sawdust had been laid along the passages. The horses all looked wonderful. It was a sort of parade.

'And all of us boys stole glances at the famous people, as they came round admiring the horses. I don't know whether we were more interested in the actresses, like Jose Collins and Ivy Tresmond, or the famous sportsmen, like Jimmy Wilde.

'Then on the Sunday morning the horses were all out on the gallops at ten-thirty, specially for the guests. After they had done their stuff, we brought them back into stables and did them up, and then we got ready for the afternoon's programme. It was always a very full one. First of all, a football match between us and perhaps Mr Paddy Hartigan's apprentices from nearby Ogbourne. Mr Paddy was our Mr Martin's brother. Then a Donkey Derby, which was really almost a team race between us apprentices and the actress guests of the party. Then we all went over to King Edward Place, which was Mr White's home and stud-farm. We used to have boxing matches there, usually with one main event which was often a local heavyweight against the amazing Jimmy Wilde – and the big man never won! And then we would wind up with cock fighting on the lawn in the evening.

'The guests used to bet on every event of the afternoon!

'I think I knew, even at the time, that every rich man did not live this way. But none of us in any way resented the goings on, probably because Mr White was a good master to all of us. It was, all the same, rather a violent change in outlook for me, thrown into the whirl of all this, straight from a strictly Primitive Methodist home, just a miner's son. I was never in any sense bitter about the obvious extravagance, but I do remember promising to myself very privately that some day I was going to make just as much money as any of these people! And that when I did, may be I'd be more careful of my money, although I'd make sure that I had a good time, too!

'On the few occasions that Mr White did not fill his house with week-end guests, we were all made to walk to church on Sunday mornings. I used to walk the two miles to Womborough.

'An example of Mr White's thoroughness was our football team. Mr White used to engage a trainer and often a Swindon professional to coach our apprentices' team. And the stable lads had a team as well, which was at least once even more effectively assisted. They had a fixture with the Kingsclere team one Sunday, and Mr White was particularly anxious to win that match. Four Swindon professionals quietly became stable lads for the day, and were played in the team. But there was no score in the first half, and still no score right up to the last few minutes. Mr White then let it be known that there was a five pound note for every player who scored a goal. The Kingsclere goalkeeper was knocked out, but still the match finished with no score. The Kingsclere stable lads never knew how well they had played that day.'

Obviously Gordon was very good from the beginning. Under Steve's enthusiastic, sympathetic instruction he was soon riding gallops and had a ride in public in his first year. In his second season he rode several winners, including a double at Lewes, before Paddy Hartigan fell to his death from his hotel room at Liverpool and Martin moved to Ogbourne to take over his brother's stables and to marry his wife Norah, daughter of the great theatrical impresario George Edwardes.

Although Jimmy White offered Martin £3,000 – a fantastic figure in those days – for Gordon's indentures, the trainer refused. A happy decision in every way. Under these kind people's care and expert tuition Gordon's talent flowered, so that, when he finished his apprenticeship in 1925, he had ridden 114 winners.

Transferring to Tommy Hogg nearby at the other great training stable, Russley Park, now, owing to the labour problem, condemned to farming – you can catch a glimpse of Foxhill and Russley from the M4 – Gordon, weighing only 6 st. 11 lbs., rode 118 winners to finish Champion in his first season as a full jockey. It was a truly remarkable performance.

However his triumph was short-lived. When the 1926 season started, he was found to have T.B. and was out of the saddle for the remainder of the year. Happily he made a good recovery and, returning to his same retainers, began his remarkable sequence of twenty-seven years as Champion, broken only by Freddy Fox, who beat him by just one in 1930, and by illness in 1941.

His loss of the title in 1930 was compensated by his first two classic successes, the Oaks on Rose of England and the St Leger on Singapore.

Although Freddy Fox won the Derby for Fred Darling in 1931 on Cameronian, Gordon not only regained the championship, but was also given Fox's job as first jockey to Darling's wonderful Beckhampton stable. He entered the most coveted job in racing, backed by his devoted wife Margery, whom he had married in 1928 and who has remained at his side, a constant comfort and support ever since.

In 1933 he shattered all records. After winning the last race at Nottingham on October 3rd, he won all six races on October 4th, at Chepstow and the first five on the same course the following day – twelve consecutive winners, easily defeating the world record of nine.

On the anniversary of Fred Archer's suicide Gordon equalled

'the Tinman's' record of 246 winners and he went on to finish the year with a total of 259, which has been beaten only twice since – by Gordon himself, in 1947 and 1949.

To get these figures in proportion we must remember two things. First, there were fewer race meetings (and no evening meetings), and travelling was inevitably more strenuous. Secondly, to balance that, Gordon never had to waste and was always considerably lighter than Lester, who has to watch his weight all the time. As a result, the opportunities are levelled out and comparisons between two great champions become as odious as ever.

Fred Darling, the little martinet of Beckhampton, was Gordon's hero. In all things he was a perfectionist, a training genius, who tolerated mediocrity in neither man nor horse. That Gordon and all his employees loved him was no measure of his charm – he had so little – but rather of his genius.

His jockey says: 'He was absolutely ruthless with horses and men. Mr Darling was always right in everything he did.'

He taught Gordon so much. Above all he instilled in him punctuality, planning, organisation and realism with horses – never to overrate an animal or put it on a pedestal, but to treat a horse as a horse. If only more English people would adopt this frame of mind.

Far be it from me to say that the great man of training overdid his severity. I can only report that some years after his death I was going round stables with that outstanding studmaster, George Harries of the Ballykisteen and Victor Studs, who had, incidentally been working for George Edwardes in those days when Gordon was at Ogbourne and managing for him and his daughter Mrs Hartigan later on.

We came to that fantastically successful sprint sire Denturius, a typically powerful, chunky chestnut son of Gold Bridge, standing chained in his box – a strange sight in this yard, where kindness prevailed and all the inmates were handled better than than anywhere else.

George explained, 'He's turned completely savage. Only one old lad, who has always done him, can really cope with him and he's away sick. The poor stallion man, who's looking after him now is having a terrible time. I'm afraid I'll have to have the horse put down. He's very old and he could easily kill someone.'

Puzzling over this as we walked to the house, I asked George who had trained Denturius. He was temporarily stumped. It was all so long ago. We went straight to the form-books.

'Of course, I should have remembered.' he said. 'Fred Darling. And that explains a lot.'

George told me that, when Fred went round stables every evening, he expected all the colts to stand to attention while he inspected them.

'They were tied up on three chains,' he said, 'and, if they moved, he cracked them with his walking-stick. He left the fillies alone, but the colts were always subject to this iron discipline. Denturius was as good as gold when he first came to stud, but I suppose that, having a fiery, courageous temperament, he had always resented this treatment and went to the other extreme, trying to get his own back when he eventually realised that it had been relaxed entirely.'

The old man sighed. 'It was probably my fault,' he said. 'Perhaps I should have been just as hard and strict, but I'm afraid I'm not made that way!'

Whenever I watch racing on the straight course at Newmarket and see jockeys holding their horses back for a late run, I think of the advice that Darling gave his jockey, who, riding a good horse with 9 st. 10 lbs., fought to hold him up and finally finished only third.

Darling said: 'Gordon, what were you doing in the early part of the race? It looked as if you were fighting him. Never do that again. Let them run their own race. Never fight a horse of mine at Newmarket. Get smartly out of that gate, get a good position and get there nicely balanced as soon as possible. Then let them do the rest themselves.'

Then typically he added: 'I and my staff are looking after them day and night. They get the best hay, and the best corn, the best of everything. If they lose, it's my responsibility. I don't want any fighting. There are occasional exceptions, but if one comes along, I'll tell you. Newmarket demands that the horse should run his own race.'

Any time you are there, you can see the wisdom of these words. If the young Australian Des Lake had not fought to hold him back and disappointed him, that outstanding colt Bold Lad would undoubtedly have won another 2,000 Guineas for Paddy Prendergast.

When Gordon retired he had won fourteen classic races. A lot has been made of the fact that the Derby eluded him until 1953. They said that Epsom didn't suit him and so on.

This was quite wrong. Gordon rode Epsom better than anyone, except perhaps Steve Donoghue and Lester, but you cannot come without the horse and on several occasions it was just bad luck that he was not on the winner of the Derby.

Riding Easton in 1934, he ran up against a rattling good Derby winner in Windsor Lad and was beaten a length – form which was confirmed to an inch twelve months later in the Coronation Cup over the same course and distance.

1936, was, in his opinion, his first unlucky Derby. The Aga Khan had three runners and, as Gordon was not required by his retaining stables that year, he was available to ride a very good little pony called Taj Akbar. Charlie Smirke, who had ridden Windsor Lad the previous year, was on Mahmoud, unlucky short-head runner-up to Pay Up in the 2,000 Guineas.

Waiting to produce Taj Akbar's tremendous finishing burst, Gordon had just started to move to overhaul Smirke in the straight, when a tiring horse rolled on to him and knocked all the stuffing out of his little colt. Inevitably unbalanced and checked in his stride, he did remarkably well to finish second, beaten three lengths by his grey stable-companion.

'Without that piece of bad luck,' says Gordon, 'I am as sure as I can be that I would have won.'

In the early part of the following season the champion was trying to help Michael Beary, who was suffering one of those bad patches which most jockeys have to endure from time to time. He got him some rides and some winners. So, when Fred Butters was looking for a rider for Midday Sun in the Lingfield Derby Trial and in the Derby, Gordon suggested Michael, who won both races on the colt, while his benefactor was still waiting to win the world's greatest race.

It really was an extraordinary tale of misfortune.

Next year was a vintage one for Beckhampton. Gordon won his first 2,000 Guineas very easily on Pasch for 'Manna' Morris.

While they were preparing the colt for the Derby on the replica of the Epsom course, which Fred Darling had laid out on the downs, Aly Khan bought the Prix Juigné winner Bois Roussel for Peter Beatty and sent him to be trained at Beckhampton.

Prevented from riding in the final gallop before the Derby, Gordon had to rely on Fred Darling's verdict that there was nothing between Pasch and the French colt. He had a straight decision between the hot favourite, on whom he had already won a classic and the 20/1 outsider. There was really no choice in the circumstances. Any jockey would have done the same.

But Pasch failed to act down the hill at Epsom and could finish only third, while Charlie Elliott, coming from behind with an irresistible run, swept Bois Roussel past the tough, staying Scottish Union to win easily by four lengths.

Behind Blue Peter in the last pre-war Derby, Gordon showed once again that it was just the horses and not the Epsom course or the big race, which prevented him from achieving his ambition. The champion somehow squeezed a remarkable performance out of the Beckhampton colt, Fox Cub, to finish second to Lord Rosebery's splendid chestnut.

Turned down by the services on account of his T.B., he bought a farm, worked on it, flew his racing pigeons for the Home Guard and kept on riding. Thank heaven he did. Throughout all those years abroad he was an inspiring nostalgic pin-up for all of us exiled lovers of racing.

Even when the Derby was run at Newmarket the hoodoo still remained. In the spring of 1940 there was nothing to choose between Tant Mieux and Pont L'Eveque until the final work-out at Beckhampton, when Gordon rode the former, beat his stable companion by a hundred yards and naturally decided that this was the one to be on in the big race. Wrong again! Tant Mieux failed to stay and Pont L'Eveque won easily, ridden by Sam Wragg.

The jinx struck in a different way the following year, when Gordon had already picked Owen Tudor out of Fred Darling's four-strong Derby team. Asked by the Duke of Norfolk at Salisbury in May to help to instruct a new Arundel apprentice at the start, the sympathetic champion was complying with typical conscientiousness when the boy's filly whipped round, lashed out and broke his leg, putting him out for the rest of the season.

He missed riding a Beckhampton classic double – the Derby on Owen Tudor and the Oaks on Commotion. Billy Nevett rode the colt and Harry Wragg the filly.

So the Derby losing saga continued. Even that remarkable year of 1942 was to prove no exception. Of course Gordon had lost his title in 1941. His Beckhampton substitute, Harry Wragg, a superb horseman and one of the coolest, most intelligent jockeys of all time, had taken the championship. The same year Fred Darling topped the trainers list, helped by two outstanding two-year-olds – Big Game and Sun Chariot, both of whom finished the season unbeaten.

In 1905 Colonel Hall Walker, later Lord Wavertree, presented his stud at Tully, Co. Kildare, to the British nation for the purpose of forming the National Stud. As well as the rich land and excellent buildings, the gift comprised four stallions, forty-five top class brood mares, yearlings, foals, hunters, cart-horses and 600 head of cattle.

This strange man, who organised his actions and the running of his horses by the movements of the stars, even included all the furniture and pictures in the house and, of course, the famous Japanese garden.

For a short while my old guv'nor Atty Persse was Wavertree's trainer at Russley Park. He told me 'One day at Ascot when the King was there we had a runner which was strongly fancied by me. I told my owner it would win.

'Unfortunately Jupiter was interfering with Venus at the time. So, when Edward VII, who, after all, was not averse to a flutter, asked Hall Walker if he fancied his horse, he forgot my advice and replied: "No, Sir, he has no chance."

'Always prepared to back my certain knowledge against the forebodings of any astrologer or soothsayer, I had a good bet, which was shortly returned to me, with interest, when the animal won by three lengths in the style of the good thing that it was.

'As he left the winner's enclosure, Hall Walker had the misfortune to meet the King again. In very acid tones His Majesty thanked him for his most excellent information, adding: "I shall not ask you again!"

'My owner was so upset that he left the racecourse immediately.'

A few years later Hall Walker made amends most handsomely by leasing to the King a cold of his own breeding, the 2,000 Guineas and Derby winner Minoru. Indeed Tully bred many great horses, including Blandford, the sir of four Derby winners. But Minoru established a precedent which was to have an enormous effect on British racing thirty years later when the sport was in desperate need.

In 1939, five years before the entire stock of the National Stud was to be transferred to England, a colt by Bahram and a filly by Hyperion were foaled at Tully. Up to the death of Lord Lonsdale all the produce of the National Stud were leased to 'The Yellow Earl' for their racing careers. When he died, it was decided that they should be leased to the Monarch and run in the royal colours.

So, in 1941, just as racing was at its lowest ebb, King George VI appeared as the owner of the two best two-year olds in training. It was a tremendous boost.

When Gordon returned, fighting fit, at a natural riding weight of eight stones, there were only twenty-seven horses at Beckhampton instead of the usual seventy. But they included the colt and the filly, who were hot favourites for the classics.

Hopelessly out of form to begin with, he was suspected of having lost his nerve – even Sun Chariot suffered the only defeat of her life on her re-appearance. But then he won a little race and swiftly dispelled all fears as his confidence returned.

Big Game and Sun Chariot won the two Guineas races with such contemptuous ease that it was impossible to anticipate anything other than another Royal double in the Derby and the Oaks.

But Fred Darling and his jockey had their problems. Sun Chariot was as temperamental as any daughter of Hyperion. Those who knew her vary only in the word they use – cow, lady, bitch – but the sense is always the same. Yet all agree that she was utterly brilliant. So, although she constantly refused to go on to the gallops and, when finally persuaded, misbehaved outrageously, even going down on her knees and roaring like a bull, it was a battle worth fighting. I often wonder how many other trainers would have been able to handle her to win even one classic, let alone three.

Unlike many Englishmen, Fred Darling never put a horse on a pedestal. However, good it was, it was still a horse, the servant of man.

Atty Persse used to illustrate this attitude with the story of that other superb filly Pretty Polly on the day that she ran her last race. When the time came for saddling, the peerless wonder refused to enter the saddling box, but dug her toes in, swished her tail, kicked and generally napped like the worst mule. Everyone was trying to coax her with pats, blandishments and handfuls of grass, when an old steward came by. Quickly summing up the situation, he raised his umbrella and shouting: 'Get in, you pampered bitch!' gave her a hearty crack over the backside. Shocked and surprised by such cavalier treatment, Pretty Polly shot into her box and gave no further trouble.

If Gordon was worried about Sun Chariot's temperament, he was even more concerned about Big Game's stamina.

'I can hardly explain it even now,' he says, 'but he gave you rather a hollow feeling, and you sensed that if something came up alongside, there might not be much left in Big Game. He was brave enough and he had plenty of guts. I suppose it was the suspicion that, if really tackled, he could not quite get the one and a half miles.'

With hindsight, trainers who have handled his progeny might be inclined to doubt the handsome horse's courage and guts.

In the Oaks Sun Chariot spoiled three starts and then, when the gate went up, ran away out to one side, so that the field had gone a furlong before she had covered fifty yards. Even when she decided to race after the others, she was so far behind that Gordon, in deep despair, thought it was hopeless.

After a mile, however, she had sauntered up to the others and a quarter of a mile out she joined the leaders to win very comfortably by a length. 'It was one of the most amazing performances that I have ever known,' says her jockey.

All was set for the odds-on Derby favourite. But others, apart from Gordon, shared his qualms. Indeed that outstanding judge of classic trials, the late William Hill, risked his all laying against the Royal colt and, by so doing, made a fortune and laid the foundation of the Hill bookmaking empire.

Gordon describes that historic race in a most instructive way. There have been many horses since, who have come into the same category.

'My own feelings were more hopeful than confident. As a matter of fact, Big Game would have had more chance if the race had been run normally at Epsom. Here at Newmarket, apart from a small short-cut just where the horses come round into the straight, it was necessary to canter the whole one and a half miles of the course in order to reach the start, and this did Big Game no good at all. By the time we reached the gate, he was sweating and had taken quite a lot out of himself already, before the race had started.

'I purposely let him go out of the gate slowly, but he still fought me for a while. However, we settled down in a nice place about fifth or sixth, and so far things were going reasonably. Approaching the Rails, where we always normally begin to move on a bit, Big Game was right up in front with Hyperides. But his head began to nod a bit, and that made me desperately anxious. Then, abruptly, the bottom seemed to fall out of everything: he just blew up, and was completely finished. Harry Wragg challenged on Watling Street, and got up to beat Hyperides by a neck.

'Mr Darling thought that I had come a little too soon, but behind that opinion was his conviction that Big Game stayed the full mile and a half. I am equally convinced that this was one of the few occasions when Mr Darling was wrong. Big Game could beat all but the best over that distance, but he was not a genuine stayer. You can tell because when this type begins to tire, they blow right up and have not got a kick left. Some horses, even if they do not quite get the distance, will battle on. But others just can't, and this is nothing to do with their guts or courage. Big Game was game enough, and there was no finer battler over a mile, but he was one of those who are incapable of any extra effort if tackled after he had already gone much over a mile. If that happened, he was done.'

Although the colt had lost condition and had been somewhat

soured off by the Derby and his preparations for it, Darling's inspired training revived his interest so that he won the Champion Stakes and was promptly retired to stud, defeated only one – in the one race that really mattered!

Sun Chariot was a very different kettle of fish. She continued to improve in ability, if not in temperament, and from the way in which she won the Leger, slamming the Derby winner and runner-up, Watling Street and Hyperides, she confirmed herself as one of the greatest fillies of all time.

'I have no doubt', says Gordon, 'that she would have won the Derby just as easily. She was certainly the greatest filly I ever rode.'

So ended an incredible year, when Gordon had won no fewer than four of the five classics in the Royal colours – but not the Derby.

Those who criticise Gordon as being only a jockey and not a horseman would do well to remember the way in which he handled Sun Chariot. Not even the greatest artists, the horseman-jockeys like Steve Donoghue and Lester Piggott could have done any better with this wonderful temperamental lady.

The following year the champion was presented with another problem horse, one who was to prove himself probably the greatest of all international stallions, Nasrullah.

Gordon believes that the best mover he ever rode owed his outbreaks of temperament chiefly to the zoned racing of the war years, which necessitated his being kept at Newmarket, training alongside the July course, where he had to race.

'If only he could have been taken off the Heath for a change, I am sure it would have altered his outlook completely,' he says. 'He hated the place. We had terrible times with him in the early morning work. He would frequently hold the whole string up and we had to dodge between the Banks and get up to all sorts of tricks with him in order to get him to work at all.'

So many horses, particularly those of the Nearco line, seem to dislike our wide, straight staring courses.

Dr Edouard Pouret, probably the world's most famous racing vet, himself a fine horseman and former amateur rider of note, has no illusions about it.

'Ir is not lack of courage which makes horses develop a

hatred of such courses,' he says. 'It is just not natural for them. They like going round bends. You will notice that on a turn an animal will frequently catch hold of his bit again and try to run away with you.'

Despite all this, Nasrullah, who had shown his dislike of the straight mile by running in snatches to finish fourth in the 2,000 Guineas, ran a good race in the Derby, just failed to stay and was beaten a length and a head by Straight Deal and Umiddad.

Towards the end of the season he won the Champion Stakes in grand style. The Aga Khan then sold the future champion stallion to Joe McGrath, who was later to pass him on to the United States, where he is now a legend.

The following year was one of those arguments for Lester Piggott's freelancing. Fred Darling, of course, had first claim on Gordon, but the second retainer was held by the Aga Khan and his trainer Frank Butters, who had been responsible for Nasrullah.

This time there was no three-year-old colt of any consequence at Beckhampton, but Butters had a splendid animal in Tehran. Gordon rode him to win his first race in 1944, but was obliged to ride Distingué in the Guineas. Tehran, hopelessly drawn, ridden by Peter Gomez, was close up third.

In the Derby Gordon had to ride the Beckhampton colt Mustang, who was well below classic standard. Eph Smith rode Tehran and, despite the firm ground, which his mount hated, was beaten only by a neck by Ocean Swell. Next time out Gordon rode him to win and again in the St Leger, when he got his revenge on the Derby winner, beating Borealis by 1½ lengths with Ocean Swell a length further away third.

Unlike most jockeys , the champion preferred to give the credit to his horse when it was due rather than to himself. He always admired Tehran's wonderful courage. Whenever anything came up to him, he would always battle on and pull out that little bit extra which made all the difference between winning and losing.

'Tehran was the sort of horse that makes jockeys. The experts would always say what a wonderful race his jockey had ridden, but it was Tehran himself who did most of it.'

Forty years old and still champion – but still no Derby.

Now a recurrence of his T.B. initiated a long persistent bout of terrible depression and nervous trouble, relieved by the end of the war in Europe and a consequent return to his beloved St Moritz, where the air and the curling restored him to form. Even so it was not until the end of 1945, the year of Dante and Court Martial, that he fully recovered. He had topped the list yet again with 104 winners.

1946 produced his first post-war double century (212), but Edward Tudor was no Derby winner – not even when the winner was the grey 50 to 1 shot Airborne.

Gordon broke his own record in 1947. He finished with the incredible score of 269. This time his Derby loser, however, excited bitter resentment and harsh criticism from the multitude of 'sportsmen', who talk through their pockets.

Later he wrote of this year: 'We were back to racing as it should be by now.' That, of course, depends on what you mean by 'as it should be'. These years were the swansong of the old brigade. It was a sort of Walter Mitty time that didn't really exist, except in the wishful nostalgic memories of returning warriors. A time of lavish spending with loose money when spivs, black marketeers and racing flourished as though tomorrow would never bring cruel reality.

Instead of pursuing the democratic progress of the war years, the gentlemen of the turf gratefully doffed their humble, revealing uniforms and gracefully resumed the privileges of the exalted civilian ranks, to which birth or wealth had raised their fathers. It was all rather pathetic and very sad. Just at the time when they could have used the know-how and camaraderie of the war to reform and rejuvenate British racing as the leader of the modern sporting world, they seemed determined on putting the clock back.

Blissfully ignorant of the practical side of the industry, they paraded the racecourse wheresoever they pleased, preferring, it seemed, to ignore all foreigners and most of their fellow-countrymen – those who were segregated in strictly defined enclosures when they sought to spend their money to watch horses racing. The plebs, so it appeared, could consider themselves damn lucky to be allowed on the Heath at all. The

Jockey Club had wide powers and there was no appeal against a sentence which removed a man's livelihood. Let Yanks and Australians, Wogs and Frogs have contrivances like starting-stalls and patrol cameras, innovations like professional stewards, overnight declarations and so on. We apparently had no need of such things in Britain, where we invented racing and where we still ruled the racing world. Even this illusion was to be shattered for the first time in 1947 when the French won three of our classics. But even then it didn't sink in. Perhaps they assumed that the French horses were doped. Not that they intended to do anything about routine dope-testing. That would have been vulgar.

This criticism does not seem to me too severe.

But Gordon rose above it all, the wonderful little champion, who won so many races, but still could not win the Derby.

Fred Darling had been very ill in the previous year and now returned to Beckhampton for what was to be his last season.

Tudor Minstrel won the 2,000 Guineas in a common canter by eight lengths. He was one of the easiest-ever winners of the classic and Gordon says: 'On that day he was the best miler I rode in all my career.'

Then the trouble started as they started to prepare the hot favourite for the Derby. Gordon takes up the story:—

'Tudor Minstrel had been quietly practising round the replica gallop of the Derby course which the Guv'nor had laid out at Beckhampton. If Mr Darling had a Classic horse, which he had any intention of running at Epsom, his routine was always the same. He would put an older horse – probably that grand old fellow Ray, which we had now bought for this sort of work – with the Epsom horse, and let them canter round the replica gallop twice a week for a fortnight. In this way he need have no fear that his winner would not act at Epsom. I rode Tudor Minstrel in the last of these canters.

'It was a severe jolt to me. On pulling up, I went straight to the Guv'nor and said to him: "This fellow's not right. He can't get on his other leg. If he does, he's all at sea."

'Mr Darling was as disturbed as I was. The left-handed course at Epsom might prove to be the only thing that could lose the Derby for Tudor Minstrel.

'In the final work, Michael Beary came down to ride Blue Train. We went up the mile and three furlongs of the trial ground, which is pretty well straight. Tudor Minstrel went splendidly, but Blue Train worked badly, and so Mr Darling took him out of the Derby.

'That left me with Tudor Minstrel and the doubts about the left-handed course, and also just a little doubt about his stamina over one and a half miles. I did not know how to ride him, and neither did Mr Darling. Whether to let him go and risk the left turns, or whether to take him right up and give him every chance at the finish. He might fight me all the way and kill his chance.

'I have never, in the whole of my life, had such an uncomfortable ride at Epsom. Every time I held him up, he fought me. Every time I let him down to go, he shot off to the right. Either way, he was making certain that he lost the race. The whole race was a nightmare, but he still finished fourth.

'Then the letters began to arrive. Hundreds of them, and telegrams as well. Some incredibly impertinent people even telephoned. I was told that I had pulled the horse's head off. The kindest suggested that I was incapable of riding a donkey.

'As a matter of fact, I find donkeys very difficult to ride.

'Although, as you now know, I had no opportunity of making the wrong choice in this Derby, since Tudor Minstrel was so much the best at Beckhampton, one pleasing reference to previous unfortunate selections was made, at this time, by Lord Woolton. I had collected quite a nice sum from my fellow jockeys to contribute to the Conservative Fighting Fund then being raised, and I sent a cheque to Lord Woolton. In his letter acknowledging the cheque, Lord Woolton's secretary had typed, no doubt at his dictation: "It is most encouraging for me to know that you of all people are backing the right horse." But when he came to sign it, his Lordship evidently got cold feet, for he altered the sentence in his own hand-writing to read: "It is most encouraging for me to know that you of all people are backing the right horse again."

'Those alterations gave me a big laugh.

'Tudor Minstrel went on to Ascot, and he won the St James's Palace in a canter. What a difference there was going round to the right! Then we went on to Sandown for the Eclipse, with Migoli the big danger. And Migoli duly won. Personally, I have always put this defeat down to watering the course. Migoli loved it soft and Tudor Minstrel liked it on top. Frankly, I do not agree with the watering of courses. Why should one type of horse have it the way he likes best all the year round? A horse that likes the going soft nearly always gets it that way in the spring and in the autumn. Surely the horse that likes it on the firm side is entitled to the summer? If we ever again get a summer, of course.'

One of the more exasperating events of that year happened at Chepstow, where Glendower, a good horse, opposed by only one other runner, started at 20/1 on, whipped round at the start, unseated Gordon and took no part. Gordon learnt afterwards that one man had a system whereby he picked the champion's most likely mount every day and backed it to win him a thousand pounds.

Those were his instructions to his bookie regarding Glendower that day at Chepstow. There were no overnight declarations then and so he was not to know that the field would cut up so badly. When the results came in, he discovered that he had lost £20,000!

Fred Darling was now very ill indeed and decided that he must retire. He would have to sell Beckhampton. Like so many old trainers, however, he was determined to keep a finger in the pie as long as possible. This was to have a profound effect on the whole of Gordon's life, although at the time no-one could have foreseen what would happen.

A friend of Gordon's had agreed to buy the place as a speculation. This would have meant, of course, that, when he retired, Gordon would have been able to train in the surroundings he knew and loved so well. Gordon recommended Noel Murless as the new Beckhampton trainer and Noel agreed with the new purchaser that he would take on the job.

However, Fred Darling decided to sell Beckhampton to Dewar, the owner of Tudor Minstrel and to persuade the other patrons to stay on. He accepted his jockey's suggestion of Noel as the new trainer. If only the original plans had come to fruition, Gordon would have been able to take over when Noel moved to Newmarket instead of finding himself in the horrible situation whereby he had to give up training because he had nowhere to train. He would never move to Newmarket.

'Once a downsman, always a downsman,' he says.

The new trainer and his jockey started well. They won the 1,000 Guineas with Queenpot and would surely have completed the Newmarket classic double with The Cobbler if a bruised foot had not prevented that handsome speedy colt from having a preliminary race. As it was he was beaten a head by My Babu.

Once again, the stable jockey had no choice but to ride the Beckhampton colt in the Derby. He should never have run because he had no chance of getting the trip and indeed won two sprints later in the season.

The French challenge was now in full swing. My Love won the Derby from his compatriot Royal Drake.

Despite the change of trainer at Beckhampton, Gordon won his twenty-first championship with 224 winners. In 1949 he nearly beat his own record, finishing with 261 winners. But once again no Derby. Royal Forest started favourite, but sweated his race away in the Epsom preliminaries, as so many horses have done before. Even so he finished fourth behind the three concerned in that first-ever Derby photo-finish, Nimbus, Amour Drake and Swallow Tail.

Time was running out, but at the end of 1949 Gordon took a fifth retainer – for Jack Clayton, who managed the stable at Newmarket, where Fred Darling's former travelling head-lad, Norman Bertie, was installed as trainer. But for this the great champion would probably have had to retire without ever winning the greatest race.

1950 was the year in which I myself started training after two years as assistant to Atty Persse. Gordon was very good to me and from the start helped me with my little string at Lambourn.

It was a year when all the classics, except the 2,000 Guineas, went to France. The Beckhampton three-year-olds were extremely moderate, but Gordon won 201 races. Far from flagging with age, he went from strength to strength, winning 227 in '51 and 231 in '52. He had won the 1,000 Guineas on Belle of

All, but still no Derby when he came to his forty-ninth year, 1953.

He was champion again in 1953 with 191 winners. It was to be the last time, but it didn't matter because that total included the one winner he had always wanted – the Derby.

Now Sir Gordon Richards, he took a house at Worthing for Epsom week as he had done so often before. As he takes up the story himself, you can hear him talking in that well modulated, crisp, clear voice. His thoughts about others, like Fred Darling and the old lady, are so typical.

'Norman Bertie asked me to come and ride Pinza for a canter round Tattenham on the Friday morning. I met him in the paddock about seven-thirty. We had one of our own lead horses, and Mr Wootton kindly lent us one of his. I told the riders to keep increasing right into the straight so that Pinza could get the feel of the ground and the roads which cross. We set off at the seven-furlong gate at the top of the hill, but neither of the lead horses was any good to me. Pinza swept along with his ears pricked, doing nothing, and he finished like that. Bertie and Mr Clayton met me in the paddock, and asked me how Pinza had gone. "Well he's done nothing," I told them. "Those horses were no good to him." They said that they would send for another from Newmarket, and that Pinza would have to work again in the morning. You see, he was such a tremendous horse, and he did himself so well, that it was essential that he got a bit of opening up.

'There was a great change on the Saturday, the morning of the race. For such a big horse, he came down round Tattenham like a bird.

'I went back to George Duller's house for breakfast and, if possible, a sleep. George is one of my best friends, and I have been doing this for years. But there was something about this year's Derby which had me even more tensed up than usual. Her Majesty's Aureole had put up a really sparkling show in winning the Derby Trial at Lingfield, and there was no doubt in my mind that he was my great danger. The fact that Aureole belonged to Her Majesty, and that she had just knighted me in the recently published Honours List, added piquancy to the situation.

'At Epsom, the jockeys are taken most of the particularly

long way from the weighing-room to the paddock in cars. I suppose that now I am a trainer, while I shall not exactly resent the lift for the jockeys, I shall wonder why trainers – with the saddles – are not accorded a similar privilege. Maybe somebody in authority at Epsom will read this paragraph!

'We jockeys got out of the cars, and started to walk the short distance left to the paddock. Her Majesty was standing with the Duke of Edinburgh, and some of the Stewards, and she stopped me. She gave me that wonderful smile as she shook hands with me, and said: "It's all terribly exciting!" The Duke also shook hands with me, and said: "You'd think there were only two runners in the race! Nobody talks of any of the others." Her Majesty wished me luck, and I wished her luck. Then I went on to the paddock.

'Pinza is of course a grand horse, but he is a real man and he took all the upsetting preliminaries in his stride. He seemed to be enjoying the noisy crowds. He was on his toes, but he was perfectly happy. I have an idea that he was far less nervous than I was.

'I was drawn number five, which is not really a good draw because the Derby course bends out to the right after a little, and so the runners are apt to bunch when this point is reached, with the result that the low numbers may get buffeted. But as it turned out, Pinza could have been drawn anywhere for all the difference it made.

'After we had gone about three furlongs, I was maybe twelfth, but I was nicely tucked in on the rails. With about six furlongs to go, on top of the hill, I had managed to work my way into fifth place, without having to leave the rails. Smirke had now taken up the running on the Aga Khan's Shikampur. As Smirke began to go on, I found myself just in fourth place behind Star of the Forest, who I realised was tiring. I had two or three horses outside me, and my only chance was to go between Star of the Forest and the rails. I gave Pinza a little kick, and he went through like a lion. I found myself, right in the middle of Tattenham, in second place about four lengths behind Shikampur. Pinza came down the hill, and round, quite perfectly, just as he had done that morning. Although I was still four or five lengths behind Shikampur, I already knew that the race was over. I let Smirke lead me until just under two furlongs from home, and then I went by and we won as we liked.

'For such a big horse, I have never known such an active horse as Pinza. Most big horses need to be driven, but not Pinza. He did it all by himself, a quality which Mr Darling used to call class. Pinza was a terrific racehorse, brimful of class.

'I have been told that my expression never changed, that I seemed to take that tremendous moment unnaturally quietly, even when I was being led in. This seems to have surprised some people, in view of the fact that I had just won my first Derby after all those years of disappointment. But I am not surprised myself.

'Frankly, my mind was in a turmoil, and my brain perhaps a little numbed. Everyone was being so tremendously kind; the reception which the crowd gave me was something out of this world. Far better to keep on a mask concealing my almost overwhelming full feelings, although I did not consciously do so.

'Her Majesty sent for me after the race, and there was no sign of disappointment in her face. Aureole had finished a gallant second, but the fact remained that – good horse though Aureole certainly is – he never had a chance with Pinza, who was one of the greats of all time. Still, before the race everyone had thought that Aureole could win, and you know how hopeful an owner always is! But Her Majesty seemed to be just as delighted as I was with the result of the race.

'After she had congratulated me, the rest of the Royal Family gathered round. We talked about the race, about Pinza, and about Aureole. The Duke of Edinburgh suddenly asked me if I was going to retire now that I had won the Derby. Before I had time to reply, the Queen answered him for me. She said: "Of course not! He's going to ride for me in the Derby next year, on Landau."

'I went back to Marlborough that night a very tired but a very elated man. Not only had I been trying to win the Derby for years, but so had that grand supporter of racing, Sir Victor Sassoon. And at last we had both done it!

'One final story about that Derby. Ever since I had first gone to Newmarket, as a little boy unable to reach up to her door-knocker, I had always stayed in a house run by a Mrs Seaman.

She was a great person, who was a mother to us all, and we soon got to calling her Ma. She was a grand cook, who used to taste everything as she was cooking it in order to be certain that it was right. She loved cooking, and had been a cook in private service of the great houses of England. She was proud of that.

'She made me so comfortable that I never wanted to stay anywhere else in Newmarket, and I very seldom did throughout all the years that followed. She and I were great friends. After her son got married, she bought a house and called it Myrobella, and moved into it. Sometimes she used to get nervy or something, and would complain about her tummy, and then I told her that I sometimes got the same. She then always felt much better, and seemed delighted that I also suffered!

'Towards Derby time, and when I was up staying with her for one of Pinza's work mornings, when she was very old and very sick and bedridden, she called me to her bedroom as I was leaving the house in the morning. I am afraid that I had been singing in the bath, and she had heard me. "I could kill you," she said, "getting up singing when I'm lying in bed here." And she almost meant it, she hated inaction so much.

'Only a few weeks before she died, she asked me if I was going to win it. "Win what?" I asked. "The Derby, of course," she said. It was almost an obsession with her. When I told her that I had been knighted, she did not approve at all, because she thought it might upset me for the race! "They might have left it till after the Derby," she said almost angrily.

'She was a great old lady. I discovered that she had asked her doctor to keep her alive until after the race, because – as she told him – she had waited nearly thirty years for the great occasion when I should win.

'She did live to know that I had won. And then, quite peacefully, she gave up the trouble of trying to stay alive.

'Just as Mr Fred Darling died, a few days after knowing of the triumph of the horse he bred.'

Gordon won the King George VI and Queen Elizabeth Stakes at Ascot on Pinza but the enormous bay, who had the St Leger at his mercy predictably broke down before that race.

Gordon finished this last season as champion with 191 winners.

His Derby ride in 1954 was to have been Landau, one of those National Stud horses leased to the Queen for its racing career – an unreliable animal, a son of Sun Chariot. Gordon rode him in a Derby trial stakes at Lingfield and thought he should have won. 'It was the same old tale again, when you asked him to do something he either would not or could not.'

Soon after this, riding Misty Night at Salisbury, an apprentice in front of the champion touched the heels of another horse and came down bringing Gordon down with him. The champion was badly concussed and, in fact, was unconscious until he woke up in Salisbury Hospital.

He was now fifty years old. He had celebrated his fiftieth birthday a few days earlier on 5th May by riding Mabledon for me to win the Rose Stakes at Sandown. By the time you get to the half-century you don't recover as quickly as in your younger days from nasty cracks on the head or broken bones.

Reluctantly he had to decide that he would not be well enough to ride Landau in what was to have been his last Derby. This was the race which Lester Piggott won on Never Say Die.

Gordon came back just in time for Royal Ascot where, riding Rashleigh, he had that unhappy contretemps with Lester on Never Say Die, which resulted in Lester's suspension.

Typically Gordon was on the side of the Stewards and of his fellow jockeys. If he were not, he would not be Gordon. He wrote afterwards 'Why do you think that the Stewards have been so patient with his youthful impetuosity? Why do you think that day at Ascot all of us concerned – Poincelet, Gosling, Doug Smith, Rickaby and myself – did our very utmost to save him when we were in front of the Stewards? Why were they so lenient, in view of all things? Because everyone knows how very well worthwhile Lester Piggott is, not merely in ability but in character.

'Incidentally, I have heard it said that all we senior jockeys were gunning for him that day. Ask Lester Piggott! Or any of the Stewards. And I have heard the ridiculous suggestion made that the Stewards' enquiries should be held in public. Ask any good jockey what he thinks about that! Everything is above-board in that Stewards' room, and it will be the doom of racing when the type of men now Stewards lose interest in racing. They are above all pettiness and malice, which cannot be said for all their critics.'

Gordon had ridden fifty-four winners and was well ahead in the Jockey List by 10th July at Sandown when he was riding a two-year-old called Abergeldie in the Star Stakes. This one, like Landau, on whom he had just finished third in the Eclipse, belonged to the Queen.

He was riding in a one pound dock and the filly may have felt it a bit cold on her back. She half reared up and then went right up on her hind legs as they went down the gravel track to the course. A colt will not come over backwards unless he is pulled over, but a thoroughbred filly, like a number of girls we all know, will flip on to her back without a moment's hesitation.

Unfortunately, on this occasion Gordon was underneath. When he was x-rayed in hospital, it was found that he had fractured and dislocated his pelvis.

It was the end of the great champion's racing career.

As I said before, comparisons between different times should be avoided at all costs. It is fair to say, however, first that with the opportunities provided at the time he was riding, Gordon rode more winners than any other British jockey. He holds the record total of winners with 4,870 from 21,834 months – not a bad average!

He himself says that his secret was the will to win and concentration on the job at all times. As one who has known him well for many years, I can vouch for both those things, as well as for his wonderful, open, honest attitude towards life.

I shall always remember telephoning to ask him to ride. Perhaps Margery would answer first. Then that brisk, happy business-like voice. 'Sorry Major, I was doing the one thing you cannot do for me. Now then, what can I do for you?'

'Could you ride Mirabelle for me at Nottingham, Gordon?'

'Sorry Major, I am no good.'

'I know you are not Gordon, but I would still like you to ride her!'

'Tell you what I will do Major; I'll ride her for you at Leicester a week later. Will that be all right? I reckon she should win there easily.' He had all his ideas and future plans so cut and dried.

Atty Persse used to say that Gordon's secret lay in the great strength of his legs, in that he could squeeze a horse so tight with his knees and hold it balanced so effectively that it would run dead straight however much he threw the reins at it and however vigorously he rode. The champion himself does not believe this to have been the case. But I remember when he rode V.C. for me when she was only half fit and still quite fat at the beginning of her career. She won all right very comfortably, but for the next week she had a large bump on either side of her withers.

Much later, when he was training, I was telephoned by the *Daily Mail* in a frenzy. 'Gordon Richards has been taken to hospital' I was told. 'It looks bad. I hope to goodness your obituary is up to date. Will you get on right away and find out all about it?' I telephoned feeling very worried. To my relief Gordon answered the telephone himself. 'Nothing to get upset about, Major. Tell your office it is the same trouble that you and I and everybody who has ever spent his life riding on wet saddles have always had. Piles!'

The *Daily Mail* were not particularly amused.

One thing is certain. There never has been and never will be a greater champion and I doubt if anyone else could have kept the racing scene as happy through all those troubled times.

2: Eph and Doug Smith

'Bastard!' In a loud, flat voice the word would ring out across the unsaddling enclosure. Eph Smith, deaf since childhood, was telling the horse he had just ridden exactly what he thought of him. Standing there with his saddle over his arm, he never made excuses to the owner and trainer like most other jockeys.

'He's still very green, sir. He needs a bit further. It might be a good idea to try blinkers. I was badly bumped early on – brought to his knees, he was,' etc., etc., always ending in the inevitable 'But I'd like to ride him for you next time, sir.'

Not Eph. He talked to the horse and to anyone else who cared to listen. If the horse didn't give, didn't even try to give when he asked for more, then Eph had no use for him. 'Bastard!' That was all, and it did not endear him to his owners, although it delighted the realist trainers for whom he rode, who knew that honesty is always the best policy which can save owners so much money in the long run.

Eph comes into this book because, with his brother Doug and Sir Gordon Richards, he bridged the gap between the old and the new; because he rode two great horses, Blue Peter and Aureole; because I had personal experience on several occasions of his jockeyship; and because he started the revolution.

Born in 1915, the son of an all-sporting Berkshire farmer who rode over fifty point-to-point winners, Eph was riding as soon as he could walk and had a lot of success in local gymkhanas. Norah Wilmot, the local trainer, inspired his love of racing, but, when he was thirteen, he was apprenticed to Major Fred Sneyd at Sparsholt.

I know old Fred fairly well. A trained vet, he had assisted his uncle, Dick Dawson for many years at Whatcombe and, for some unaccountable reason, was always jealous of the great man's success. He had a terrible chip on his shoulder and was always hard up. This was obviously the reason why he concentrated on the production of apprentices. These were the days when indentures, which were all lodged with Weatherby's, bound a boy body and soul to his master for five years or, as in Eph's case, until his twenty-first birthday.

When I started training in 1950, the indentures were exactly the same as Fred Archer and his father had signed with Mat Dawson eighty-two years earlier, viz:—

'Frederick Archer now or late of Prestbury near Cheltenham of the age of eleven years or thereabouts does put himself apprentice to Mathew Dawson of Newmarket All Saints in the County of Cambridge training groom to learn his Art . . . to serve from the day of the date hereof until the full end and term of Five Years from thence next following to be fully completed and ended.

'During which term the said apprentice his Master faithfully shall serve his secrets his lawful commands everywhere gladly obey . . . he shall not commit fornication nor contract matrimony during the said term he shall not play at cards or dice tables or any other unlawful games whereby his Master shall have any loss . . . he shall not haunt taverns nor playhouses nor absent himself from his said Master's service day or night unlawfully. . . . He the said Mathew Dawson will pay unto the said Fred Archer the undermentioned wages that is to say seven guineas for the first year nine guineas for the second year eleven guineas for the third year and thirteen guineas for the fourth and fifth year respectively and his said apprentice in the Art of a Jockey and Trainer of racehorses which he uses by the best means that he can and shall teach and instruct or cause to be taught or instructed finding unto the said Apprentice sufficient meat drink and also hat coat and waistcoat in each year and lodging during the staid term. . . .'

Believe it or not, the 'fornication, playhouses, taverns' etc., were all still there. As for the money: when I went to Atty Persse in 1948, the apprentices were still being paid half-a-crown a week. And Archer was lucky. All Atty's boys had to provide their own clothing for the first year. This meant that many of them were nearly in rags. It was a licence for slavery. Dick

Dawson was Atty's oldest friend and Fred Sneyd naturally took over his uncle's indenture forms.

The conditions were that the apprentice rode any horse trained by his master free, which meant that the trainer was credited with the jockey's fee. This was fair in the early years because most owners don't like boys on their horses. They have to be persuaded and every trainer who tries to get his boys on in the world, loses so many races in the process that he deserves compensation.

For rides on horses from outside stables the trainer shared the jockey's fee with the boy and built up an account in the apprentice's name. If you could produce a fashionable apprentice, he was often the best horse in the yard. The same applies today, but the wages are very different.

So a rich trainer like Atty never worried about giving a boy a chance. He didn't need the money and, preferring to employ them as cheap labour, grudged any time they spent away riding in races.

Living conditions with Sneyd were deplorable and Eph recalls that the food was execrable. Eddie Larkin and Jimmy Lindley, who were apprenticed there after him, left because they could not stand the conditions. But the Smiths and Joe Mercer, who stuck it out, certainly received a good start in their profession.

Indeed Eph had already ridden in a number of races when at the age of fifteen, weighing 6 st. 7 lbs., on his home course at Windsor, he got up on Gordon Richards' inside to beat the champion by a short head and record the first of 2,313 winners.

Ironically, some years later, when my good apprentice, Taffy Thomas, who was so tragically killed at Warwick, came up on the younger Smith's inside at Ally Pally, I was had up and warned by the stipe 'Your boy was menacing Doug!'

The words may have been ridiculous, but the warning was not, in those days when there was no patrol camera to make jockeys keep a straight course. The same Taffy Thomas had a horrible fall at Bath when he tried to execute the same manoeuvre inside Gordon at the distance. He was lucky to escape serious injury. My filly, High Chair, galloped loose all over Lansdowne, was caught up in barbed wire, which should never have been there, and was cut so badly that she had to be destroyed.

And it was at Bath towards the end of the 1930 season, after he had ridden several winners, that Eph's career was nearly ended. He fell three furlongs from home, was dragged, thrown over the rails and broke his leg so badly in two places, that the doctors wanted to amputate. He was saved by Fred Sneyd's brother George, who, besides owning racehorses, was a very successful surgeon and insisted on calling in a top-class orthopaedic surgeon from London.

When he had fully recovered in 1932, two gusts of ill wind for Harry Wragg blew a great deal of good for Eph. First, he won the Great Metropolitan at Epsom on Roi de Paris because Harry could not do the weight of 6 st. 7 lbs. Then, when Harry, who was retained by Jack Jarvis, broke his leg, Eph was retained by the famous Newmarket trainer as light-weight jockey. He was only seventeen, but he had 561 rides and fifty-two winners.

I have never forgotten that Goodwood Cup (I was twelve years old and taken there as my annual 'birthday treat' by my parents), when Eph rode Sans Peine as pacemaker to Foxhunter, the stout-hearted stayer, who was ridden by Joe Childs. It was a field which included Brown Jack and Brulette, but Foxhunter was favourite and there was a gasp from the stands when the horse broke down on the final turn. Eph, waiting for his stable-companion to come by, realised something was wrong and had the good sense to ride his horse out to win at odds of 20 to 1.

When Eph reached the age of twenty-one, his long apprenticeship to Fred Sneyd came to an end at last. He had had over 2,300 rides, which had produced 215 winners. In addition to half the outside riding fees, he should have been credited with half the winning presents from the owners. There were some big races involved, including several triumphs at Royal Ascot. Clearly his account should have contained several thousands of pounds. Instead he received only about £1,000.

It is as well to recall the general scene of British Racing as it enjoyed its last period of supreme world dominance, complacently basking in a fool's paradise three years before the outbreak of the second world war. It was like the last days of Pompeii.

The Jockey Club at that time was omnipotent. Apparently

convinced of the divine right of peers, some of its members treated trainers, jockeys and all owners except their intimate friends with condescension and occasionally downright rudeness. The Press were generally subservient. They had to be. Any journalist who stepped out of line and criticised the rules of the Turf was liable to have his Press pass withdrawn, quite arbitrarily, and there was no appeal against the sentence.

The standard of local stewards was appalling. Lacking practice in race-reading, general experience of the sport and dedication, they were either disinclined to make a burden of their honorary duties or just failed to notice incidents in running, which, to more experienced observers, seemed to call for official enquiry. You could, if you were brave enough, write about this unhappy state of affairs without risking all, because the local stewards at run of the mill meetings were seldom members of the body.

So criticism mounted until in 1931 Lord Rosebery initiated a discussion on the matter at a meeting of the Jockey Club. His suggestion was not the replacement of local stewards by stipendaries, but the provision of paid secretaries to assist and advise the local stewards. Three years later the Jockey Club decided to proceed on these lines if the necessary finance could be provided from the grants forthcoming from the operation of the Tote. The scheme was passed before the beginning of the 1936 season. The time lags are typical and significant. It was a perfect compromise, because, of course, as paid servants, the stewards' secretaries had to toe the line or risk dismissal.

Unhappily the standard of local stewarding is still far too moderate. Some years after the war came the Francasal ringing scandal, when the telephone wires were cut at Bath. The late Brigadier Wyndham Torr, for whom I trained, acted as steward at Bath and recalled that notorious day. 'As we walked into the paddock,' he said, 'I pointed to a jockey reeling slightly and shouted to the senior steward: "That jockey looks drunk!" The old man turned to me indignantly and said: "There's no need to shout at me. It's my brother who's deaf. I'm blind!" He took no action.'

Reading patrol films and the correct interpretation of the rules is far too expert a job for amateurs. I hope this reform will soon come about; that the paid steward will have the casting vote and that he will receive his salary from the Levy Board instead of the Jockey Club.

To revert to 1936. The average apprentice jockey came from very humble origins, lacked education, was entirely dependant on his master and would have taken Eph's thousand pounds without question and indeed with gratitude to the trainer.

The Smiths were different. By no means rich, they were nevertheless comfortable farmers. See the picture of Eph as a boy, who won hundreds of show-ring prizes, superbly turned out in boots and breeches on his own perfectly made pony. So at twenty-one this deaf, independent young man was not overawed by the trainer. Not only did he summon the family solicitor to extract his rightful dues, but he immediately bought his nineteen-year-old brother Doug out of his apprenticeship with Sneyd.

Years were to pass before the effects were felt, but this action undoubtedly sowed the seeds of the racing revolution ahead.

To Eph, as first jockey to Jack Jarvis and Lord Rosebery in 1939, came the distinction of riding one of the great classic winners, Blue Peter, to win both the 2,000 Guineas and the Derby.

A glorious chestnut by Fairway out of Fancy Free, Blue Peter had inherited more of his sire's sweatiness and had a magnificent temperament. In the parade and at the start of the Derby he was as calm as if he had been on Newmarket Heath. He gave Eph a copybook ride to win hand-ridden going away by four lengths.

Eph was to write: 'With just under two furlongs to go I felt now was the time to clinch it. I changed hands, gathered the reins in more tightly, and Blue Peter took hold of the bit without the slightest hesitation to lengthen his stride instantly. He swept past the second horse and then Perryman's mount in less than twenty yards as though they were standing still.

'The winning post seemed to be coming to meet me instead of me going towards it and when I kicked my horse gently on with hands and heels he swept on like an express train. He never showed any signs of weakening, he was never challenged, I never had to touch him with my whip.'

Blue Peter, who had already taken the Blue Riband Stakes, went on to win the Eclipse and was undefeated as a three-year-old.

Unquestionably an outstanding racehorse. He did a marvellous trial before the St Leger, in which he would have met the unbeaten French champion Pharis, but the outbreak of war prevented the final classic from being run. Both colts were, of course, members of the male line of Phalaris. In the arguments about which would have won I find myself speaking with the bias of a trainer. Blue Peter, who died aged twenty-one in 1957, had not lived up to expectations as a stallion. He sired one Derby winner, Ocean Swell, and two Gold Cup winners Ocean Swell and Botticelli. But his produce were soft. They were anathema to a National Hunt trainer, because, for some strange reason, they were all super natural jumpers, but they could stand neither the inevitable rough and tumble of a jumping race, nor the pressure of a hard fought finish. However, he's been a wonderful sire of broodmares.

As the war ended, there were three outstanding colts among the high-class animals in Jack Jarvis's yard, Ocean Swell, Honeyway and Royal Charger. The last two both had their problems.

Sir Jack Jarvis must have been a great trainer. He gave his charges so much work, that they frequently looked like animated clothes-horses, lean and herring-gutted with poverty lines down their quarters.

Atty Persse used to say contemptuously: 'Harry Rosebery must have a wonderful breed of horse to stand up to the treatment they get.' True. But they and the other horses at Park Lodge not only stood up to it, but kept on winning from the beginning to the end of every season. Moreover, they trained on, which is more than could be said of many brilliant Persse two-year-olds.

I asked Rosebery the secret. The elder statesman has always had one great advantage over most of his fellow members in the Jockey Club, which he ruled for so long. He was a fine horseman, who knows horses and has always understood every facet of the game. At ninety, he is still as bright and knowledgeable as ever. He answered. 'Jack certainly worked them very hard. But he would make them ready early, race them through until the July meeting and then give them a rest in order to get them up again for an autumn campaign.'

Of course individual horses required different treatment, but that was the general rule and it worked.

Honeyway and Royal Charger, like Blue Peter before them, were such superb, high-class animals that not even Jack could alter the tremendous condition which they always carried.

Back in this country in the spring of 1944 for three months between Italy and D-day in France, I spent a day with Jack at Newmarket while on an exercise in East Anglia and I have never known a man so thrilled with any horse as he was with magnificent brown three-year-old Honeyway, who will always remain my beau ideal of a flat-racehorse. It was incredible to find this man, who always thought of Blue Peter as the champion of champions, saying that he believed Honeyway to be at least as good if not better than the Derby winner. As he had Ocean Swell in his yard at the same time, his judgment cannot have been far adrift. Unhappily one of Honeyway's testicles was only half-way down during this vital classic year and he pinched himself when galloping so that he could never give of his best. It was enough to sour off most colts, but not the great-hearted Honeyway, particularly when Eph found he should be ridden from behind.

Put back to short distances the following year, he became champion sprinter. Then in 1947, after carrying Eph to victory in the Victoria Cup (with 9 st. 7 lbs.) and the Cork and Orrery, he justified his trainer's faith by winning the 1¼-mile Champion Stakes after being left ten lengths. His last success before going to stud was over one and a half miles. What a great horse he might have been.

Chubb Leach once said to Eph: 'A good jockey doesn't need orders and a bad jockey can't carry them out, so why give orders?'

Royal Charger was a brilliant but temperamental horse. He did not like racing alone in front and had to be covered up until the last possible moment. He ran in blinkers.

One day in a small field at Newmarket Jarvis ordered Eph to stay close to the stands rails, where he was drawn, and on no account to hit the horse. The remainder of the runners raced in the middle of the track, leaving Royal Charger under the impression that he was on his own in front. Just when the horse needed a couple of cracks to ensure victory, Eph remembered his orders, rode out with hands and heels and was beaten a short head.

'Why the hell didn't you give him a smack?' bellowed the trainer when his jockey returned.

'You told me not to hit him.'

'Well, you could have waved your whip at him.'

Eph shouted back: 'What's the bloody good of waving a stick at a horse that's wearing blinkers?'

Hitherto, jockeys would have never spoken to a trainer like that. Even Charlie Smirke, that fine, tough, likeable jockey, would have hesitated before swearing at a trainer of Jack Jarvis's stature. However it was that very stature which made Jack forgive Eph the next day, when the stable jockey seriously believed he had earned the sack, even though they both knew that he was in the right.

He wrote: 'It may not appear to have been a serious incident, nor one which I should have worried about too much, but in those days not even a senior jockey was expected to answer back when spoken to by the boss. Times are different now, but in the thirties and forties jockeys were still very much accustomed to discipline. It was tradition, really. As apprentices they had been brought up sternly by their bosses, always subject to the strictest discipline, and it became steeped in their minds that to obey was the absolute criterion. Any thoughts of rebellion could only lead to instant dismissal, a hiding or both, and it became second nature to take all the kicks without answering back. It might sound all rather Dickensian, but it happens to have been true. Jockeys never, never retaliated when spoken to sharply or unjustly criticised. They took it and suffered in silence.

'I don't know if it was my answering back or the fact that I rode the same horse in 1945 to win the Newmarket Challenge Stakes, but next season my retainer was doubled to £3,000 a year. Then Royal Charger, covered up, ridden with the other horses and given a tap with the whip, went on to win the 1946 Ayr Gold Cup in easy fashion.'

I was very lucky with Eph – he rode me a number of winners – and I am a great admirer of him as a horseman and jockey. The latter was more obvious. Modelling his style, perhaps subconsciously on the jockey whom he most admired, Michael Beary, who, in turn, had been taught by Steve Donoghue, he rode in the classic British style, which so admirably suited his ideal jockey's build.

In addition he was immensely strong, had the independent seat of a horseman who has ridden all his life, and the hands which combine a sympathetic understanding of the horse. But for his deafness (he rode in races with a deaf aid), he could well have been champion as often as his brother. It was this understanding that earned him his most famous post-war triumphs on the Queen's Aureole.

Eph had first worn the royal colours in 1950, when he rode the late King's good, brave mare, Above Board, to win the Yorkshire Oaks and the Cesarewitch in which the royal jockey, Harry Carr, could not do the weight. Cecil Boyd-Rochfort's confidence in the mare was well justified. I have seldom seen an easier big race winner.

Three years later in the first year of her reign the Queen ran her Hyperion colt Aureole in the Cumberland Lodge Stakes at Ascot because once again Harry was too heavy.

Eph had just won the Leger for the Captain on Premonition – a race in which Aureole had finished third. But the bright chestnut with white socks, who had run second to Pinza in that Coronation Derby, was a bit of a lad. In fact he was so temperamental, that a famous doctor with a reputation for extraordinary powers was called in to 'lay hands' on him to soothe and settle him.

Before accepting the ride Eph asked to ride the colt in work at Newmarket and insisted on a neck strap to avoid pulling on his mouth. This was the mark of a real horseman. When a two-year-old, full of the joys of spring, was ducking and diving, jumping and kicking, someone would shout to the unfortunate apprentice on top: 'Let go your neck strap, you windy little sod!' Old Atty Persse who had once been one of the bravest and best jumping jockeys in the world now sitting with me in the jeep, would mutter: 'You hang on to it, boy! Anyone can tell that feller's never been much of a horseman. A neckstrap's the best thing there is for horse and rider. Just keep your finger in it and you can let him dart away without ever risking hurting his mouth by jerking the reins.'

Aureole worked kindly thus equipped and won his Ascot race very comfortably.

The following season the remarkable Eph turned down the royal retainer out of loyalty to Jim Joel, but, with that owner's permission, accepted an invitation to ride Aureole in all his races. It was a wonderful combination. This highly-strung, difficult colt was tamed sufficiently to win the Coronation Cup, the Hardwicke Stakes and, despite dropping his jockey when frightened by an umbrella at the start, the King George VI and Queen Elizabeth Stakes to earn full recognition as a splendid racehorse worthy to be a leading stallion and so to change the fortunes of the royal studs.

In 1963 Eph was involved in one of the most sporting gestures I have ever seen. At the last moment he had accepted a ride in the Derby on a 100/1 outsider, Hullabaloo, an unruly colt, who refused to line up at the start. Backing right away from the gate, he indulged in every sort of antic, delaying the start of the classic by a quarter of an hour.

The twenty-four other jockeys rode round or stood by the gate, minding their own business. But twenty-one-year-old Yves Saint-Martin on the hot favourite and eventual easy winner Relko quietly showed all the signs of a great natural horseman and a most unselfish young man. He rode back to where Eph was struggling with his stubborn mount and tried to lead him back into line. Unfortunately Hullabaloo, living up to his name, refused to take any part and was left.

With what cool confidence Yves rode that Derby winner, always in the first three and switching smoothly to the centre of the track two furlongs out to win with contemptuous ease.

Relko looked a great Derby winner that day – very different from the poor little woebegone pony he looked at the Curragh, when, withdrawn through sudden lameness from the Irish Sweeps Derby, he hobbled back to the stables just as his nine lengths Epsom victim Ragusa cantered home to £49,152 victory. Alone with the Turf Club vet Bob Griffin, I inspected Relko when he returned. Although he had looked magnificent in the paddock beforehand, the favourite, his head hanging, was now lathered with sweat and trembling violently. Bob's immediate diagnosis – 'I think he's pulled a muscle in his quarters' – was probably right. But there was never a truly satisfactory explanation, and it will remain one of those unsatisfactory mysteries which were to become all too familiar in succeeding years.

Eph's Derby ride the following year was Oncidium, a brilliant, but wayward colt, who had won the Lingfield Derby Trial so easily by six lengths, that he stayed second favourite to Santa Claus at Epsom at odds of 9/2.

The handsome horse was owned by Lord Howard de Walden; then Senior Steward of the Jockey Club, who dreamt up the Turf Board before handing over that office to Major-General Sir Randle Feilden. Announcing the change, he said that Fielden would not only be Senior Steward of the Jockey Club for an unprecedented period of five years, but would also be Chairman of the new Turf Board, which would hold supreme control over the whole racing industry. Immediately under him would be eight other stewards of the ruling bodies, the Jockey Club and the National Hunt Committee, and a permanent secretariat. In addition he would have the full-time co-operation to the chairman and one other Government-appointed member of the Levy Board. The Chairman then was still Field Marshal Lord Harding.

Howard de Walden gave three reasons for the formation of the Board.

1. The stewards were becoming overloaded and there was insufficient time for forward planning.

2. Even closer liaison was needed on all policy matters between the Jockey Club, the National Hunt Committee, the Levy Board, Government departments and all other racing associations; and

3. The traditional yearly change in stewards did not give the continuity in administration now needed.

Two vice-chairmen, a steward from each of the ruling bodies, would serve on the board for two years. Stewards of the Jockey Club and the National Hunt Committee would now serve for a period of three years.

While such bodies as the Trainers' Federation and the Racecourse Owners' Association would not be represented on the board, an advisory council would be set up within the board to consult organisations when necessary.

Weatherby's would continue to privide the secretaries for the Jockey Club and National Hunt Committee, but they would not provide the secretariat for the Turf Board.

Howard de Walden talked about broadening the base of the Jockey Club. Membership would become more catholic, he said.

The scheme looked good and received an excellent press. It has indeed, with additions and modification, formed an excellent working framework ever since. The author of the scheme himself duly retired at the end of the year and has not served as a steward since. He has many business interests.

As for his horse, Oncidium, who started second favourite in Santa Claus's Derby and lost much more money for many people when he just refused to race, Eph wrote later: 'If he had shown a consistent interest in racing, he would have been among the great. As it was, the only thing you could do was try to forget him and hope never to get another like him. He had a kink.'

'Oncidium was a pig of a horse.'

Which is just about where we came in.

'Bastard!'

Doug has always been as much an admirer of Eph as his elder brother was of him. He recalls with amusement:

'In the jockeys' changing room, where he was generally liked and respected, his friends used to laugh and say "Here's another for the farmyard," as Eph came in after a race calling the animal he had just ridden a "cow" or a "pig". He had far too much regard for the truth to be diplomatic.'

He rated his brother as undoubtedly one of the finest characters he met in his life and, as a jockey, among the best all-rounders. Bearing in mind his handicap of deafness, he was amazed that Eph got as close to being champion as he did.

Life was naturally easier for Doug, who was brought up in the same way as his elder brother, riding and hunting all through his childhood, serving his time with Fred Sneyd and having his first ride at the age of thirteen.

Remember Eph's horrible fall at Bath in May 1951? That was on the day before Doug was due to make his début at Salisbury on Hullo Marten in the City Bowl. Already scared at the prospect of his own ride, the little boy, who boxed at 4 st. 7 lbs., was terribly upset and shocked when he read in the evening papers of his brother's broken leg.

Sneyd found him crying in bed. 'If your brother had cried like that,' he said, 'I'd have broken the other leg too!'

It is hard to imagine any man behaving like this to a child who has just left a happy home and whose adored elder brother has been badly smashed up.

Not surprising Hullo Marten, who finished last but one, was his only ride that year. The following year he won the same event but this was his only success from twenty rides.

With some justification Doug has more time for Fred Sneyd than his brother had. I think that when the old trainer fully realised the value of this pair of goslings, he probably decided not to jeopardise the future flow of golden eggs by falling foul of a horseman father of a very different type from the usual apprentices' parents. By the time that Doug came along, he had already learnt a lot through Eph.

In his third season Doug had over a hundred rides. The five winners, which they produced, included a most significant one at Chepstow on the day when Gordon Richards was setting up an incredible new record. The champion had won all six races on the first day and, with five already to his credit on the second afternoon, was all set for a whitewash as they went out for the last.

In a desperately close finish Gordon's mount, 3 to 1 on Eagleray, was beaten a head and a neck. The winner was Lamont, ridden by tiny apprentice Douglas Smith.

For the majority of his riding life Doug has had to be content to play second fiddle to Gordon and it was only when the great man finally retired that he came into his own. Nevertheless they became and remained close friends, particularly in the winter, when they enjoyed shooting together and formed a most successful curling team in St Moritz.

In early life Doug's mentor was another quiet, stylish, much respected light-weight, Fred Fox, who won the Derby on Cameronian and on the triple-crown winner Bahram.

'Remember,' he told Doug, 'however good you are, there's always someone better.'

Doug tried to model his riding on Harry Wragg, that outstanding tactician, who was particularly brilliant on stayers. And it was in the riding of stayers that Fred Sneyd instructed his pupils best. He instilled into Doug that a long-distance horse must be taught two things by his rider. First to relax and to lob along in the early stages of a race as though he was quite uninterested; secondly to get his second wind before making his final effort. The jockey's responsibility was to check the horse and then, when he felt him fill his lungs, to go all out for the winning post.

Doug's brother-in-law Fred Winter, greatest of jumping jockeys, asked Pat Taaffe about riding the four and a half miles of Aintree in the Grand National. Fred said: 'Pat himself was taught by Dan Moore, who said that at Liverpool you want to hunt and hunt and hunt until you come on to the racecourse and then you can start thinking about being a jockey.'

It's the same approach and there is no doubt that it must be the right one, as you will see today when Lester Piggott settles his horses so beautifully in long distance races.

I like the story of the day in 1934 when Doug rode his first treble at Ripon and was presented by Lyons with a 7 lbs. Dundee cake for the week's best sporting performance. 'The Major promptly appropriated it,' said Doug, 'but was kind enough to allot me one thin slice. "You write and thank them," he told me. "It was a good cake, you know!" '

Very few apprentices, particularly of such a low weight, are used by their trainers for schooling hurdlers. Fred Sneyd, however, knew the Smiths' ability and made them school even the most difficult animals until they began to earn too much money to risk a fall. Furthermore he used to hire them out to ride important gallops for other trainers in the neighbourhood.

In 1936 Sneyd got Doug the job as light-weight jockey to Frank Butters, who was training for the Aga Khan. In May the following year, after the family row with Sneyd, the nineteen-year-old lad finished his time. By his twentieth birthday he had ridden a winner on every course in Britain.

During the war Doug continued to ride with conspicuous success. Despite his size, he had been accepted in the Veterinary Corps, but was down-graded because of a 'lazy eye' and so was not liable for service abroad.

From 1943 to the end of 1946 he was royal jockey and, although he relinquished the job to sign for Lord Derby in 1947, he was to wear the royal colours regularly throughout his career. His first classic winner was the late King's Hypericum in the 1,000 Guineas.

As temperamental as we had come to expect of Hyperion's daughters, this speedy filly started at 100 to 6. As she arrived at the gate, she suddenly charged the tapes, depositing her jockey and cantering the whole way up the course at Newmarket to be caught in the car park. I was abroad at the time and heard the race on the wireless. I remember wondering then whether the start of a classic would have been delayed for a quarter of an hour for an outsider belonging to an ordinary owner.

Certainly Gordon, riding the favourite, Neolight, was under no illusions. Fillies, particularly, hate being kept hanging about at the start and get very worked up. When Doug, reunited with Hypericum, returned to the start, the champion jockey rightly declared that the royal filly had an unfair advantage. These somewhat 'treasonable' thoughts were not dispelled by the race, in which Hypericum beat Neolight by 1½ lengths.

From 1947 until his retirement Doug rode for Stanley House – first for the old Lord Derby and, on his death, for his grandson. The twenty-one years association with the famous 'black, white cap' brought him 350 winners. Unfortunately, as happens with so many studs, the fortunes of Stanley House were slightly on the wane, when Doug took over from Harry Wragg. Nevertheless the retainer was to provide him with considerable happiness, immense respect from all, and Alycidon – advantages, which outweighed many other considerations.

Oddly enough, although he was to be champion five times, that 1947 season produced the highest total of winners in his entire career. With 173 victories he was second on the list. But

Gordon, the champion, chose that year to break the all-time British record with 269 successes.

Doug was always a firm believer in the retainer system and made no secret of his feeling when Lester turned freelance. But one of the oldest sayings in racing is that you can't come without the horse. The result was that his record in the classics was extremely moderate for one who reached the exalted height of champion jockey five times.

He excelled at Newmarket, particularly in long distance races 'Across the Flat', and he won each of the mile classics twice. In 1959 Lester chose the wrong Murless filly so that Doug won the 1,000 Guineas on Petite Etoile, that superb, lean, greyhound-like racing machine. Incidentally, I often wonder whether some of these brilliant race-mares have an excess of male hormones and whether this could explain their stud failures.

He won the 2,000 Guineas first on David Robinson's Our Babu in 1955 and again three years later on the Queen's Pall Mall.

The nearest he ever came to winning the Derby was in 1949 when he rode Lord Derby's Swallow Tail. The colt had trotted up in the Chester Vase – most horses love going round sharp bends – but had pulled himself up in the straight in Liverpool's Knowsley Dinner Stakes to be beaten by a 33 to 1 outsider. So Walter Earl decided to try blinkers in a home gallop with immediate success. They kept the colt's mind on the job and he worked like a train. This was the first time that Epsom had been equipped with a photo-finish camera to decide the result of the Derby. It was to prove its worth. In retrospect it was one of the most consistent (or, as the French would say, 'regular') classics ever. The first four favourites in the betting filled the first four places, although not in the correct order. They were Royal Forest, ridden by Gordon Richards, the 2,000 Guineas winner Nimbus, the mount of that outstanding jockey Charlie Elliott, Amour Drake with Franco-Australian Epsom specialist Rae 'Tojo' Johnstone in the saddle, and Swallow Tail.

Elliott, who could ride any sort of race, decided to fox the opposition with unheard-of tactics. He would make all the running to win the Derby. Doug, obeying orders, kept Swallow Tail close up and brought him up the straight in the middle of the course. Under pressure Nimbus hung away from the fence towards his challenger and a furlong from home the two colts bumped. Clearly Swallow Tail suffered more and his jockey could not get him balanced again in time. Right on the line Johnstone, who had been forced to switch to the inside shot Amour Drake up on the rails to snatch second place. The camera showed that Nimbus had won by a head with Swallow Tail third the same distance away. If he had finished second, Doug would have objected and would probably have been awarded the race. But there was no patrol camera and, in any case, far from interfering with anyone, Amour Drake would have been the likely winner, if the stewards had held an inquiry, because he must have been crossed by the winner.

Blinkers were the making of the best horse Doug ever rode, Alycidon, a lazy colt, who could so easily have turned sour if they had not been fitted.

So much nonsense has been spoken and written about blinkers in this country, that a few words may not come amiss. My old guv'nor, Atty Persse, who was already leading amateur rider in five countries, started training at the turn of the century when the American Tod Sloan had just successfully introduced the practice of riding with short stirrup leathers. With the exception of Lester, Freddy Head, Terry Biddlecombe and a few others today, who have found it preferable to carry short leathers to a new extreme, we have all used the Sloan seat under both rules ever since. It is more comfortable, and more effective in every way, keeping the weight off the horse's back, correctly positioned at the point of balance while at the same time proving far less tiring for the rider.

The disadvantage, as Atty had already learnt in America, is that a short-legged jockey, riding in this way, cannot use his legs effectively to drive and guide his horse. Big, lazy English colts soon discover that there is little reason to exert themselves for the slight irritation on their backs. You might as well have a monkey on an elephant. There was nothing ungenuine about such an animal if its mind wandered from the job in hand.

'You couldn't have jockeys whipping their horses all the time,' said Atty, 'so we had to find some other means of supplying the missing impulsion. By preventing a horse from looking behind or to either side, they keep his eyes straight ahead and thus his mind on his job.'

He added: 'After all, we fitted blinkers to our carriage horses to prevent them from looking and shying at strange sights in the hedges and thus to provide a safe conveyance.'

The first time you fit them, you give the horse a good crack round the hind legs with a 'long Tom' (or hunting whip) so that he associates the idea of blinkers with being made to go. Occasionally they can make a horse too free and hard to settle, but in general they are an invaluable aid, which saves horses from being flogged by frustrated jockeys. In the United States, where riders have affected ultra-short leathers for many years, the majority of horses seem to wear them. No stigma whatever is attached to blinkers in any other country but England. Unfortunately, however, some journalist referred to them as 'the rogue's mask' and earned his anonymous self the loathing of trainers ever since.

It's all right if, like Atty, you have owners of the Basset, Berry, McCalmont, Sefton type, who understand horses. The vast majority of owners today do not. What do you get when you telephone your patron in Sunningdale or Stratford-on-Avon?

Trainer. 'I hope you'll be able to get up to Warwick on Monday to see Lemon Pip run, John. He's wonderfully well. Jorrocks rides and I'm sure he'll win.'

Owner. 'But I thought we agreed after Kempton that the horse had run so badly he needed a rest. What's made you change your mind?'

Trainer. 'We galloped him in blinkers today and he went like a bomb. You can have a bit on him if you like. He's a different horse.'

Owner. 'Did you say blinkers? I'm damned if I'll have any animal of mine running in those things. If you can't do better than that, I'll have to take him away and send him to someone who knows how to look after horses properly.'

The answer then depends on the trainer's independence and the length of his pocket. Either he sticks to his guns and lets the horse go to someone else, even though he bought it, broke it and has lived with it in sickness and in health so that he loves it like a child; or he submits and agrees to run the animal without blinkers again.

In both cases the poor creature is due for some quite unnecessary hidings from the jockey, who will only be obeying orders.

So much for the ignorant owners, who prefer to listen to the know-all-know-nothing-never owned, trained or ridden friends in their clubs than to their trainer who is looking after their interests and is usually subsidising them by charging far less than the horse actually costs him to keep.

Oddly enough Doug was associated with two of the most outstanding cases of blinkered horses in recent times, Alycidon and Durante.

The latter, a big, strong liver chestnut, bred in Kilkenny by his owner Major Dermot McCalmont, was first put in my care when he arrived from Ireland with the usual batch of home bred yearlings. At that time I was in charge of Atty Persse's bottom yard in Upper Lambourn. By the Derby winner Dante, Durante was out of Lapel, one of the most prolific winner-producing mares in the stud-book. Among those that I remember during my time at Kingsdown were Over the Border, Red Carnation, who I used to ride myself, the Irish Leger winner Cassock, and the Hunt Cup winner Val d'Assa, a very full sister to Durante. They all wore blinkers – a fact which finally persuaded Peter Walwyn to fit them to Lapel's great-grandson Linden Tree, enabling him to finish second to Mill Reef in the Derby of 1971. Peter, one of our finest trainers today, learnt his job with Atty's brother-in-law and long-time assistant Geoffrey Brooke, who was Durante's final trainer.

Soon after we had broken the yearlings – a fascinating, though often frightening period – and ridden them away, we found that Durante was lame behind. He partially recovered, but developed a kind of string-halt, lifting a hind-leg unnaturally high in the air when he walked or trotted. He was impossible to train.

With the help of the vets we persevered for months to no avail. He appeared to be lame somewhere up in his quarters, though where and why we could not discover.

Finally in despair Atty advised his cousin Dermot McCalmont to have the colt castrated and take him back to Ireland to turn

Sir Gordon Richards on the 1953 Derby winner Pinza. 'There never has been and never will be a greater champion'

Eph Smith on that great horse Blue Peter. 'He rode in the classic British style, which so admirably suited his ideal jockey's build'

Doug Smith wins the 1949 Ascot Gold Cup on Alycidon. 'By his twentieth birthday he had ridden a winner on every course in Britain'

out in the paddocks where he had been reared. I have often wondered whether, if the vet, who performed the operation, had treated Durante as a special case instead of just another to be 'added to the list', we would have learnt the truth. Probably one of the balls was slightly hitched up. Maybe the castration released some unsuspected adhesions or possibly it was just the rest which brought about his recovery. I was never able to find out.

Suffice to say, however, that when Durante was sent back into training, he was as sound as a bell, but, of course, being 'two stone lighter', he was not eligible for the classics, which must surely have been a tragedy in view of his subsequent performances.

Nevertheless, when Atty first started to train him, he thought Durante was still a hopeless case – a big, clumsy horse, who could not go fast enough to keep himself warm. Many trainers would have given up, dismissing him as still too backward and he would have been sold for a song as a potential jumper. Not so Atty, who was always a firm believer in blinkers and, moreover, knew the breed.

Equipped with blinkers, Durante became the most popular horse in the country, winner of three Liverpool Autumn Cups, two Jubilees and many other races carrying enormous weights. Doug talks at length about the courage and prodigious strength of the horse. He was as honest as the day is long, but he just needed blinkers to make him work. The old man reckoned that blinkers improved Durante as much as two stone – possibly more. Over distances of ten to twelve furlongs 28 lbs. is the equivalent of about 14 lengths. So you see why I campaigned so long and hard for overnight blinkers.

Doug says: 'Alycidon was a lazy horse and a horse of intelligence who could see no point in unnecessary exertion.'

The turning point in the colt's career came when Doug was still convalescing after a serious operation and brother Eph was standing in for him on Alycidon's first appearance as a three-year-old at Hurst Park where the 1¼ miles start was all too close to the race-course stables. Alycidon consequently refused to face the starting gate and when Eph gave him a crack with the whip to send him about his business it had entirely the opposite effect. The colt was hopelessly left and his trainer Walter Earle was summoned by the stewards to explain this behaviour.

Earle told the officials that he would try blinkers next time and from the moment that he fitted them Alycidon went from strength to strength. Two weeks later he won the Thirsk Classic Trial ridden by the stable apprentice Dick Shaw and, although he was beaten in the Chester Vase, he promptly went on to win the Royal Standard Stakes at Manchester.

Then, with Tommy Lowrey in the saddle, the chestnut won the Princess of Wales Stakes at Newmarket, beating the previous years St Leger winner Sayajirao convincingly by two lengths.

By now Doug was ready to take over and at the end of July he rode the colt in the St George Stakes at Liverpool. There were only four runners and although the field included the good stayer Riding Mill, Alycidon started at 7 to 4 on. It was an extraordinary race. Doug had taken the lead going very easily a furlong from home and was only 100 yards from the winning post when a violent thunder clap suddenly rent the air causing the leader to sprawl so badly that he nearly collapsed from fright. Doug had to ride him all out to win by a head. The cloud burst immediately after flooded the enclosures and caused the abandonment of the meeting.

There is no doubt that Alycidon should have won the Leger. Unfortunately they went so slowly in the Doncaster Classic that Doug had to make his own running. Alycidon propped whenever he saw spectators leaning over the rails and nearly stopped dead when a dog ran across the course. It was only when Black Tarquin had shot past him into an unassailable lead below the distance that he started to gallop and was finally beaten only 1½ lengths. Clearly, blinkers or no, he had to be provided with a pacemaker.

I have never understood why the Rules of Racing are not modified to authorise pacemakers. Of course they are used and in this case they were employed by no less a person than Lord Derby. But because the rules stipulate that every horse must run on its merits, we have always been discouraged from referring to pacemakers and I believe that this has caused British horses to lose a number of good races which they would have won if they had had leaders. Furthermore, far too many big staying races have been and still are run at a ludicrously slow crawl because none of the jockeys are prepared to make the running.

I had a funny experience in a far humbler sphere one day at Folkestone. At the time I trained a very bad three year-old filly called Lyon's Delight who would have richly deserved every one of Eph's farmyard epithets. Apart from the fact that, given the slightest opportunity, she would kick any horse or human being like lightning, she also hated racing with other horses. She had, however, just a little turn of foot.

I had entered her for a $1\frac{1}{4}$ mile apprentice event at Folkestone and sent her down from Lambourn when I discovered that the race had cut up so badly that there would be only two other starters.

At the time I had a very experienced apprentice, Taffy Thomas, who had served his time with Atty Persse and was later to be killed when riding at Warwick.

Our two rivals were ridden by young boys having only their first or second rides in public. Lyon's Delight was equipped with breast girth, blinkers and everything bar the kitchen stove. I told Taffy to keep her behind at all costs until under a furlong from home when he could bring her wide of the other two runners with one final burst. Luckily both the other boys had been instructed not to make the running. The result was a farcical crawl which earned the headline in the following morning's papers, 'Apprentices Ride Cup Race.' Taffy obeyed my orders to the letter. The others had played right into his hands and Lyon's Delight to her great surprise and annoyance actually won her only race.

We were all summoned before the stewards and, although the other boys and their masters were given a rocket, Taffy and I were laughingly let off. Lord Abergavenny said 'I don't suppose I can say anything to you. After all you have won the race!'

This was a perfect example of how, without pacemakers, good stayers can be beaten by bad non-stayers. Alycidon was given a pacemaker for the first time in the two mile King George VI Stakes at Ascot on 9th October – his last race of the season. Benny Lynch in the Derby second colours set a good gallop until coming out of Swinley Bottom when Doug sent Alycidon on and beat a very high class field contemptuously by five lengths.

During the winter, faced with the problem that in the big Cup races Benny Lynch would run out of steam too soon, Derby, Earle and their jockey decided to provide their colt with a second pacemaker and bought Stockbridge for that purpose.

Just as Chattaway and Brasher paved the way for Bannister's first four minute mile a few years later, so Stockbridge for the first part of the journey and Benny Lynch for the second, won the Ascot Gold Cup for Alycidon. It was a memorable race. Stockbridge led up the straight and, passing the stands first time round, was two lengths in front of Benny Lynch with Alycidon close up third. As Stockbridge weakened running down into Swinley Bottom Doug shouted to Lowrey to get on. Benny Lynch quickly took it up from Stockbridge closely tracked by Alycidon. Threequarters of a mile out in the $2\frac{1}{2}$ mile race Black Tarquin, just behind the Derby champion, was going so easily that Doug shouted to Lowrey to increase the pace. But Benny Lynch was all out, and if he was to win, Alycidon must go on and make his stamina tell. Entering the straight Edgar Britt beat Black Tarquin upsides but, gamely as he struggled, the Leger winner could not match the devastating power and superb stride of Alycidon who beat him by five lengths with Heron Bridge ten lengths away third.

Despite the fact that Walter Earle became too ill to carry on training, Alycidon won the Goodwood Cup and completed the great staying treble by taking the Doncaster Cup on his final racecourse appearance. Although he could not enjoy the final triumphs, this magnificent horse's success was entirely engineered by Walter Earle, who brought the colt to fitness by working him over short distances, kidding him and combating his laziness by working him towards his stable on the Stanley House private peat moss gallop. Alycidon was indeed a champion. Doug says 'He was nearer to a galloping machine than any other horse I have been on in my life. A horse in a million.'

Both the Smiths have been franker than most jockeys about the darker side of racing in their memoirs. Eph talks about jockey's races – those that are fixed beforehand usually in small fields – and Doug dwells on doping. In particular he mentions the knobbling of Sing Sing, the brilliant sprinter. First before the King's Stand Stakes at Ascot when he was beaten by Sound Track and then before Newmarket's July Cup when the colt was given such a heavy overdose that not only was he unable to run in the race, thereby defeating the object of the criminal's exercise, but he very nearly died.

I believe that Doug is right when he deplores the rule which allowed apprentices to carry whips in boys' races. 'If an apprentice has no whip,' he says 'he is bound to try and get behind his horse and ride it with hands and heels, however tired he may be, and in being so he may be learning something about keeping the horse balanced and getting the best out of it without indiscriminate use of the whip. The natural reaction of a tired boy eager to achieve the honour and glory of riding a winner is to turn round and give the horse a cut with the whip, if he has one. As he is incapable of concentrating on more than one thing at a time, he tends to let the reins go loose as he uses the whip. Now only one man in my time has been able to keep a horse running straight with the reins hanging loose on its neck and he was a genius. The effect when an apprentice does so is that the horse immediately swerves away from the whip, and in a moment is completely unbalanced and running all over the course.'

Doug suggests that apprentices should be allowed to use whips after having ridden five winners. Since his retirement at the end of the 1967 season, during which, following that horrible fall the previous year he had shown exceptional moral courage, Doug has been training with the considerable success which perhaps one could expect from a man who has been riding all his life. After his retirement, Eph seldom went racing and died in tragic circumstances in 1972. They were both good jockeys and they bridged the gap between the old and the new in British racing.

3: Scobie Breasley

Sunny Cove's victory in Doncaster's Park Hill Stakes – the 'fillies' St Leger' – was the first major success for Michael Sobell since he had bought up Dorothy Paget's racing stock.

Perhaps it was just as well for his health and peace of mind that a board meeting prevented the radio and television magnate from watching this triumph in the first week of September 1960.

For, after riding a perfectly judged race and taking the lead from the favourite, French Fern, a furlong out, Scobie Breasley on Sunny Cove was one and a half lengths clear and coasting in quite comfortably. Sir Gordon Richards, the filly's trainer, watching the race with me high in the stands, lowered his glasses and heaved a sigh of relief. This first big victory for a filly who could become a foundation mare, was a boost for his new owner and for the stud.

So comfortably that, with a hundred yards to go, Scobie dropped his hands. Galvanised to fresh effort, Geoff Lewis rallied French Fern to such purpose that the judge had to call for a photograph before delivering his verdict. Sunny Cove had won by a neck.

Gordon, badly shaken and going through the familiar motions of riding a finish, said: 'I wish he wouldn't do that. I was in agony! The only time I was asked to win cleverly by not more than a head, I won by six lengths. I couldn't do it the other way.'

We hustled down from the stands into the winner's enclosure, where the former champion stood, hands on hips, waiting for his filly and jockey to return.

Scobie rode in, wearing his normal imperturbable smile and didn't dismount at once. He took his feet out of the irons and sat there, looking at Gordon, knowing just what his trainer was thinking. Then he said simply: 'She pissed it!'

This hand-dropping business had got Scobie into trouble before in his native Australia, where they dole out long suspensions very readily and where they insist quite rightly on every horse being ridden right out to the winning-post no matter what his position in the field.

For years the enforcement of this rule in Britain has been one of my chief campaigns, but, for some obscure reason, the stewards refuse to oblige. Any animal, worthy to be entered for a race, must be fit enough to be ridden out with hands and heels for the full distance of that event. This is only fair to the public, who make the whole thing possible, who bet each way and in forecasts. Imagine the feelings of the casual racegoer who sees his money, which was sure to be second or third, dropped contemptuously out of the first three with no questions asked.

Scobie, on the contrary, only ever dropped his hands when he was winning comfortably so as not to subject a horse to too hard a race when it had already given all that he asked for to win. It was understandable and was one of the only two faults of this superlative horseman-jockey. The other was that certain horses just didn't seem to hit it off with him. The same applies to all jockeys to some extent, but, in my limited experience with champions, I have found it applied more to Scobie than to, say, Gordon, Lester, Fred Winter or Terry Biddlecombe. Even if they were not ideally suited to a horse, those chaps would still get a lot out of it. But the odd horse that didn't go for Scobie, performed really poorly.

Having said that, I agree with Lester that Scobie was one of the greatest jockeys of all time. In twelve years he topped the hundred mark eleven times and, in each of the four seasons that he was champion jockey, rode more than a hundred and seventy winners. And by far the majority of horses went better for him than anyone.

Born in Wagga Wagga on 7th May, 1914, Scobie served his time for six years from May 1928 to 1934 and rode his first winner, Noogee, at Werribee, Melbourne, only three months after starting his apprenticeship at the age of fourteen.

With his lovely hands and cool, fearless, unflappable character, he inspired his horses so that he soon won every prize worth winning in his native country before coming to England in 1950, to ride for Noel Cannon. He adapted himself brilliantly to our very different courses and was not long in achieving a life's ambition to win an English classic race. This he did in the 2,000 Guineas of 1951 on the 100 to 8 chance Ki Ming, trained by Michael Beary.

Disliking the British climate, Scobie returned temporarily to Australia, but fortunately he was soon back amongst us for good, and in 1954 he won the One Thousand for Druid's Lodge on Festoon, beating eighteen-year-old Lester on Big Berry.

In 1958, Vincent O'Brien paid him the supreme compliment of inviting him to ride Ballymoss in the Arc de Triomphe, where he beat sixteen rivals in this toughest of races, including the 1,000 Guineas and Oaks winner, Bella Paola.

Those of us who watched Scobie every day as part of our jobs – in my case, both as a trainer and a journalist – soon realised that this level-headed, unemotional, business-like and dedicated professional was at the same time a master of his craft. More – to use one of the most abused words in the English language today – he was a true artist.

Moreover, he was always as brave as a lion. With the jumping jockeys we saw how the true natural horseman never loses his nerve. It's the same on the flat. I remember Michael Beary riding over hurdles at the age of sixty. No matter how many falls Scobie had – and latterly he had some nasty ones – he always managed to come up smiling that slow infectious grin. He had nerves of steel.

I suppose it's wrong to generalise. But I have always loved Australians and I'm sufficiently 'square' to be thrilled by the genuine, unashamed simple pride of so many of them in the 'old country' and in their achievements there. When Scobie took the championship from Doug Smith in 1957, he was the first Aussie to hold the British title for forty-five years. Although he didn't ride under both rules like his predecessor, the great Frank Wootton, Atty Persse, who knew them both, and many others, including Brownie Carslake, reckoned that Scobie was the equal of that Australian who was champion from 1909 to 1912.

The next season, 1961, produced one of those close-run

battles between the Australian and Lester, which were to be such a feature of the sixties. On 4th October Scobie was seven behind his rival – 148 to 155. Both were keen to win the title, but the older man never lost his cool. When I telephoned May Breasley at her Roehampton home to tell her that Lester had won at Nottingham on Impelo, whom her husband had been booked to ride, she exclaimed: 'Good for him!'

She explained: 'If Ryan Price had asked Scobie earlier, he would have spent the night in Nottingham. But he didn't want to do the journey again. In any case, he wanted to take a day off to play golf. So, as soon as he got home he telephoned the trainer, who didn't mind.' May laughed. 'This Scobie's impossible. You'd have to put a bomb under him to get him going!'

But he didn't need a bomb. Three weeks later, with only twelve days of the season to go, Scobie had scored 158 to Lester's 159 and was 11 to 10 on for the championship. With three days left he was five ahead.

Finally the forty-seven-year-old maestro, who rode his first winner seven years before his rival was born, clinched the title with a treble in the Lingfield mud. He had ridden 171 winners.

In 1962 he was Champion again with his highest total – 179. I talked to Gordon Richards about his jockey, as Scobie and May flew back to Melbourne for a richly deserved holiday. Who better to assess the new champion than the man who had held the title twenty-six times and was now his employer.

'A great artist – a natural rider like Danny Maher and Steve Donoghue – box-office all the time – and a grand fellow.' That was Gordon's verdict. 'Results speak for themselves. Look at his number of winners.'

What is his real secret? I asked.

'He's riding with his head the whole time, and he's a natural horseman. Me, I was a more thrustful rider. Scobie is persuasive. He has this gift which makes horses run for him.'

What is the effect on the animals he rides?

'Wonderful. They thrive on their work with him. And when they come back after a race you can train them at once. You don't have to ride them up and down the lanes for several weeks to get them over it, like you do when they have been ridden by some other jockeys.'

Breasley has sometimes been criticised for dropping his hands before the winning post.

'That is one of his few faults – and one which you can't forgive when it happens. He sometimes does take things a little too easy and drops his hands after he's apparently got the race won. Then Doug Smith or Lester Piggott comes and pips him. This happened to Lohengrin at Sandown. It's bad luck on the horse and on the owner, because the handicapper must act as if he had won.'

Scobie is forty-eight years old now (1962). *How long will he go on riding?*

'He says he'll carry on as long as I'm training, and will pack up when I retire. Like all Australians, he's got all the guts in the world. On those sharp tracks over there they've got to be quick out of the gate, get a position, keep it and go the nearest way. Sometimes they get into trouble with those tactics. But if they make a success out there, then they are natural riders with cool heads and guts.'

How do you account for the current Australian supremacy?

'It's like soccer today. Our fellows seem to be just about a yard slower than the continentals. English jockeys won't get anywhere by complaining. Competition is an essential part of life. They ought to pull their fingers out, watch the Aussies and learn to beat them at their own game. That's how I train my apprentices.'

The admiration was mutual. When Scobie returned tanned and fit in search of his third championship, he gave me this verdict on his guv'nor.

'He's the nicest fellow I've ever worked for. The horses look a picture – you can always pick them out in the paddock. And he's so good at placing them.'

As we have seen, Gordon could never grow accustomed to his jockey's dangerous hand-dropping when he thought he had won. So I asked Scobie about it. He was typically frank about his failing: 'I don't know why I do it,' he said. 'I ought not to – I've had enough rebuffs for it. It cost me the Australian Derby and the Melbourne Cup and earned me a month's suspension when I dropped my hands on Chanak in the Guineas and was just caught on the line. I suppose I just think instinctively that there's no point in giving a horse a hard race when he's won.'

At the start of that winter Scobie and I had lost a friend. Neville Sellwood was nearing the end of his greatest season when, on 7th November, he was killed on Lucky Seven at Maisons-Lafitte.

At thirty-nine Neville, another Australian, was the complete jockey. He had won that year's English Derby and was about to be acclaimed champion of France to receive the famous *Cravache d'or*.

I was with Atty Persse at Lambourn in the spring of 1951 when dark, wavy-haired Neville arrived from Sydney to join the stable. As always before the start of the season the Persse horses were at their freshest. In the paddocks, where they knew every blade of grass, they were dynamite.

The first morning, in front of a critical audience of owners, Neville, unfit after the long sea voyage from Australia, was put up on the giant chestnut colt, Bob Cherry.

A jump and a kick from those immensely powerful quarters and the new stable-jockey was hurled into the air. He picked himself up quickly and was re-united with the colt. But not for long. Bob Cherry repeated the performance with even more gusto. Neville was unseated four times that morning, but he was such a quick learner, that, once he had adapted himself to English horses, it never happened again.

He rode four winners at Royal Ascot that year – three for Atty, including Val d'Assa in the Royal Hunt Cup and, appropriately, Bob Cherry, who was later to go as a stallion to Australia.

When George Moore returned to Australia at the end of 1960 and Alec Head asked my advice about engaging a successor, I was able to give him Atty's appraisal of Neville. Alec had no cause to regret his decision to engage him.

It was Neville's jockeyship that won the Derby for Vincent O'Brien. As eight horses and their riders crashed on Tattenham Hill, his horse, Larkspur, jumped over the fallen favourite, Hethersett.

More forceful than most of his countrymen, he was still a brilliant stylist with lightning reactions – and courage. At a time when masters of their craft were scarce in racing, Neville Sellwood was irreplaceable.

This time we were treated to an even more dramatic finish to the jockeys' championship between Scobie and Lester. On the final day of the season at Manchester, Scobie had won 176 races against Lester's 174. Each had four rides. A few days earlier, Scobie had apparently clinched the title with a treble at Lingfield. But Lester had fought back and, with a double on Friday, was right back in the game. His mounts looked the most attractive.

Sure enough Scobie didn't ride a winner. But Lester could only manage one. So 'Sco' had won his fourth and, as it turned out, last championship.

The loss of Manchester, both as a flat and jumping track, was a tragedy. It was a fine course. But I shall always believe that the sale of Birmingham to developers was the greatest tragedy of all, reflecting sadly on the whole system of English racing until Gerry Feilden, George Wigg and others brought some sanity into the sport.

I can speak with some authority about Birmingham because I ran many horses there under both rules with my fair share of success. I actually saddled a double one day in 1956, winning the first and last races with first-time-out two-year-olds owned by that great Australian sportsman, Sir Frank Packer. I think every trainer agreed with me that it was a wonderful racecourse. A splendid, level, galloping track, which could take any amount of racing in all weathers.

Unlike most of our racecourses, the draw made no difference in short races. A straight mile, undulating only slightly, not less than thirty yards wide at any part. The round course was a few yards under a mile-and-a-half with a straight run in of half-a-mile. It gave every horse a chance. A novice chaser or hurdler always had time to see the obstacle before he was asked to negotiate it.

You saddled in your box in the racecourse stables – a tremendous advantage for a trainer and his staff – and led out straight into the paddock situated right beside the excellent stands. The crowd had perfect viewing of every race from stand to ground.

Although attendances dropped away, they were falling everywhere at the time and, although the trend has been towards racecourses in the country a few miles away from big towns, I have no doubt that, glamourised to suit the vast modernisation of what is now Britain's second city, and helped by many sponsors available in the midlands, Birmingham could now have been one of Europe's finest racecourses. To my way of thinking it should never have been sold.

So, as Lester won Manchester's last ever race, he received the cheers for a gallant loser from an ironically near-capacity crowd as Castle Irwell. His final total of 175 had beaten his previous best by five but was still one short of his rival's tally.

It had been a bad year for English racing. Paddy Prendergast was champion trainer for the first time. His patrons, the Mullions, were leading owners in front of American Gertie Widener, who topped the breeder's list with the help of Hula Dancer. The leading sire was Italian Ribot in front of America's Native Dancer and France's Chanteur.

Add to all this the extraordinary muddle over the suspected Derby doping of Relko and the inescapable fact that four out of five Classics, plus the King George Stakes, the Eclipse and the Champion Stakes had gone abroad and it was easy to see why many writers described 1963 as a year best forgotten. They added that England was fast becoming a second-class racing power.

I wrote: 'I disagree, but only if the lessons of this season are learnt and acted upon. . . .

'If the new-found co-operation of police and Jockey Club leads to the formation of a permanent anti-dope squad.

'If England's fantastic new gambling spree through the betting shops can be channelled by the Levy Board to keep the sport on which it depends.

'The sufferings of 1963 will then have been well worth while.

'By 1970 England could once again have resumed her place at the top of the racing world.'

Soon after the end of the season, the Marquess of Abergavenny spoke at Cheltenham on the improvements scheduled for the headquarters of jumping.

He said: 'This scheme will cost in the region of £1 million. When we can start will depend on support from the Levy Board.

This will, in turn, depend on whether the Board can persuade off-course bookmakers and betting-shops to make a realistic contribution to the levy instead of the ridiculously wretched pittance they produce at present.'

When the Derby market opened just before Christmas, Irish trained Santa Claus was appropriately installed as favourite. Described by Paddy Prendergast as by far the best two-year-old in Europe, the English-bred bargain colt, a 1,200 guinea yearling, had beaten the Chesham Stakes winner, Mesopotamia, by a contemptuous eight lengths in the National Stakes at the Curragh.

On New Year's Day 1964, shortly before his daughter, Loretta Swift, was due to make him a grandfather for the second time, the champion jockey was engaged to ride the Irish-trained colt in the Derby on 3rd June. The Australian went on his holidays in the West Indies with his life's ambition in his sights.

During that winter more and more people at the top, and organisations in racing, demanded a tote monopoly as a solution to the problems of the industry. But Lord Harding, the Chairman of the Levy Board, now promised a £2½ million levy for 1965. This was £1 million more than the 1963–64 target, which was not to be realised.

As the flat season got going, Santa came in for steadily increased support. And when, ridden by the little known Curragh rider, Jimmy Burke, he appeared for the Irish Guineas, it was obvious that even a narrow victory in this, his first race of the season, would slash his Derby odds from 7 to 1 down to a very short price indeed.

It was clear that Mick Rogers had left just enough room for improvement in the angular bay Chamossaire colt before the Epsom classic on 3rd June. At half-way in the Irish Guineas Santa Claus was last of the sixteen runners, yet Burke, who had appeared in public only twice that year, was not in the least worried.

Threading his way through the field, he was still eight lengths behind the leader, Young Christopher two furlongs out, when he went for a gap that closed.

Young Christopher's jockey, Jimmy Lindley, was making his

best way home and the supporters of even money Santa were gowing frantic when Burke finally found his gap a furlong out. Santa Claus engaged overdrive and stormed past the leaders to win as he liked by three lengths from Young Christopher with Crete half a length away third.

Jimmy, a future partner for the winner, although he didn't know it then, said: 'I thought I was going to skate in, but I was beaten by a very good horse.'

It was hardly surprising to find the Derby favourite's price cut to 2 to 1.

Mick Rogers understandably dodged the nobblers, keeping his colt's travel plans and whereabouts a mystery. He was actually stabled secretly at Kempton. Although I am one of them, I am sure that the Press do the sport a grave disservice in these sort of circumstances by their all-out efforts to trace the favourite, who is, after all, being kept hidden in the best interests of the betting public, who would lose their money, if he were got at.

Santa's triumph in the 1964 Derby was due to the superb riding of the fifty-year-old champion jockey, who, from a good break, coolly kept his mount tucked in at the rear of his field. Coming to the top of the hill, he was four from last. Running down to Tattenham Corner, the favourite moved quietly into eighth position – 'I had a lovely run down the hill,' said Scobie.

Then, still a long way behind the leaders, he asked his horse one little question. The response was electric.

'I just clicked to him,' he said, 'and immediately I had to say "Steady on, there, you're a certainty." '

Nevertheless, a furlong from home, with Indiana going strongly in front, it looked as though the favourite would be beaten as he hung towards the inside rail. Quick as light, Scobie pulled his whip through and straightened Santa Claus, took the lead inside the last fifty yards and won by a length.

Paddy Prendergast, who had saddled the third, fourth and sixth, said: 'It was one of the finest races I have ever seen ridden at Epsom.'

I shall always remember the Melbourne maestro, a grandfather twice over since Loretta's daughter a week before, coming on the best ground down the middle of the course and just picking off his rivals one by one.

May said afterwards: 'After Scobie had won, I expected him to say he would retire. But he didn't. He just loves racing. Now he won't go chasing after mounts and try to become champion again. He intends to leave that to Lester Piggott and the others.'

In 1966 Scobie received a tremendous welcome from the crowd at Longchamp after winning his first French classic, the Poule d'Essai des Pouliches (1,000 Guineas) on Right Away. Etienne Pollet declared: 'What a wonderful rider.'

This compliment from the winner's trainer was richly deserved. The fifty-two-year-old Australian, only just recovered from a heavy shaking at the Epsom Spring meeting, had made the young French champion, Yves Saint-Martin, on the second, Tonnera, look like an apprentice.

Waiting in front, particularly in a classic on a stiff, unfamiliar track, is a most difficult race to ride, entailing superb judgment of pace.

Scobie jumped out of the starting stalls in front of his seven rivals. He was still leading but apparently uneasy, as Yves on Tonnera, a recent easy winner, started a confident run soon after entering the straight. The former British champion, in full command of the situation, delayed until Tonnera's head reached his filly's girths. Then suddenly he sprang into action and showed that Right Away still had plenty in reserve. Riding with the energy of a man half his age, grandfather Scobie drove Right Away through to the post to win by a length from Tonnera.

It was swamp fever year, when French owners and trainers raged because our Minister of Agriculture acted on 14th May to prevent the spread of the frequently fatal disease to these islands. From midnight on that day Fred Peart banned the import of all horses from the Continent. It was just over a fortnight since Chantilly-trained Kashmir II had won the 2,000 Guineas. Already Nelcius was strongly fancied for the Derby. Now he and the other French candidates for the big Epsom races were banned.

Favourite at 3/1 was Vincent O'Brien's gawky brown Right

Noble, a caricature of his splendid sire Right Royal. Charlottown, a powerful bay son of the 1960 French Derby and Grand Prix winner Charlottesville, and Meld, heroine of the 1,000 Guineas, Oaks and St Leger five years earlier, was under a slight cloud. Unbeaten as a two-year-old, the Wernhers' colt had been lame early in the year and had not appeared until the Derby Trial at Lingfield on 13th May.

I think it is fair to say that he should have cantered this race. Ridden by Ron Hutchinson, the staying-bred colt was tucked in at the rear of his field until half-way. He improved his position up the hill, but challenged much too late to catch Brian Taylor on the 20/1 outsider Black Prince. In the circumstances it was an excellent performance from a colt who had not seen a racecourse since October, and his trainer, Gordon Smyth, said: 'I don't think his Derby chance is any the worse.'

The stewards questioned trainer and jockey. Ron said that Charlottown was checked round the first turn and then threw up his head several times in the straight. His explanation was accepted. Lady Zia Wernher was emphatic. 'Charlottown should never have been beaten,' she said.

One bookmaker, who offered Charlottown at 12/1 for the Derby after the trial, was swamped by would-be takers and quickly adjusted the price to 8/1. Another made Charlottown 7/1, while Right Noble varied from 4/1 to 5/2 with different firms.

When Scobie was announced as the Derby rider of Charlottown and rode him a gallop at Lewes six days before the classic, the odds shortened dramatically to 4/1. 'It was the first time I had ridden the colt,' said Scobie. 'He worked well and I was very pleased with him.'

Since the pre-Derby newspapers were full of Lester's break with Noel Murless, this swamp-fever classic was probably one of the least publicised in Epsom history. Nevertheless it was to provide a thrilling climax.

Even without the favourite Right Noble, winner of his only race that year and the mount of Lester Piggott, the Irish challenge looked formidable. Paddy Prendergast's Khalekan, John Oxx's Northern Union (Johnny Roe) and Mick Rogers's Radbrook, ridden by Bill Williamson, all had their supporters. Moreover Vincent O'Brien ran two other colts, Ambericos, a first foal of Ambergris, and Grey Moss, who had won Chester's Dee Stakes by twenty lengths.

Nevertheless all the late money came for England's second white hope, Pretendre, trained by seventy-nine-year-old Jack Jarvis and the mount of his youthful jockey, Paul Cook. The fine big chestnut out of a staying mare who had produced several winners, was by the Queen's stallion Doutelle, whose untimely death was one of the greatest tragedies, not only for his owner, but for British breeding. Pretendre had won four of his six starts the previous year including the 7-furlong Deerhurst Stakes and Britain's answer to the Grand Criterium, that splendid mile contest at Doncaster, the *Observer* Gold Cup, which was originally the brainchild of *Timeform's* enthusiastic expert boss, Phil Bull.

Jack Jarvis, who had won the Derby with Blue Peter and Ocean Swell, had always worked the colt with the Derby in mind. When he reappeared on 19th April to win the 1 mile 110 yards Blue Riband Trial Stakes at Epsom by an impressive six lengths, the veteran trainer felt compelled to train him for the 2,000 Guineas eight days later. From a bad draw at Newmarket he ran adequately to finish eighth.

As the twenty-five runners paraded and cantered down to the start, Pretendre, despite his twenty-year-old jockey, who had won that year's 1,000 Guineas on Glad Rags, shared favouritism with Right Noble at 9/2. Third favourite at 5/1 was Charlottown. The punters had given their verdict. They believed that this first-class colt, good enough to win most normal open Derbys on all home and public work, should have retained his unbeaten record at Lingfield. Now we were to see whether the officials were right in blaming Charlottown or whether his connections were unjustified in substituting Ron Hutchinson's friend and countryman Scobie in the great test.

Most Derby's have their moments of drama. Just as the runners were about to leave the paddock, thirty-nine-year-old Gordon Smyth, who was saddling his first Derby runner as a trainer, summoned his farrier. Charlottown, who had pricked his off-fore foot and missed the Brighton Derby Trial through lameness, had been uncommonly difficult to shoe. As he was on his way to the parade, it was found that he had spread that plate. The start was delayed for a quarter of an hour while the farrier did his work.

Still no starting stalls, but Alec Marsh let them off first time to a fair break, and within two furlongs Right Noble, on the rails was disputing the lead with Pretendre's stable-companion, St Puckle. At half-way Right Noble had a slight advantage over Lord Rosebery's colt with Black Prince third and Sodium fourth.

Coming down the hill Scobie was tracking Lester, always close on the rails. As the field rounded Tattenham Corner, Right Noble was obviously labouring and Jimmy Lindley took the lead on Black Prince only to surrender it two furlongs out to Pretendre. Now, just as it looked as though Paul would win his second classic, we saw the inspired riding of a great master.

Right Noble sprawled away from the rails leaving the gap, which Scobie had anticipated. With lightning reactions the fifty-two-year-old former champion shot Charlottown to the front. Now dignity and impudence, age and youth, were sharply contrasted as the Australian veteran and English youngster fought a thrilling battle up the hill. Though riding honours were equally divided, Scobie's experience had taught him to use every type of ground to his advantage as well as ever Napoleon did. As we had seen so often at Newmarket, Brighton and Epsom the split-second timing at the exact moment of that spurt out of the dip had given Charlottown the momentum, and the big bay kept going up the hill to defeat his chestnut rival by a neck. Black Prince ran well to finish third, five lengths away, and Sodium, who was later to triumph in the Irish Sweeps Derby, was fourth. The result had given English racing and breeding the boost we so desperately needed after four lean years of failure in our premier classic. And Lady Zia Wernher, the winning owner, had proved against all arguments that the mating of two great horses, like Charlottesville and Meld, can produce a classic winner. She who, with her husband, Sir Harold, had taken the decision to 'jock off' Ron, although he was the stable-jockey, in favour of Scobie, declared: 'Breasley rode such a beautiful race, I can't get over it.'

My final memory of the 1966 Derby will always be the impeccable artistry of Scobie and the coolness of his young rival, Paul Cook, who, within inches of every jockey's greatest ambition, never thought of going for his whip but rode Pretendre out to the end with hands and heels.

Scobie was to win two hundred more races and suffer falls which would have daunted many a younger jockey before he retired in 1968. A natural perfectionist with a unique understanding of horses, he is already a successful trainer.

Thank you, Sco, for the real privilege of watching you ride.

4: Geoff Lewis

There is said to be one major difference between English and Australian jockeys. When the Englishman returns from an off-season riding tour abroad, he is asked by his fellow jockeys: 'How many winners did you ride?' The Aussie in similar circumstances is asked: 'How much money did you make?'

Geoff Lewis, married to an Australian, appropriately bridged the gap in his greatest year, 1971. Although a lay-off through injury from a Newmarket fall may have cost him the championship, his many wins included the Derby, Oaks, Coronation Cup, Eclipse, King George VI and Queen Elizabeth and the Arc de Triomphe. On percentage alone he made an immense amount of money. More important still, the popular Epsom golfer had finally 'arrived'.

At thirty-five, Geoff had started the season poised to take over the champion jockey's crown. 'I have a very, very good chance,' he said with that attractive slight hesitation, 'and I'll be trying a bit.'

As first jockey to Fred Darling's successor, Noel Murless, he had stepped into the shoes of those other champions, Steve Donoghue, Sir Gordon Richards and Lester Piggott.

And, built in the same stocky mould, it is on Sir Gordon, the greatest champion of them all, that Lewis has modelled himself. The same neat, spruce appearance in silks or civvies; the same brisk, square-shouldered walk into the paddock; the same bright-eyed, extrovert outlook.

In a race, if you half-close your eyes, you're twenty years back in time, thrilling to Gordon's bustling, upright, whip-swinging, irresistible style that his hypnotised rivals feared for twenty-five glorious seasons.

'It came naturally,' says Geoff. 'When I began, I was always told to ride my horses on a long rein, allowing them to drop their heads and relax like Gordon, who was the master of the upright style. I thought, if it's good enough for him, it's good enough for me. And if I'm half as successful as him, I'll be very happy.'

The similarity does not end there. Lewis keeps himself superbly fit all the year round. Where Gordon spent his winters curling at St Moritz, or shooting, Geoff rides in India until the end of February. Furthermore, he has another Richards-type advantage over the hungry champion, Lester Piggott, who has had to watch his weight constantly to keep down to 8 st. 6 lbs.

'I ride at 8 st. 2 lbs. all the time without ever wasting,' says Lewis.

He served his time with Ron Smyth and rode his first winner, Eastern Imp, on his home course, Epsom. Although he won good races like the Hunt Cup and the Stewards' Cup, he was slow maturing, like many of the best horses, and was in his thirtieth year before the winners started coming in abundance. That was 1965, when he finished the season with ninety-seven victories to his credit.

Six years earlier he had made the wisest move of his life by marrying Noelene Munro of the famous Australian racing family. It has been an outstanding success. They are one of the most popular couples in the sport.

Like Gordon, Geoff is naturally intensely loyal and is much happier as a retained jockey than as a freelance. It has paid amazing dividends.

Still maintaining his association with the Kingsclere stable, taken over by Ian Balding after the death of Peter Hastings-Bass, Lewis elected to ride as first jockey to his young Epsom friend John Sutcliffe in 1969. It was this decision that finally earned him his rightful place among the world's leading riders.

When the Newmarket Guineas meeting opened on April 29, he was already a long way ahead in the jockeys' table with eighteen winners. Sandy Barclay had ten and Lester at this stage only nine. As so often happens, the Epsom horses had been well forward from the start of the season.

Geoff, who had never ridden a classic winner, was on Sutcliffe's Right Tack in the 2,000 Guineas. Stable confidence was infectious even though the champion's mount, Ribofilio, had been backed throughout the winter as though there was no settling day. In the end it was a shame that Lewis's thoroughly professional triumph should have been obscured by the sensation that followed the debacle of the Engelhard colt.

For those of us who love British racing this must always remain one of the blackest days in turf history.

Before the mile classic, bookmakers fielded strongly against the favourite, who was sweating slightly in the parade. He cantered down 'like a dead duck', according to Piggott, was never going at any stage, was pulled up before the winning post and finished in a distressed condition. Nevertheless, the bay colt, who had been guarded for forty-eight hours prior to the race, ate up his feed that night and Helen Johnson-Houghton said, 'It's a complete mystery. We are all terribly worried.'

The mystery deepened three days later when the Jockey Club reported that Ribofilio had not been doped.

Major-General Sir Randle Feilden, the Senior Steward, said: 'Michael Moss of the Equine Research Station at Newmarket has completed exhaustive tests on Ribofilio. There is no trace of any suspicious substance.'

And David McCall, the best racing manager in the business, reported that the bay colt was back at Blewbury apparently normal. He was particularly puzzled because Ribofilio was in tremendous form on Wednesday morning at Newmarket – 'full of the joys of spring' – but, completely out of character, was as quiet as a mouse a few hours later as he was saddled for the race.

'Normally he is a handful. Sometimes he almost kicks his trainer out of the box,' he said. 'Cantering down to the start, he is usually a runaway type, but this time he never took hold of the bit. He was not the same horse. In the race, if Lester had gone on riding him he might have fallen down.'

The stable's vet, Charles Franks of Lambourn, inspected Ribofilio in the Links stables after the race while the rest of us were wandering about in a stupefied daze. He reported that the horse appeared to be an animal that had had a great shock. The heartbeat was faster than normal and the eye membranes were inflamed. Subsequent electro-cardiac tests, however, revealed no abnormality. After starting erratically, they became quite regular.

The Jockey Club were now keeping quite quiet about this scandalous affair. Perhaps in the circumstances they could do nothing else. I imagined the Club as a steel-shod octopus desperately trying to find its way out of the middle of an ice rink and finally in despair flopping down in the hope that some outsider would come to the rescue. Well, of course they were right. Time inevitably came to their aid. Harold Wilson's saying that a week is a long time in politics is even more applicable in racing, as the fixture list moves relentlessly along.

The Derby is, after all, only five weeks after the Guineas. The public, still reeling from the shock of the first classic, were now wondering about Ribofilio's prospects in the great race, for which through sheer weight of money, he had so long been the anti-post favourite.

I demanded a public trial, staged as a race by the stewards. In the *Daily Mail* of May 20 I wrote: 'It now appears that an unhealthy situation can be averted only by a full-scale timed public trial for the American problem colt. Just as the Jockey Club always used to scrutinise the weights and supervise all trials at Newmarket, so now they must take charge of affairs and ensure that the horse is rigorously tested.'

The colt's connections, who had behaved in exemplary fashion throughout, stepped in and organised a public gallop themselves. It took place over one-and-a-quarter miles at Sandown on 27th May and proved very inconclusive, although Ribofilio's time was two seconds better than the average for the track and four seconds faster than that put up later in the day by Trumpeter and Remand. After a long conference with his trainer and jockey, David McCall said: 'Piggott doesn't think the horse is really back to his best. He is not yet quite what he was. But we have another week. His owner definitely wants him to go at Epsom. He won't win any races at home in his box.'

The gallop at least allowed the more knowledgeable an opportunity of warning the punters against the colt. I wrote 'I think Ribofilio will not be sufficiently fit to do himself justice next week. On yesterday's evidence he will be about 90 per cent, so that the Irish Derby on 28th June will probably see him at his best.'

I have recalled the Ribofilio affair at some length because it helps to recreate the scene of Geoff Lewis's first big year. Moreover it is a vital factor in the evolution of modern British racing. The colt's connections and almost all trainers were – and still are – convinced that he had been got at during the last two hours before the classic. Moreover Lester Piggott told me recently: 'I am absolutely certain that Ribofilio was done. But they found no trace, did they?' Europe's leading vet, Dr Edouard Pouret, says: 'Such an infinitesimal amount of dope is needed nowadays. It could so easily have been administered by someone brushing against him as he went into the pre-parade ring.'

Without knowing the details of their investigation into the case, it is hard to see what the Jockey Club could have done. Nevertheless I believe that they were badly advised in their public relations. Although Michael Moss had drawn blank, the colt's millions of supporters would have been happier if they had been told that he had tested a blood sample instead of just saliva and urine. They would like to learn that the Jockey Club had inspected the books of all major bookmakers to discover where and by whom the favourite had been laid for both the Guineas and the Derby. For the good of the sport it is so essential to keep everyone in the picture.

Meanwhile Geoff had won his second classic, when he took the Irish 2,000 Guineas on his Newmarket winner Right Tack. It was a splendid double and, with Sandy Barclay required for Paddy's Progress in the Derby, Geoff was asked to ride Blakeney for Arthur Budgett in the Lingfield Derby Trial. Breeder, owner and trainer of this beautiful colt, Arthur has been my friend for many years. He is the kindest, straightest, most honourable man in the world and an outstanding advertisement for his profession. But on this occasion when his colt was running for the first time that season, I believe that he was unfair to Geoff.

Blakeney made up so much ground to take second place that he emerged as the hero of another disappointing race. Geoff told Arthur when he came in after failing to catch Lester on The Elk by only three-quarters of a length, 'I was hampered down the hill.' It was the understatement of the year. Even though the champion jockey had ridden a superb race, taking the lead after half a mile and judging pace beautifully to make his best way home, his rival had no chance. He was hopelessly interfered with and nearly stopped in his tracks.

The late William Hill, always a great judge of pre-classic form, said: 'Blakeney should have won by ten minutes. The Elk will never beat him again.'

Instead of giving Geoff another chance, Budgett announced on the spot that Blakeney's Derby rider would be the young Northern jockey Ernie Johnson, who had formerly been understudy to Lewis at Kingsclere. It was a bitter blow.

The following day saw Prince Regent, a handsome black colt trained by Etienne Pollet, winning the Prix Lupin by a head from Noel Murless's Caliban, beautifully ridden by Sandy Barclay. This Derby trial was worth no less than £44,000 to the winning owner, the Comtesse de la Valdene, whose brother, Raymond Guest, had already won the Epsom Derby twice with Larkspur and Sir Ivor. Any enterprising sponsor who cares to subsidise one of the British trials, preferably either the Lingfield race or York's Dante Stakes, by another £10,000 will be doing a great service to the sport and to its followers, who are usually left confused before Epsom because a number of colts have been avoiding each other to win sub-standard events.

Pollet, who had previously won the Derby with Sea Bird II, declared immediately: 'Prince Regent will definitely run at Epsom.'

Piggott, naturally worried about Ribofilio, had shown interest in the colt, so that Pollet added, 'If Deforge does not want to ride, we would like to have him.' There was no mention of Geoff at this stage and our hero had to be content with the Irish colt Agricoltore on the big day. Caliban had performed so brilliantly that Murless decided to go for the French Derby.

At Epsom Ernie Johnson seized his opportunity and shot Blakeney through on the rails to win from Shoemaker and Prince Regent, but Jean Deforge rode the Lupin winner so erratically that at one stage he veered right over to the stands rails and just as sharply back again. The French jockey said: 'I had to snatch him up to avoid a beaten horse coming down the hill. Otherwise I would surely have won easily.'

However, Prince Regent's owner and trainer were in no mood

for excuses. They had lost the one race in the world which could have increased their horse's value to at least a million pounds. In seeking consolation at the Curragh they would also seek another jockey.

Piggott, who had reported 'Ribofilio was not even 90 per cent in the Derby. I didn't think he'd run as well as he did,' was approached. He replied, with justifiable satisfaction, 'It's rather nice to be asked to ride the two favourites in the Irish Derby. But I'll definitely stay with Ribofilio.'

So Geoff got the coveted mount and, despite Ribofilio's remarkable recovery, rode a copy book race to beat Piggott and the ill-fated Engelhard colt.

As the season went on, Geoff rode more and more winners, leading the way in the jockeys' championship. Whereas his previous best season, 1965, had yielded ninety-seven winners, he had already noticed 124 by 11th September, when he was finally collared by Lester. He finished the season with 146 – exactly double his total for 1968.

The following year produced 135 successes and heralded the great days to come. It was for many the year of Nijinsky. To Geoff, however, it was the year when he took over the most coveted job in racing. It was more than that. When he accepted Noel Murless's offer, he made one stipulation – he must ride Mill Reef in all his races.

The greatest thrill at Royal Ascot was the way in which the charming little bay American two-year-old spreadeagled his field in the Coventry Stakes.

Dismounting after his eight-lengths victory in front of a 31,000 opening-day crowd, Geoff enthused; 'He's the best two-year-old I've ever ridden – a very, very good one indeed.'

So it was not surprising when the top French two-year-olds were completely outclassed in the Prix Robert Papin at Maisons-Laffitte in July. But on this one occasion Geoff and his wonder colt, drawn on the outside and racing on their own, had to be beaten a short head by Lester on My Swallow, taking full advantage of the stands rails from a No. 1 draw. The nearest French horse was four lengths away.

The following day I wrote: 'I believe Mill Reef will reverse the placing when he meets the winner again.' That meeting was not destined to take place until the 2,000 Guineas. In the meantime My Swallow broke all French two-year-old records by winning the Morny, the Salamandre and the Grand Criterium, while Mill Reef slaughtered his opponents in the Gimcrack and in the Dewhurst.

In 1971 Paul Mellon's colt justified all Geoff's loyalty. Trained for the Derby, he was entitled to be defeated in the Guineas by John and Jean Hislop's Brigadier Gerard, who had not only been trained for the early mile classic, but was also a rattling good colt.

Thereafter Mill Reef came right into his own. Geoff grew in stature and confidence with every triumph and it seemed only right and proper that he should win that remarkable Epsom treble – on Mill Reef in the Derby, Lupe in the Coronation Cup and Altesse Royale in the Oaks. His sense of balance and judgement of pace increased so that he even went into the world's hardest race, the Arc de Triomphe, with a cool which he never would have possessed three years earlier.

After Mill Reef had won the King George VI and Queen Elizabeth Stakes at Ascot, we asked Jean Romanet, the charming sympathetic French Secretary General: 'Is that good enough for the Arc, Jean?' He shrugged. 'Is the Arc good enough for him?'

There was just one moment entering the Longchamp straight when he looked as though he might have been shut in as Geoff had been on Prince Regent two years earlier. But the colt's brilliant acceleration and his jockey's new-found ability quickly settled the issue to beat Pistol Packer by three lengths and win for Paul Mellon the £105,000 winner's prize.

Geoff had certainly earned his favourite dish that night. 'I don't speak the lingo, Tim. Would you order me a large plate of frogs' legs, please!'

Although he has ridden only one actual classic winner for Warren Place, he says: 'I'm thrilled to be riding for Noel Murless.'

He rides out there on Wednesdays and Saturdays, spending the previous nights in Newmarket. On Tuesdays and Thursdays he is on his home gallops with John Sutcliffe. Between these two and Ian Balding he has a lien on more than 200 horses.

Basically Geoff shares Gordon Richards's dislike of riding abroad, except for his retaining stables. 'I don't go much for travelling,' he says.

Thinking back over the last four triumphant years, he comments: 'The only thing that has made me unhappy has been replacing Sandy Barclay. That's racing, I suppose, but it was a pity that it had to be him. I like him very much.'

There are few people whom Geoff dislikes and I have yet to meet anyone who does not like this charming, happy little man, who, with Noelene and their two children, will always be a credit to the British racing scene.

Of Lester Piggott, he says: 'If that big, long fellow spends too much time riding in France, he could well find himself losing his title.'

Nobody in the racing world would be surprised to find Geoff following once more in the steps of Sir Gordon. Certainly not Lester. When I asked him at the start of 1972 whom he considered to be his most formidable rival in the world, the champion replied: 'I have no doubt that now it's Geoff Lewis.'

5: Bill Williamson

They call him 'Weary Willie', this lithe, lean horseman, who rode his first winner on the great Flemington circuit just after Lester Piggott's second birthday, and who has been described by the British champion as the best jockey in the world.

Just as Fred Archer feared George Fordham ('the yellow man'), so Lester had reason to respect the mastery of the seemingly dour Australian, who suddenly sparkles when a party gets going and who explodes into superlative action towards the finish of a big race. The world's most coveted prize, the Prix de l'Arc de Triomphe has eluded Piggott because on Sir Ivor and Park Top he was out-generalled and out-ridden by the weary one.

Born on 12th December, 1922, Bill was already established as champion of Melbourne and renowned as one of the greatest jockeys ever to ride 'down under', when he followed Scobie Breasley to these islands in 1960 at the shrewd invitation of Seamus McGrath. 'Williamson is a great loss to us,' I was told by a senior Australian steward. 'He's one of the finest riders we've ever produced, as brave as a lion and as straight as a die.'

Indeed, whenever his prowess as a jockey is mentioned the word honesty will soon be included. In a sport that is fraught with temptation Bill has always been the personification of integrity.

His first ride in Europe, Lucky Guy in Sandown's Coronation Stakes on St George's Day 1960, was a winner. Few racegoers, however, realised that they were watching a maestro when he shot away to beat Garnet Bougoure on Barclay and Jimmy Lindley on Aggressor.

Dermot O'Brien remarked: 'Bougoure and Lindley were so

busy waiting on each other that they let Lucky Guy go.'

Bougoure certainly knew different. An extremely effective rider, hailing from Melbourne, he had suffered before from the genius of Weary Willie.

We could do with so many more Bougoures. Although he was never in that happy little band of international stars who can win races which they have no right to, snatching victory from defeat in the most miraculous way, he was at the top of the second class. He would seldom lose a race which he ought to have won.

Like nearly all Australians, he was a splendid judge of pace. On Newmarket Heath or the rolling Berkshire downland gallops, a trainer will usually instruct his work jockeys: 'I want you to come five furlongs at a nice half-speed,' or 'a good, working three-parts speed on the bridle,' or, as per the late Atty Persse's normal orders, 'Come the whole way, Michael. You boys lay with him.'

Working on the Australian tracks is utterly different. Governed by the stop-watch, accuracy is the key word. From his earliest days an apprentice is ordered to gallop a certain distance in a given time and woe betide the boy who is too far out in his judgement. They very soon learn.

The great trainers reported that Garnet was a wonderful work-rider. Moreover he would never hurt a horse, so that, after he had ridden it in a race, it would always eat up its feed and could have run again the next day. Sitting still and always well-balanced, he was grand when a horse was still on the bridle, but not so good when he had to let one down and ride it out in a close finish.

A strange, incongruous, little known sidelight on this charming, very quiet, apparently colourless man was his winter relaxation. Bougoure was an enthusiastic gambler at the Tables and was seldom happier than in the chip-chinking, smoke-laden, green baize atmosphere of Las Vegas.

For Paddy Prendergast he had considerable success, winning the 1,000 Guineas on Pourparler, the Oaks on Noblesse and the King George VI and Queen Elizabeth Stakes, the St Leger and the Irish Sweeps Derby on the Mullions' brave little bay Ragusa.

Despite his extra brilliance, Williamson was not to be quite so lucky for Prendergast, because the horses which he had to ride were not in the same class.

Nearly ten years were to pass before the ever-popular, gifted Irish trainer was to say: 'Bill's a wonderful jockey, but he just doesn't seem to be as lucky for me as he is for Seamus.'

For it was Seamus McGrath who brought Bill over and Seamus who was to be rewarded with the greatest triumph ten years later at Longchamp.

The sad truth, however, is that there is not enough racing and insufficient prize-money in Ireland for top international Australians. By the time that the Dublin Sales of 1961 came round Bill had decided to move from the McGrath stable to Harry Wragg in Newmarket.

He started off the 1962 season on the right foot, winning the One Thousand for his new stable on the Kildangan filly Abermaid. This was one of those dramatic Williamson finishes that have thrilled us ever since.

Bill, who had won all the Australian classics, the Irish Leger and Oaks, was having his first ride in the 1,000 Guineas, but he rode the tricky Rowley Mile as though he had spent his life at Newmarket. Three furlongs out Display led, followed by Jim Joel's favourite West Side Story. Once again Bougoure, who had just moved from Vincent O'Brien to Paddy Prendergast, was the victim as Williamson pounced with a devastating last minute run out of the Dip. On the rising ground Display's stamina gave out and she went under by half a length with West Side Story three quarters of a length away third.

Nevertheless, no sooner had the placed horses entered the unsaddling enclosure than a stewards' objection was announced. In living memory there had been only one stewards' objection in a classic – the Derby of 1913, which Craganour lost to Aboyeur. Now it was officially alleged that Abermaid had interferred with Display and West Side Story. Fortunately the patrol camera, still a novelty in England, was in operation, although the Press were not to be allowed to see the films for some years. It revealed that the incident occurred on the finishing line and so had no bearing on the result.

Eph Smith thought West Side Story would have finished second but for the interference. Garnet Bougoure on the other

Santa Claus, ridden by Scobie Breasley, wins the 1964 Derby. 'It was one of the finest races I have ever seen ridden at Epsom'

Geoff Lewis on Mill Reef. 'Geoff grew in stature and confidence with every triumph'

Mill Reef and Geoff Lewis coast home to victory in the 1971 Derby

hand said, 'Display rolled about a bit coming up the hill and, although I was squeezed right on the line, it made no difference.'

The winning jockey had no doubts. 'Half-way up the hill,' said Bill, 'I knew I was going to catch Display and West Side Story. While they were fading, my filly was finishing fast. Nobody touched anybody else and I must have won in any case.'

The Wragg colt Miralgo was already strongly fancied for the Derby, but Bill was to win another classic before that fateful day at Epsom. This was undoubtedly a bad year. Vincent O'Brien's Sebring was strongly fancied for the Derby until the Irish Guineas saw his failure without semblance of excuse. His American owner, Townsend Martin, stranded at Shannon because of gales, had dashed across Ireland by car and arrived on the Curragh just in time to see the defeat of his favourite.

Drawn No. 1 on the stands side, Sebring jumped off well, but was tucked in behind the leaders by O'Brien's new Australian, dour, long-legged perfectionist Pat Glennon. Three furlongs out, as England's Catchpole, who had finished sixth in the Newmarket classic, led on the far rails, Glennon brought Sebring out for his effort. The big bay only ran on at the same pace.

A furlong from home Williamson came into the picture on the 20/1 outsider Arctic Storm. With a beautifully timed run he brought his colt between Catchpole and the fence to win by one and a half lengths from 25/1 St Denys with Catchpole, another 20/1 chance, third.

Although Arctic Storm, as game a colt as ever there was, came from humble origins and did not quite stay one and a half miles, he would probably have won at Epsom, if he had held the engagement.

As it was, the favourite, after winning the Brighton Derby Trial was Major Lionel Holliday's charming quality colt Hethersett. There seemed every reason to believe that this lazy, unimpressive home-worker would avenge his unlucky sire, Hugh Lupus, who injured his back jumping one of the Epsom roads before the 1955 Derby.

Since Brighton is virtually modelled on Epsom, their trial might have been expected to succeed. Unhappily the very similarty of the two tracks was to prove its downfall. As one trainer said: 'It's bad enough taking a horse to Epsom once – let alone risking him twice on those gradients!'

By now the form for the 1962 Derby was completely topsy turvy. Tony Askew's Pindaric, trained by Tom Masson, held off his former stable companion Miralgo by a short head in the Derby Trial at Lingfield, where the Guineas' runner-up, Charles Engelhard's Romulus, was just 'not at the races'. And the late William Hill, whose expert pre-classic judgement will be sorely missed by his many friends on the racing press, declared: 'If you can find a decent pony at Hawthorn Hill, he might have a chance in the Derby.'

I became personally involved in these Derby preliminaries when I engineered the sale of a half share in the French colt King Canute to Ryan Price's patron Enid Chanelle. The bay colt was owned by his breeder, my old friend Dr Edouard Pouret, now President of the French vets.

For once the Prix du Jockey Club was run before the Epsom Derby. It was won by a very good colt, Val de Loir, in record time and prompted the Epsom appearance of Le Cantilien, Crossen and Arcor, for whom Roger Poincelet, surprise 66/1 winner of the previous year's Derby on Psidium, was engaged at the last moment.

The extraordinary build-up to this strangest of classics continued when, on the eve of the race, the Stewards of the Jockey Club suspended Young Lochinvar's rider Lester Piggott, after an inquiry into his riding of Ione at Lincoln the previous week. I have dealt with this case in another chapter. Suffice to say here that fortune favours the brave and that Lester's guardian angel may well have done him and the sport a great service by keeping him out of this particular Derby on the course, where he was already acknowledged as the greatest living exponent.

I left home early on Derby Day, because I had arranged to meet Dr and Mrs Pouret at Heathrow and drive them to Epsom. Imagine my disgust when, on our arrival at the course, the doctor and his charming blonde English wife, Jean, were refused owners' badges despite the fact that they had paid the full entrance fee for their horse, a runner in Britain's biggest race. Having come all the way from Normandy that morning and changed into morning coat, top hat and the female equivalent, they were told by the executive that they would have to go into Tattersalls.

Only after an imperial row did I manage to get an owner's badge for Edouard. I had to pay £6 for Jean's badge out of my own pocket – or, in the event, Lord Rothermere's, because it made a first class story for my paper, the *Daily Mail.* But that's not the point. Foreigners do so much for us and we do so very little for them that it's horribly embarrassing. I have known delightful members of the Australian turf hierarchy who have looked forward all their lives to the day when they could watch the Derby at Epsom. After the treatment they have received they have sworn that they would never go near the place again.

Although these criticisms still apply to a number of other courses, Epsom is now happily under the umbrella of United Racecourses and is supervised by Peter Beckwith-Smith, who, as a truly professional Clerk of the Course, is fully alive to all these problems and ensures that the charge of inhospitability can never be laid at his door.

So it was even more horrible that in the most sensational Derby in history, the third victim in three years claimed by Epsom's Black Hill should have been King Canute.

At almost the identical place where, two years earlier, the French favourite Angers died and Vincent O'Brien's Exchange Student was killed at exercise, King Canute had to be destroyed after a mêlée that brought down six of the other horses, including the 9/2 favourite Hethersett. Ryan Price said Canute's leg was 'smashed to pulp' – exactly the words used by the veterinary surgeon to describe Augers' accident.

After the event many racegoers asked why the race was not declared void. But the stewards cannot take such drastic action – even for an accident of this magnitude. Moreover the fatal spot was just out of view of the patrol camera that covered the runners coming down to Tattenham Corner. A senior official said: 'We hoped that the TV cameras would have been able to help, but it's a blind spot for them.'

So much has now been achieved since the improvements to the track. The going is incredibly different and every inch of the running is covered by the patrol camera. So Harry Carr, Wally Swinburn and King Canute did not suffer in vain.

It has always struck me as interesting that the Australians, reared on some of those tight little circuits of the bush meetings, all finished the course in a race won by Larkspur from the French pair Arcor and Le Cantilien.

Did the best horse win? That will always be debated, but certainly tiny Larkspur – he stood only 15 hands 2 inches – did nothing wrong and was himself seriously hampered.

The winning jockey Neville Sellwood said: 'When Hethersett fell, my horse had to scramble between his legs.' Only giant American Raymond Guest, who won a second Derby with Sir Ivor and then won two Cheltenham Gold Cups with L'Escargot ('He's no snail!') after the last minute fall of his chief rival on both occasions, could have had the wonderful luck to win a great classic in such circumstances. Ten years later any verdict is that Hethersett must have won his only Derby for England's finest owner-breeder Major Lionel Holliday, with whom Bill Williamson was to establish such a splendid, but all too short-lived, rapport a few years later.

On this occasion Bill was 'most disappointed' with Miralgo, 'He was lying sixth coming down the hill,' he said 'and was in a nice position when he suddenly seemed to lose his action.'

The last comment on this dreadful Derby came from the previous year's winning rider, Roger Poincelet, who had adopted the same waiting tactics on Arcor and was nearly last when the accident occurred. 'These bad horses were tired when they got to the top of the hill, and a tired horse can't get out of trouble.'

So we came to the first Irish Sweeps Derby, worth £50,027 to the winner, in which Bill was back on Arctic Storm and Poincelet was booked for Mrs Howell Jackson's good bay colt Tambourine II, trained by the maestro Etienne Pollet at Chantilly, while Pat Glennon stuck to Sebring and the British champion jockey Scobie Breasley was on Larkspur. The ill-fated Neville Sellwood, of whom I have written elsewhere, was busy in France riding for the Aga Khan and Alec Head.

We enjoyed the first taste of the superlative organisation that has characterised this great Irish prestige event. Despite Williamson's brilliant handling gallant Arctic Storm just had not the stamina to last out that stiff Curragh 1½ miles against a top class horse, which Tambourine proved himself to be. Etienne Pollet speaks no English, although he understands it well. Imagine my amazement when, immediately after the announcement 'Winner all right' an official asked me: 'Would you please tell Mr Pollet that we have his owner, Mrs Jackson, on the transatlantic telephone in Virginia!'

Hethersett duly won his Leger from Monterrico with Bill third on Miralgo, a disappointing chestnut son of Aureole, who would probably not have been as successful as he was without the Australian's gentle handling of his inherited temperament.

This reward was as richly deserved as Arctic Storm's victory in the Champion Stakes. And Major Holliday's pleasure at Doncaster was matched by the happiest moment of 1962, when Zelma Williamson, as pretty as a picture, arrived just too late for the race at Newmarket, dashed into the weighing-room enclosure, asking all and sundry: 'Where's that clever husband of mine?' Then when Bill reappeared, she kissed him fondly, an action which caused certain eyebrows to be raised! Remember this was 1962, long before the reformation of Newmarket and the relaxation of pomposity were enforced to halt the alarming decline in attendances at the headquarters of racing.

The next three years belonged to Paddy Prendergast. Not only was he the first Irish-based trainer to win the English trainers' championship, but he held the title for three successive years. Thanks to Noblesse's runaway victory in the Oaks and the classic successes of brave little Ragusa, Paddy topped the £200,000 mark in 1963.

Beaten horses are forgotten all too easily with the passage of time. Garnet Bougoure, riding as Paddy's stable jockey, was enjoying a fabulous season, but at Sandown on 13th July it was only weight that came to his aid when Bill Williamson produced Miralgo's greatest effort in the Eclipse.

It was a real Australia day. Jockeys from Down-Under scored five wins and four seconds in the first five races. Scobie Breasley and Ron Hutchinson both rode doubles.

But the palm of a great afternoon was earned by that other Melbourne pair, Bougoure and Williamson, heroes of a connoisseur's Eclipse. Two courageous colts, Khalkis and Miralgo, battled to the last stride, giving of their utmost. Yet both would have been fit to run the next day. At that time there were still too many English jockeys flogging cruelly and clumsily in their finishes. One wished they would imitate the coaxing methods of the Australian artists so that they would win more races and there would be far fewer equine rogues. Fortunately the new generation of top jockeys, fortified by the example of our own champion Lester Piggott, have done just that and the standard, as a result, is higher than for many years.

The victory of Khalkis was due to Miralgo's seven pound penalty for winning a race worth more than £4,000 – a most unfair impost which was abolished before the following year's Eclipse. Harry Wragg's horse and his jockey were undoubtedly the heroes of that memorable afternoon.

The year when the Jockey Club and National Hunt Committee in the person of Lords Howard de Walden and Cadogan demanded a Tote Monopoly ended, with Bill still riding for the Wragg stable. It was never an entirely happy partnership, however; chiefly, I believe, because both men think too much. Harry, the famous 'head waiter' of an earlier generation, was a better jockey than most of those who have ridden for him in his role of trainer. Bill, on the other hand, is at least the equal of the old maestro.

Like many owners and trainers Harry sometimes seems over optimistic about the prospects of some future classic hope. I remember going round stables with Atty Persse when Lord Sefton's new draft of yearlings had just arrived. We went into the box of a massive brown colt by Nearco out of Red Garter. The old man gazed long and hard at the animal. 'Hugh has won the Derby with this one already,' he said. 'I reckon the great soft sod will be lucky if it ever wins a seller at Newton Abbott!' He was not far wrong. Named Titian, he had a most inglorious career.

There are all too many Titians in every yard each season. One such colt prompted two of the best Wragg-Williamson stories. Bill went down to Newmarket to ride this wonderful animal in its first serious work as a two-year-old over five furlongs.

Harry, one of the few English trainers to use the stop watch consistently, was beaming as Bill and the work riders trotted back to him.

'No good,' said the stable jockey. Harry frowned. 'What d'you mean – no good? You came up there in 60⅖ seconds. That must be good.'

Bill looked at the trainer pityingly. 'I don't care if we came up in ten seconds flat. He's still no bloody good!'

Nevertheless the same animal was still believed to be a real future Derby prospect when it appeared for its first race. Pulling out all stops, Bill galvanised the ungainly colt and somehow forced him to finish close up behind the placed horses.

He was greeted with happy anticipation by his owner and trainer. In silence the Australian dismounted and took off his saddle.

'Well, what do you think of him now?', demanded Harry as though saying: 'I told you so.'

Unfortunately most owners would rather that you insulted their wives than that you told them their horses were no good. They take it as a personal affront even though you are only doing it to save them money. But, like Lester and Eph Smith, Bill never minces words. Looking straight at his questioner, he said quietly: 'I wouldn't let that get on my cow. Or, if it got on my cow, I'd have to shoot my cow!'

The end of a beautiful friendship was not far away.

Before the end of 1964 Bill was already being recognised as the ideal jockey for the big occasion. 'He's so incredibly cool,' said Harry Wragg, who, in his riding days, had been one of the coolest customers of all time.

Paddy Prendergast booked him to ride Patti in the St Leger. The filly had been backed down to favourite for the Oaks only to finish a disappointing fourth behind Homeward Bound. However, like so many of her sex, she appeared to be coming into her own for the autumn, winning the Galtres Stakes at York very easily.

Right up to the eleventh hour there had been doubts as to whether the English and the Irish Derby winner Santa Claus would run. Finally two days before the final classic Mick Rogers, whose year had been constantly harassed by journalists, announced: 'The colt was not striding out normally in his home work this morning and I have decided not to run him.'

Those who still believed in Santa Claus, rushed to back Indiana, who had finished second in the Derby at Epsom and also the French colt White Label, who had defeated Indiana in the Grand Prix. Charles Engelhard's candidate, the mount of Jimmy Lindley, was backed from 25s down to 100/7 and, taking the lead from I Titan two furlongs out, he finally earned the just reward for his consistency.

Noel Murless's plan had looked like working out when Impact took the lead after two furlongs and set a good gallop right round the turn into the straight. At this point Lester Piggott, who had always been lying handy on I Titan, went clear of his stable-companion only to surrender the lead to Lindley.

Now Indiana looked like coming home alone until suddenly the Williamson magic began to work again. With a brilliantly timed run Patti challenged fiercely. Colt and filly fought out a memorable battle until right on the post Indiana stuck his head out to gain the verdict. Prendergast was delighted. 'If only she had shown this form at Epsom,' he said, 'she must have won the Oaks.' But, of course, Williamson had not been riding her on that occasion.

Incidentally it is worth recalling the extraordinary riding of the French star, Jean Deforge, on White Label. This wealthy, gifted young man was like the girl with the curl right in the middle of her forehead. When he was good, he was very, very good, but when he was bad he was undoubtedly horrid. In this classic he was bad, adopting completely contrary tactics to the front running which had won the Grand Prix de Paris.

The colt, who had defeated Indiana when ridden by Heurteur at Longchamp, was still lying two lengths last 5½ furlongs from home. In the circumstances he ran a good race to finish sixth.

Deforge said: 'It was a terrific gallop. I couldn't follow' – a remark which was not borne out by the time, which was good but 3⅖ seconds outside Windsor Lad's record of 3 minutes 1⅗ seconds set in 1934.

As the year closed, we were treated to another of those vintage Williamson displays. This time the scene was Ascot on 9th October and once again Bill was riding for 'P.J.'

The Ascot going was perfect, but still not soft enough for Meadow Court, the big, backward bargain two-year-old, bought by Prendergast for Bing Crosby, Max Bell and Frank McMahon for only 3,000 guineas. His success in the Sandwich Stakes was due entirely to his jockey. I shall always remember it. Switching him on to the other leg in the last hundred yards, the Australian drove Meadow Court past Foothill with all the star quality and insistence of Gordon or Lester at their very best.

Paddy said: 'That was real classic riding. Williamson is a truly great jockey.'

On to Doncaster a fortnight later, when the Murless colt Leonardo looked a certain winner of the £24,830 *Timeform* Gold Cup until Williamson unleased a furious finishing burst from the Mullion's, Prendergast-trained, Hardicanute. Paddy left the scene of his triumph, declaring: 'Williamson will be my first jockey next season whenever available.'

However, there's many a slip and, by the start of the next season Paddy had taken a short-lived retainer on Paul Cook, was using his own young rider Peadar Matthews and, most important had second claim on Lester Piggott, who was still first jockey to Noel Murless.

However Dandini, a big soft grey colt, failed to come up to expectations and neither the Curragh trainer nor Lester had any say in the finishes of the first two classics.

It was different for Bill, who formed a new partnership, which was to have the most far-reaching effects in the years to come.

Major Lionel Holliday was seventy-five years old. Unpopular because of his outspoken curtness and his insistence on having his own way in everything, he was still a great breeder, who really loved and understood horses. From where I stood, he was a most admirable old man.

A master of foxhounds for many years, at Leicester sales he bought a charming, brave ten-year-old horse that I had known and hunted for some years – a tough bay cob, happily named Bobby, whom you could turn off a tarmac road and jump a gate from a standstill, who would go all day and never turn his head.

Bobby had been fired. But this made no difference to old

Holliday. He saw the character in that little gelding's eye, knew at once the sort of horse he was and bought him for his whipper-in for 200 guineas.

Several years later, when I was talking to him about his horses, the old man could tell me every bit as much about Bobby as about Hethersett or any of his other beautiful horses. And they really were beautiful horses. You can pick out the horses of certain trainers, Fred Darling, Atty Persse, Noel Murless, Paddy Prendergast, by the distinctive way in which they are turned out in the paddock. The Holliday horses stood out as a breed. They had lovely heads and they radiated quality. He may have been a martinet, but he knew just what he was doing.

Of course it must have been maddening for a trainer with the lifelong experience and expertise of Geoffrey Brooke to be telephoned before first lot at Newmarket by his owner in Yorkshire.

'Where are you taking the horses this morning?'

'The Limekilns.'

'No, you're not. I want you to go to Start Side' (or one of the other gallops).

Geoffrey found this intolerable. However the Major, after changing trainers several times, was lucky first with a much younger man, Dick Hern, who left to take over the Astor stable, and then with Walter Wharton, a charming, skilful man, who had handled the Holliday horses in the north of England until he moved down to Lagrange at the end of 1962. A true horse-lover, Walter and his owner understood each other and they both, like the Irish and the French, immediately recognised the value of Bill Williamson.

The season started with a problem. England's leading filly, Night Off, was coughing and for a long time it looked as though she would have to miss the 1,000 Guineas.

But, after winning the Major's first race of the year at Ally Pally on 12th April, Walter said he was very hopeful that Night Off would be fit to take her chance at Newmarket sixteen days later. The big bay filly, who had beaten the hot French favourite Fall in Love on the Rowley Mile in September, had been less seriously affected by the cough than most.

'She has never left her manger,' said the trainer. 'Lately I have been able to give her some good half-speed work.'

It was just sufficient because the riding of the 9/2 favourite was entrusted to Williamson and Night Off beat the French, the Irish and the Cough to keep the Newmarket Classics double in Britain. After two depressing years this boost was sorely needed by our bloodstock industry.

Rose of Mooncoin, Mabel and the big grey sprinter Attitude were the pick of the paddock, where the poverty lines on the tall bay favourite's quarters bore witness to the difficulties that Walter Wharton had overcome since she stopped coughing a month earlier. Nevertheless the filly showed her appreciation of the soft, testing ground as she cantered down extravagantly.

From then on it was up to Bill, who gave us a world-class exhibition of jockeyship to win the 1,000 Guineas for the second time in four years.

First Quita II on the far rails, and then Ruby's Princess in the centre, made the running, while Miba, Long Look, Night Off, Free Time and Night Appeal were all well there on the stands side.

Two furlongs out Rose d'Or momentarily took up the running from Quita, only to surrender it to Rose of Mooncoin. But, as his nearest rivals faded, Williamson was forced to hit the front a little sooner than he intended. Watching that now so familiar style, with the elbows in the white and maroon colours going vigorously, we thought that the favourite was all out. So did twenty-two-year-old Jean-Claude Dessaint, winner of the last two French Champion Hurdles, who forced Yami up to challenge Night Off coming out of the Dip.

But once again the Australian master of Kidology had kept a little bit in hand. Now driving in earnest with all his tremendous power, he got the necessary response from his courageous mount to win by a neck. 'She fought well,' he said as he returned, full of admiration for the filly.

It was a triumph for Major Holliday, who bred both the sire and the dam of the winner of this, his third classic. He had won the 1951 Oaks with Neasham Belle and the St Leger of 1962 with Hethersett.

'If I live long enough, I'll win them all,' said the old Yorkshireman. Unfortunately it was not to be. Nor was he to live long enough to witness the greatest triumph for his breeding, with which Bill was again to be associated.

The racing air in Sea Bird's year was laden with dope and suspicions of dope. In her next outing, the Musidora Stakes at York, Night Off, now favourite for the Oaks and ridden this time by Joe Mercer, walked past the post tailed off, last of five runners.

'My filly is desperately ill,' said Major Holliday. 'She's in a terrible state, almost dead. I think she has been got at – doped, poisoned. I feel sure of it.'

His fears were reinforced by the betting. Night Off, forecast a strong favourite at 11/10 on, had been easy in the market, slipping from even money to 11/10 against as support came for the eventual winner, the Irish filly Arctic Melody. After the race she was led in for an official dope-test in a very distressed state with her head hanging. The Major said: 'I thought there was something wrong with her beforehand. She didn't seem herself and was sweating in the paddock.'

These were exactly the same symptoms exhibited the previous day by the strong Derby fancy Look Sharp in the Dante Stakes, when for no apparently valid reason the Stewards failed to order a dope-test. It is incredible how bad public relations in this respect have been over the years. They have improved, but still leave a lot to be desired. The public must not be treated like children. They should surely be told everything possible, consistent with security.

Furthermore, although, in the case of Night Off, the result of the test was returned as negative, it seeemed extremely likely that a new drug was being used. The only real answer to this kind of situation must surely be a detailed inspection of all big bookmakers' books to discover by whom the favourite has been opposed in the market. Detection can start from there. On several occasions the bookies have said that they would be only too willing to co-operate. The pitiful performances of Ribofilio and another brave Holliday filly in the Newmarket classics three years later were to highlight this problem.

As Dr Edouard Pouret has pointed out, 'You need such a minute quantity of some modern drugs, that it must all too often be possible to escape detection. Blood tests, as well as saliva and urine, should undoubtedly be taken in all doubtful cases.'

Fortunately Lord Wigg and Sir Randle Feilden were alive to the problem and, with the backing of extra money from the Levy Board, there is hope of reform on the horizon.

Pat Glennon duly won the Derby on Sea Bird and finished up by winning the Arc de Triomphe on Etienne Pollet's colt, a brilliant but temperamental chestnut, whose faults were to be transmitted, multiplied, to his son Gyr to the discomfort of Pat's countryman, Bill Williamson.

It was a strange combination. Pat, as dour as the gloomiest Aussie music hall comic, spoke no French. Pollet refused to speak English, although he had an American wife.

Whenever there were essential orders, Glennon would stand, looking at the gesticulating French trainer for some minutes. Then he would say in the broadest Strine: 'Shershee Madam Polly.' As long as she was at home, Mrs Pollet had to act as interpreter. However, it worked and, if Glennon had not had family troubles back in Australia, the association would probably have lasted indefinitely.

Pollet said: 'French jockeys hate making the running. Australians, trained to judge pace expertly, are very good at it. As a result Glennon has won me many races, which I would have not otherwise have won.'

Of course on Sea Bird Pat was able to ride a model race on that sunny afternoon in October, but the chestnut would have won the Arc however he had been ridden.

There were no fewer than four Derby winners in the field – Sea Bird (English), Reliance (French), Meadow Court (Irish) and Tom Rolfe (American) as well as Anilin, the previous year's Russian Derby winner.

Sea Bird and Reliance were the two horses to sweat up in the parade. Tom Rolfe cantered down to the post in true American fashion, accompanied by a hack.

England's hope Oncidium was reluctant to enter the stalls and the last to leave them. From an otherwise good break the Italian challenger, Marco Visconti, and the blinkered Irish colt, Khalife, disputed the lead for the first mile with Anilin third close up. Piggott moved Meadow Court into third position as the Russian colt took the lead entering the straight.

But suddenly in one dramatic moment the race was all over, as Glennon, riding with the supreme confidence of a jockey who knows beyond all doubt that he is on a champion, dashed Sea Bird into the lead.

From that moment, even though he was hanging to the left all the way up the long straight, it was just a matter of by how far the Epsom Derby winner would win. Reliance, swishing his tail in response to Yves Saint-Martin's frenzied riding, struggled gamely but had no chance of reducing the leaway. Sea Bird passed the post six lengths clear. Five lengths behind Reliance the Rothschild pair, Diatome and Free Ride, fought out a photo-finish for third place. Anilin was fifth behind Free Ride, Tom Rolfe sixth and Meadow Court, the best of the Anglo-Irish contingent, eighth.

Although I never liked Sea Bird as a horse, he was obviously one of the greatest race horses of all time. If further proof were needed it was provided a month later when Diatome won the Washington International.

Meadow Court had been the best horse in these islands during this unhappy first year of the Turf Board's reign – a year which had been so seriously blighted by the spread of equine 'flu. Vets reported that many animals, either because they had the disease worse than others, or because they were brought back into work too soon, had been permanently affected. Unfortunately compulsory inoculation was not to be introduced for five years, during which time all too many trainers were to declare, as they did at the end of 1965, 'Thank goodness that's over.'

There were rays of sunshine in the gloom, however, as Jockey Club member, Jim Philipps, blamed our breeders and trainers for the decline in British racing, and the trainers' federation decided to go all out for the tote monopoly.

The Jockey Club's handling of the Les Hall case was a major step forward. The Hampshire trainer was suspended by the Stewards of the Jockey Club after his filly Littleton Queen had run moderately at Salisbury. Hitherto this would have been a sentence which would have ruined his chance of ever pursuing his profession again.

But after only fifteen weeks, the shortest disqualification ever inflicted on an English trainer, he was reprieved. The chestnut filly, who had brought about his downfall, bought by Ken Cundell for 1,450 guineas at Sandown, had not shown on three subsequent outings and fetched only 280 guineas when offered for sale at Ascot in September. Although this established a wonderful precedent, it was hard to dispute the argument that the authorities were still picking on the little men. Five years were to pass before this impression was corrected.

On the same day that the ban on Hall was lifted the Jockey Club, acting on the recommendations of the Norfolk Report, decided to encourage owners and trainers to give more opportunities to apprentices.

From the start of the 1966 season the apprentice scale of allowances would read as follows: 7 lbs. until an apprentice had won ten races (instead of six); 5 lbs. until he had won fifty races (instead of twenty-five) and 3 lbs. until he had won seventy-five (instead of forty).

Writing now with hindsight, time has already proved the immense value of the new rule, which has played an enormous part in the resurgence of British jockeyship. The production of such as Tony Murray, Pat Eddery and Philip Waldron would have been far more difficult without it.

On the debit side we were still suffering badly from the lack of starting-stalls. Not only had Oncidium been left in the Arc, but Solstice, our other hope, had had to be withdrawn after showing violent dislike for the stalls in the pre-race trials of this unfamiliar method of dispatch.

The stalls experiment in the Chesterfield Stakes at Newmarket on 8th July had been an unqualified success. In the 50 seconds that it took to start the race from the moment Alec Marsh called in the twelve runners until he pressed the button and they flew out straight and true, the many critics were silenced except for the frustrated rumblings of some of the old brigade.

The late Sir Jack Jarvis said: 'Regardless of the result I think stalls are awful.' Afterwards he said grudgingly: 'Well, I suppose they might be all right for short races.' The Duke of Norfolk was reported as saying that horses wouldn't like the stalls any more than his cattle at Arundel would like to be mechanised. As machine-milking is now the order of the day throughout the country, this hardly seemed a valid argument.

Predictably Lester Piggott won on Ron Mason's Track Spare and declared: 'This is now the sixth country in which I have ridden a winner from starting-stalls. They will succeed and I am in favour.'

Unfortunately, although the Jockey Club decided in principle to go ahead with the introduction of starting-stalls after seven highly successful experimental races at Newmarket, they still had not decided on the most suitable type and were further delayed through shortage of money.

From Bill Williamson's point of view the big news had come in mid-September, when he had accepted the retainer as first jockey to Major Holliday in 1966.

The new year opened with a surprise move when breeding expert Peter Willett, introduced by the Turf Board Chairman, Major-General Sir Randle Feilden, gave a warning – at, of all places, the Royal Society of Arts – that only far more revenue from betting could save the British racehorse breeding industry. For the first time in its history of more than 200 years the Society discussed racing. Peter pointed out the faults which had led to the impoverished state of this industry, once a national asset and the envy of the world.

'No fewer than thirty of the 100 English classic races run from 1946 to 1965 were won by horses bred outside England and Ireland,' he said, giving as his main reasons for the unhappy condition of the industry 'complacency, disregard of unsoundness and over emphasis on precocity'.

'How much happier a lot have the breeders in France, where the leading owner received more than £250,000 in stakes and more than £25,000 in breeders' prizes last year in contrast to this country where the leading owner – a Frenchman – won £61,000.'

Since the second world war air transport had steadily opened up international racing, ruthlessly exposing the limitations of the British breeding industry.

Strange to think that it was only in 1966 that Peter read this paper to the Royal Society. Since then, although American bred horses have formed a habit of winning our Derby, British horses have been sweeping the board in France to such an extent that the French authorities have changed the conditions of many races.

That same emphasis on precocity has once again come to the rescue. Remember Atty Persse's one essential quality for a racehorse – 'speed, more speed and still more speed?' The French ignored this principle to their cost. The Americans and British are reaping the rewards of sticking to it.

Now Paddy Prendergast came out in favour of a tote monopoly and signed up a new Australian, Des Lake from Sydney, who surprised the Curragh by riding work in a shiny white crash-helmet, but was to prove to have been thrown in at the deep end when still too young and brash for export.

France was having troubles this year. Cross-channel owners and trainers were very upset when an outbreak of swamp fever on the continent caused our Ministry of Agriculture to ban French horses from entering this country for any reason.

For Bill Williamson this was a lean year. He ended the season with only twenty-nine winners and not even a place in the classics. Obviously he was still not fully appreciated by our trainers. At the end of a troubled year, which had seen his parting from Lester Piggott, Noel Murless engaged another Australian, the great Sydney rider George Moore, as first jockey to Warren Place in 1967.

At last we had starting-stalls at the opening of the 1967 season. Unfortunately there were – and, for that matter still are – not enough stalls to go round. I am convinced that the big racecourses should be instructed to buy and man their own stalls. Newmarket and Newbury could draw on local stable-lads, while United Racecourses, Epsom, Sandown and Kempton, must be wealthy enough to share a set of stalls, operated by Epsom lads.

This was the year when George Moore and Noel Murless set the Turf alight. It was also the year when Lord Harding retired from the Levy Board and Lord Wigg was appointed as his successor.

Walter Wharton, Bill Williamson and racing in general suffered a severe loss with the death of Major Holliday, who had so belatedly been elected a member of the Jockey Club.

They speedily made his son Brook a member, but the guiding light had gone out and, although some outstanding horses have still carried the white and maroon silks, the empire seemed already on the wane when Bill unleashed Vaguely Noble's challenge to win the *Observer* Gold Cup most impressively.

Unhappily the colt had not been considered good enough or well enough grown as a yearling to be entered for any of the classics. Besides, as a son of the late Sir Winston Churchill's Vienna, he was not considered real classic material.

Nevertheless, when the large Holliday draft of horses in training was offered at the December Sales at the end of this foot-and-mouth season, there was betting on the amount that Vaguely Noble would fetch and certain confidence that he would break the previous British auction record for a horse in training of 47,000 guineas. Favourite in the betting at 4/1 was a price between 85,000 and 89,000 guineas.

But this figure was soon left far behind when the bay colt, who had been closely inspected by innumerable experts, entered the ring looking magnificent.

The sale climaxed a day of hectic selling dominated by the dollar and the franc in Tattersalls' ring. Bidding opened at 80,000 guineas and rose quickly.

'He could still be cheap,' shouted the auctioneer Ken Watt to the packed ring as the bids rose above 130,000 guineas. French bloodstock agent Godolphin Darley, who had made the running, hesitated and in stepped the splendidly loud extrovert American dealer, Albert Yank, conspicuous among the sheepskin uniformed crowd in a bright fluorescent orange ski-suit. Pandemonium set in when the hammer fell at a new world record price for a horse in training of 136,000 guineas to Mr Yank, who was apparently acting on behalf of his 'buddy', Hollywood plastic surgeon Dr Robert Franklin 'and his beautiful wife Wilma'.

It was late in the evening and we were all desperate to get this sensational story into our first editions. We cornered Mr Yank outside the ring – a little tight posse of journalists under the arc lights now quite oblivious to the cold of that winter night and the deep, damp straw underfoot.

Yank was acting in conjunction with the Anglo-Irish Agency and naturally the colt went to the Curragh to be trained by

Paddy Prendergast. This was an admirable arrangement because Williamson, who had done so much to help Wharton in the making of Vaguely Noble, had just signed up as first jockey to Rossmore Lodge in 1968.

However, Texas oil tycoon, multi-millionaire Bunker Hunt, who soon bought a large share of the colt, knew more about racing than the beauty surgeon. He quickly realised that if this colt was to justify his purchase price, there was only one chance. He must win the world's greatest and richest race, the Arc de Triomphe. Nothing else would suffice. This was what the whole gamble depended on. So he decided to send Vaguely Noble to Chantilly to be trained by Etienne Pollet. It was a bitter blow for Prendergast and for his jockey.

After Sir Ivor had proved himself an outstanding horse by winning the Guineas and the Derby, Vaguely Noble appeared at Chantilly on French Derby day. I have never seen such improvement in so short a time. He was big and superbly powerful, but his jockey was that controversial figure Jean Deforge in the 1½ mile Prix du Lys.

Although boxed in on the turn, the ex-Holliday boy broke out with a tremendous burst to win cantering by eight lengths from Nightshade. A stewards' inquiry into the manner of his breakout, in which Deforge had appeared to hit another runner, allowed the result to stand.

Said Pollet: 'I have never known such acceleration in any horse.' Praise indeed from the trainer of Right Royal, Sea Bird and Hula Dancer.

So here at last was an English-bred champion fully capable of holding his own with America's Irish-trained Sir Ivor.

However, he was now a massive, heavy-topped colt and not so easy to train. He had cantered in at Longchamp and Chantilly. These had been comparatively minor events. The opposition was different in the Grand Prix de St. Cloud, run in that damp thundery heat typical of mid-summer Paris in July. As I have written elsewhere, this was Sandy Barclay's weekend. He and his trainer Noel Murless were fresh from beating Taj Dewan and Sir Ivor in the Eclipse when they challenged with Hopeful Venture, and in a thrilling contest scored the Queen's first victory on French soil.

Deforge at his most unpredictable, kept Vaguely Noble well in the rear, continued to lay much too far out of his ground, came too late and finished third. He said: 'Vaguely Noble lost his race when he slipped and failed to act on the first bend. He came too wide.'

The colt, who had started at 2–1 on, appeared to have lost weight and was sweating in the paddock. Things would have to be different next time. They were, thanks to the wisdom of his owners and trainer, who decided to re-unite him with his former jockey Bill Williamson. In his come-back at Longchamp he reproduced all his old brilliance to win impressively.

So on 6th October when we came to Longchamp, the English bookies were offering 5/2 Vaguely Noble, 5/1 Sir Ivor, 8/1 Dhaudevi and Roseliere, 16/1 Ribero, who had defeated Sir Ivor in the Irish Sweeps Derby.

What a day it was when Vaguely Noble restored the prestige of British racing and brought off the bloodstock gamble of the century by winning this £83,400 Prix de l'Arc de Triomphe. Thousands of British visitors had earlier been rewarded by the sight of Peter O'Sullevan's Be Friendly, equipped with blinkers like his sire Skymaster, proving himself Europe's champion sprinter by winning the £16,000 Prix de l'Abbaye de Longchamp at odds of 100/30.

Seventeen runners paraded for the big race. Sir Ivor, ridden by Lester Piggott – who had so brilliantly won the previous day's Cesarewitch on Major Rose – looked the pick of the field.

As the runners were entering the stalls, Ribero was kicked hard in the groin. 'He lost a pint of blood,' said Brian Taylor, 'and had no chance after that.' David McCall said afterwards that they tried desperately to withdraw the poor lame Englehard bay but to no avail. So strong is the hold of the Tierce throughout France that there would have been dreadful ructions if a candidate were to be taken out at the last minute. This seems utterly ridiculous as well as being cruel and it is high time that the French authorities altered the practice.

The Russian colt, Zbor, led for two furlongs. Then Luthier took it up from the French Oaks winner, Roseliere, Arjou, Luciano and Sir Ivor. Luthier and Roseliere disputed the lead on the turn.

As the field swung into the straight, Williamson, riding with ice-cool confidence, loosed Vaguely Noble's head and took the lead, chased by Sir Ivor. Riding only with hands and heels, the great Australian artist came right away and, despite all Piggott's strenuous driving, Sir Ivor could make no impression on the winner, who scored by three imperious lengths in the style of a true champion. Carmarthen was four lengths away third, a length in front of Roseliere with the runaway English Oaks winner La Lagune fifth.

Vaguely Noble had beaten no fewer than seven individual classic winners. Williamson said: 'He was going so well, that I knew I was going to win after we had covered two furlongs and never had an anxious moment.'

Piggott said. 'I was always with the winner, but he was pulling over me all the time. That's the best race Sir Ivor has ever run.'

Some tribute. And the irrespressible Albert Yank declared: 'We stole the biggest bargain of all time. He is now worth £2 million on the international market.'

Dr Franklin was full of gratitude to England. 'He's a credit to his country,' said the surgeon, 'and to his late breeder, Major Holliday. We take off our hats to English breeding, which has shown it can produce the best horse in the world.'

On the whole it has been a most satisfactory year for Bill. He had ridden a Royal Ascot double for Paddy on Hunt Cup day with the Mullions' World Cup and Bill Stirling's Grizel in the Jersey and the Queen Mary Stakes, and won the Warren Stakes at Goodwood on Karabas owned by Lord Iveagh and Rory More O'Ferrall. In the St Leger, however, riding the one-paced Canterbury, he went under by a short head to an inspired Piggott on Ribero.

However, despite his big race triumphs, true recognition in England still eluded forty-four-year-old Bill. He didn't really worry. 'I've signed up again for Paddy Prendergast and for Etienne Pollet in Paris on Sundays,' he said as the year came to a close.

Unhappily, as has so often been said, you cannot come without the horse. Every stable, however well managed, has its ups and downs. Bill had come to Paddy just after the Curragh trainer's great years. The pendulum had swung and the horses on the whole were not up to the standard of those wonderful days in the mid-sixties. Furthermore the stable suffered severely from a bad lot of vaccine in the inoculation for equine 'flu, which was now causing such havoc in the sport.

Bill won the Irish 1,000 Guineas on the Mullions' big bright bay filly Wenduyne, but now, in Geoff Lewis's first big year, 1969, it was the Australian's first trainer in Europe, Seamus McGrath, who came to the rescue with a vengeance.

Levmoss, a handsome son of the miler Le Levanstell, must be the most versatile horse for many, many years. He won the Prix du Cadran (the French Gold Cup) and came to Royal Ascot for the Gold Cup, the world's greatest staying race, backed by the supreme confidence of his jockey, who had already taken the Coventry Stakes on Paddy's stylishly speedy colt Prince Tenderfoot.

'Since I brought him over from Australia, I have never known Bill so confident,' said Seamus.

For the first half of the 2½-mile race Bill was content to dispute last place with Riboccare and Mount Athos a long way behind Coolroy, Fortissimo and Torpid. He was just starting his effort entering Swinley Bottom, when Mount Athos suddenly stopped to a canter. Ron Hutchinson said afterwards: 'My horse just refused to race any further.'

Quite undeterred, Bill brought Levmoss smoothly through his field to win by four lengths from Torpid with Fortissimo, as game as ever, three lengths away third. Starting at 15/8, Levmoss was only the second Irish winner of the Gold Cup (Gladness had won for Vincent O'Brien in 1958). Moreover, the McGrath colt was the first horse to win the French and English Gold Cups since Marcel Boussac's Arbar twenty-one years earlier. A fine stayer, we thought, discussing him. We were even more wrong than usual.

The next day Bill rode his third winner of the Royal meeting on stable-companion Laurence O (an abbreviation of Dublin's patron saint, Laurence O'Toole) in Britain's longest flat race, the 2 mile 6 furlong Queen Alexandra Stakes, which will always be associated with my boyhood hero Brown Jack. In spite of a ludicrous crawl in the early stages, it now produced a stirring finish and Bill was seen at his rousing best. He had to work really hard to drive his lazy mount a short head clear of Valoroso. As he was greeted by the owner-trainer, he gave him that familiar quizzical look through half-closed eyes. 'Don't ever do that to me again Seamus, I'm worn out!' His friend laughed. 'Do you good,' he said, 'it'll make you fit for dinner tonight.'

Bill earned that dinner. Although he had been fourth favourite for the Ascot jockeys' championship, he clinched the title with Executive in the King's Stand Stakes, bringing his score to four winners.

September saw Bill winning the Doncaster Cup for Paddy Prendergast on the previous season's Leger runner-up Canterbury, beating Laurence O by a comfortable five lengths. He was riding more frequently in Paris, but, as the bookmakers offered short odds about Irish Derby winner Prince Regent and Park Top for the Arc, nobody guessed that his greatest moment was close at hand.

Nobody had given it a second thought when Levmoss, carrying a jumping weight, had won a high-class handicap over a mile at Baldoyle. Certainly no-one, except Seamus McGrath, gave him any chance of winning the Arc when the twenty-four starters paraded on a day when Lester Piggott rode four winners and was re-united with his favourite mare Park Top.

But it was Bill, riding Levmoss with masterly brilliance, who stole the Arc for Ireland in record time. By sheer jockeyship the Australian on the 51/1 outsider foiled the gallant bid of Park Top. And Lester, who received special cheers from the vast crowd whenever he cantered down, was the first to admit that for once he had been out-generalled. He couldn't have been more sporting and I realised then that the one-time 'wonder boy' had become a very mature man.

'I blame myself entirely,' he said. 'I should have won. I came too late.'

Levmoss, winner of those Gold Cups over 2½ miles, was believed to have little chance in the 1½ mile championship, worth a record £89,000, on fast ground hardened by hot sunshine. Although Ribofilio was sweating in the parade, both Park Top and Prince Regent looked superb.

The English and Italian Derby winners, Blakeney and Bonconte di Montefeltro, were soon disputing the lead, closely attended by the Grand Prix winner Chapparal. Shoemaker and Levmoss were always handy. Park Top and Prince Regent were in the middle of the field. On the final turn Bonconte di Montefeltro led from Chapparal, Shoemaker, Levmoss and Goodly. The maestro was poised to pounce.

Once in the straight, Bill sent Levmoss into the lead just as he had done when winning on Vaguely Noble the year before. But that brain was working overtime in a way that only Lester's of the English riders does today. He would be expected to 'do a Vaguely Noble', particularly on a staying, dual-Gold Cup winner, who would surely be found lacking in finishing speed.

So this time he kidded for fully half a furlong. Green clad elbows flapping, he appeared all out to the other jockeys.

Suddenly the Australian pulled out all the stops, and, catching them unawares he hurtled Levmoss into an unassailable lead. Lester, who had been waiting coolly, weaving through the field so that he had Park Top perfectly poised for her famous late burst, was taken by surprise.

Seeing the danger too late, he rose frantically and the mare responded to his calls with the utmost gallantry. Eating up the ground with great strides, she failed by only three quarters of a length at the post.

Only the previous week the Jockey Club Senior Steward, Major-General Sir Randle Fielden had said: 'Piggott has told me that Williamson is the best jockey in the world.'

Seamus, owner-breeder-trainer of the winner, said, 'I brought Bill over from Australia in the first place. He is the best jockey who has ever ridden for me. Levmoss must be the best in the world to come back from Cup distances and win the Arc de Triomphe.'

He must surely be right. Of all the stallions in the world Levmoss is the one I would most like to use, combining, as he does, breeding, guts, quality, stamina and utter blinding brilliant speed over any distance. Just think of the great horses, who have raced over that Longchamp mile and a half. The time test showed that he beat them all. I said originally that it was sheer jockeyship which won the Arc. Perhaps future Turf historians may decide that, in fact, Lester rode a wonderful race to get Park Top so close to a supreme champion.

The rest of that fabulous day belonged to Lester, as we shall see in his chapter.

Only a week after the Arc Bill and 'P.J.' decided not to renew their partnership the following year. Paddy engaged Melbourne champion Johnny Miller to follow in the steps of his countrymen Ron Hutchinson, Garnet Bougoure, Des Lake and Williamson as first jockey to the Rossmore Lodge stable. Bill would go riding for Gordon Smyth, who had held second claim in 1969.

Earlier I had been asked to offer him the job of riding for Madame Elizabeth Couturié and Etienne Pollet. He had thought the matter over before saying: 'Thank them very much indeed for the invitation. But I don't speak the language and I have my family here in England. Besides there's more to life than just racing, isn't there?'

I frequently wonder whether there is another jockey in the world who would have made that remark.

Nevertheless at the start of 1970 it was abundantly clear that Bill, already naturally the idol of the French crowds, would be required in Paris regularly. Etienne Pollet had cut his string right down and had sent most of his owners and their horses to his former assistant, François Boutin, who had, in his first season, sent out the Oaks winner La Lagune from the new stables built by Dr Edouard Pouret between Chantilly and Lamorlaye. One horse had kept Pollet in the game, the giant chestnut son of Sea Bird, Gyr.

In a few short years the Guest family had made an enormous impact on European racing. Raymond had won the Derby twice, his sister Diana, the Comtesse de la Valdene, had won the Irish Sweeps Derby with Prince Regent and now their brother Winston, one of the all-time polo greats, had bred this extraordinary animal.

Pollet, a master of his profession if ever there was one, had, of course, trained Sea Bird and knew all the horse's peculiarities. They were magnified several times in this enormous gangling colt, who was often rudely described as a camel. His trainer knew, however, that he had quite exceptional ability. Perhaps the most remarkable feature of this horse was the size of his head, an enormous affair with a white blaze, which would have been more appropriate on one of James Pigg's hunters than on a high-class racehorse.

When the £35,000 Grand Criterium arrived a week after the Arc, Geoff Lewis, who had won the Irish Derby for Pollet on Prince Regent, had the mount on Gyr. I think even Lester would have had his work cut out to wagon the chestnut that day. Nevertheless Gyr was even money favourite to win Pollet his eighth Criterium since 1956. He was even provided with a pacemaker in Silver Table.

The danger, however, was already clearly the neat dark bay Relko colt Breton, owned by Yorkshireman Peter Butler, trained by Mick Bartholomew and ridden by Lester. As the ten runners for Europe's richest two-year-old event left the gate Silver Table took up the running and led from Breton with Gyr close up third on the inside. Geoff was shut in on the turn so that his long-striding mount was repeatedly checked and dropped right back.

As soon as they entered the straight, Lester sent Breton into the lead and, galloping strongly, made his best way home, followed by Freddy Head on stable-companion Baroque.

Meanwhile poor Geoff, desperate to get to the outside, bumped Bill Pyers' mount Faraway Son. Hopelessly unbalanced Gyr sprawled and floundered. With only two furlongs to go he was in seventh position. A furlong out he recovered his stride and fairly ate up the ground to finish third only two and a half lengths behind Breton, who had beaten Baroque by a length.

Immediately the objection hooter blared out. At the enquiry Geoff was shown the film of the race and was suspended for four days. Gyr was relegated to fourth place and Faraway Son promoted to third. The ever-popular English jockey explained: 'Gyr ran a very good race indeed. I had a lovely run. But Mr Pollet had instructed me to come on the outside. It took me some time to get him out and by then the race was over. He is still a big baby, mentally and physically. There is no doubt that next year over 1½ miles I will definitely beat Breton. Mine will be a super horse over a distance of ground.'

He was right. But it was Gyr's misfortune to have been foaled in the same year as Nijinsky. Furthermore, Geoff had ridden the Sea Bird colt for the last time. Pollet decided that there was only one man for this colt with the one-sided mouth, who hung so badly that he was a menace to himself and to others – Bill Williamson.

The new partnership appeared at Longchamp in the £15,000 Prix Daru on 19th April. Their victory was due more to Bill's superb horsemanship, however, than to the courage of Sea Bird's son, who was still hopelessly hemmed-in a furlong out. There seemed no possible way through as, full of running, he tracked the weakening grey pacemaker Rolig Fan and Lester on The Swell. Bill's lightning reactions dictated a desperate move. He pulled the long-striding chestnut back and started a new run on the outside.

It still looked 1,000 to 1 against, yet somehow he got Gyr balanced and that tremendous stride beat Armos by a nostril with The Swell third. While the photograph was being developed, Bill alone of the large crowd believed that the 5/4 on favourite had won this 1 mile 2½ furlong test. He just smiled wryly.

'It was that great big head of his that did the trick,' he said. 'It's early to say Gyr's a champion, but he's certainly accelerating like a very good horse indeed.'

Although no horse placed in the Darn had won the Derby in twenty-nine years, Pollet still had great expectations of rounding off a wonderful career with Sea Bird's son, despite his awkward conformation.

'This colt is only half fit,' he said. 'He will run in the Prix Hocquart over the Derby distance before Epsom.'

The bookmakers immediately made Gyr favourite for the Derby at 3/1 six weeks before the race. It was as good as a notice telling punters not to bet until much nearer the day. Nijinsky, destined to run in the Guineas ten days later was on offer at 5/1.

After Lester had won the two Newmarket classics on Nijinsky and Humble Duty, we assembled in Paris once again to watch the British champion's bid for a third classic victory in five days through Breton in the French Guineas. But Lester became the meat in an Australian sandwich and once again lost out to Bill.

As pacemaking Cordobes dropped back at the entrance to the straight, Bill Pyers sent Faraway Son into the lead on the rails, tracked by the odds-on Breton. Before Lester could challenge he found Bill and Caro going strongly on his outside. Had Breton accelerated at this stage, he would surely have got through. But, driving for home Faraway Son began to drift away from the fence, completing the sandwich. Even as Faraway Son crossed the line half a length in front of Caro with Breton three quarters of a length away third, that hooter sounded again. And the stewards speedily decided to award the race to Caro, place Breton second and Faraway Son third. Bill had won another classic.

Lester said: 'I would not have won the race, but as the rules stand I should have been given it. Faraway Son came away from the rails and Caro leaned on me all the way up the straight.'

Back again a week later for the Hocquart, as the pace really warmed up.

Although Gyr won the £18,040 traditional trial over the full Derby distance, he eased in the classic betting. He had dwarfed his rivals in the paddock and was backed down to 5/1 on.

Carrying his head on one side, he gave a roughish ride to Bill, who already had a black eye and a bandaged hand from a minor accident the previous day. Gyr improved steadily from the entrance to the straight to win by two lengths. Those who expected a sensational burst were disappointed, but the big chestnut kept faithfully to a straight course and was only slightly shaken up to win in average time.

Winston Guest was thoroughly satisfied. 'Etienne Pollet is deliberately timing the colt's preparation for Epsom,' he said, adding, 'Williamson is getting to know Gyr well and, although he is a difficult ride, they are getting on splendidly.'

Like Sea Bird, who had hung so badly to the left at Longchamp, Gyr was expected to be far more at home on Epsom's left hand circuit.

Bill, riding David Robinson's Yellow God, had finished second to Lester and Nijinsky in the Guineas at Newmarket. He was determined to go one better at Epsom and the papers boosted the Piggott-Williamson rivalry.

Nijinsky napped on the way down and, in the stalls, Gyr, increasingly harassed during the preliminaries reared and plunged striking his great head, cutting his forelegs and possibly losing his race.

But on the way down the hill after Tattenham Corner Bill brought Gyr fast on the outside and took the lead from Great Wall two furlongs out, raising his own hopes and those of Nijinsky's critics. But entering the dip Lester swept the big Canadian colt between Gyr and Stintino to win by 2½ lengths. Stintino was third three lengths further away.

Bill, bitterly disappointed, said: 'All that horse had to do was to get the trip – and he got it. Although Gyr tried all ways to get out of the stalls, he settled beautifully and acted perfectly on the track. He would have won any normal Derby.'

What a judge he is. Sassafras, who had finished third to Stintino in the Prix Lupin seventeen days earlier proceeded to win the French Derby at Chantilly. Notwithstanding what was to come, the formbook said that Gyr would have won that Prix du Jockey Club by about five lengths.

Despite his Derby set-back Bill was on the crest of the wave in 1970. On 14th June he flew to Chantilly for a typically cool, smooth two lengths winning ride in the French Oaks on Seamus McGrath's Sweet Mimosa. This 23/1 victory from England's Highest Hopes, who returned 11½ to 1 for a place was the most shattering Tierce buster since Levmoss's Arc. And Sweet Mimosa was a full-sister to that great horse! What a gold-mine he must be.

Three weeks later we saw Bill reach a new peak when he overcame all the problems of Gyr – and the opposition – to win the Grand Prix de Saint Cloud. Worn out and pouring with sweat as he dismounted from the huge chestnut, our Australian maestro said: 'It was difficult to say the least.'

Then, walking in through French owners and trainers acclaiming him as 'the greatest', he added: 'It was like riding two horses.'

After his Epsom experience many doubted whether Gyr, taut

and excited, would ever enter the stalls. But, although Bill rode him straight in, he came out last and remained in that position, clearly unhappy on the turning, left-handed circuit.

Meanwhile the signs were ominous for the 10–9 on favourite, because Gary Moore on Durango, pacemaker to Lester Piggott's mount Yelapa, was cutting out the running smartly from Gyr's leader Potamockere. Once your rival's pacemaker collars yours, you are apt to be in trouble.

At halfway Durango still led as Lester moved Yelapa up into third place. Yves Saint-Martin on Tapalque and Maurice Philipperon on Grandier were right there. But Gyr was still a long way last of the eight runners.

As they turned into the straight, the favourite was still in that position and Bill was obviously having all his work cut out to keep the Derby runner-up balanced.

A furlong out, however, he rallied his colt with a superhuman effort, picked him up and swept past the field in the middle of the track to win by two lengths from Grandier with Hallez a short head away third and Tapalque fourth. The time, 2 minutes 36.8 seconds, was the fastest for twenty years.

Etienne Pollet was thrilled with his jockey. 'Gyr got very excited,' he said, 'because he remembered how he had hurt himself in the stalls at Epsom.'

British Jockey Club member, Jim Philipps, who had won earlier that afternoon with Welsh Saint, said simply: 'He is wonderful, Williamson.'

And the former leading French jockey, now a top trainer, George Bridgland, said: 'it is marvellous to watch classic riding again. All apprentices should be made to watch the film of this race. I don't believe any other jockey in the world today could have kept Gyr on the course – let alone won the race.'

We will leave Bill on that note, because Gyr, chased round the Longchamp paddock by a score of photographers, was to lose his chance long before the start of an Arc de Triomphe, whose story is told elsewhere in this book.

Bill rode for the Aga Khan in Paris in 1971. In 1972 he returned to England as first jockey to our leading owner, David Robinson, the man, who, like Major Holliday, is unpopular with the Establishment because of his forthright views, but is recognised as the punters' friend because his splendidly managed horses are always having a go.

It is an ideal partnership with Bill Williamson, the quiet Australian, whose guts, wit, shining integrity and great horsemanship have decorated the British racing scene so admirably. Long may it last.

6: George Moore

George Moore streaked across the English racing firmament like a turbulent meteor, so that even those of us who knew what to expect, were once again amazed at the sheer star-quality of the little prima donna from Sydney.

I have written that he was the greatest and I'll stick to that opinion, not simply because it has been endorsed by no less a judge than Lord Rosebery, but because of George's unique record, spanning his entire adult riding career, of one winner in every three rides.

Nevertheless, I think that this verdict may be unfair to Lester and Scobie, who had stuck it out, working with absolute dedication in every kind of adverse condition on all the worst, as well as the best tracks, while our restless glamour-boy would upsticks and fly off to the next assignment. The consistent brilliance of the other two probably gives me the lie.

But even Sir Gordon Richards was mesmerised by George in that fabulous season of 1967. Gordon told me – and I was so struck that I wrote it down that evening in the Garden House Hotel at Cambridge during a Newmarket meeting: 'This George Moore's the greatest today because, like Steve Donoghue, he's got something the rest of us haven't got – and Steve was the greatest I ever knew or rode against.

'It's unfair really. The rest of us – Lester, Scobie, Saint-Martin or I – have our horses perfectly balanced, ready to slip through a gap the moment it opens up, always ahead of the next fellow.

'But this chap, like Steve, is different. With a wall of horses in front of them, they go for a gap which isn't there. But always, just as they go for it, it opens up.'

I knew Steve, but I only write about what I have seen with my own eyes when they were sufficiently experienced to appreciate what they saw. And the Steve I watched as a boy in the late twenties and thirties was still a great jockey with wonderful hands. But he had badly injured his arm and was a long way from the little master, who won six Derbys, rode The Tetrarch through his unbeaten career, and was described by the 'Spotted Wonder's' trainer, Atty Persse, as the greatest jockey of all time.

George was another natural horseman and he rode, like Steve, in the classical English style. An Australian champion, he rode for Tommy Smith, one of the best and nicest trainers in turf history. Even with this charming man temperamental George had constant rows, which enlivened the Sydney racing scene.

During 1958–60 he rode in France for Alec Head and Prince Aly Khan, who described him as the world's greatest rider. He won the 2,000 Guineas on Taboun. When Gerry Oldham wanted a jockey for Miralgo in the 1962 Derby, he summoned George, who gave the colt a great ride to finish fourth before flying straight back to Sydney.

After the break with Lester, Noel Murless first signed the outstanding Scottish apprentice, Sandy Barclay. Then in early December he offered George the job as first jockey to Warren Place. On the telephone from Australia George expressed his delight.

'One of the big factors,' he said, 'is that I would have the great honour of riding for the Queen. I would only have to do nearly as well as I did in France for Prince Aly for this to be better than that job.'

Soon after his acceptance of the Murless retainer George's reputation as racing's stormy petrel was strengthened when he was summoned before the Australian stewards, following an alleged changing-room brawl with Athol Mulley. The Sydney *Sunday Telegraph* reported that an argument broke out as the two jockeys were pulling up after the Frank Underwood Cup at the local Canterbury Track. George had finished unplaced on the odds-on favourite and Athol Mulley was third. Subsequent blows in the changing-room, stated the report, resulted in scratches on the chest for Moore, a cut lower lip for Mulley and a report of the 'scuffle' to the stewards by the jockeys' room supervisor. George was seldom out of the news for long. Wherever he was, something always seemed to be happening.

So to England on 14th April, with his lovely wife Iris and three children, he came, he saw, and, my word, how he conquered!

He had 1,973 winners to his credit when he arrived and a look at the Murless horses revealed that he would not be long in passing the 2,000 mark. They had wintered better than any other string in Europe, I discovered on my tour of the stables, looked superb and more than usually forward in condition. In particular our leading colt and filly, Royal Palace and Fleet had made staggering improvement.

Jim Joel's Royal Palace, rated second, only 3 lbs., behind Paddy Prendergast's Bold Lad in the Free Handicap, had always been a handsome colt. Now the bay son of Ballymoss and Crystal Palace had strengthened considerably. His coat glistened with well-being. 'I don't think he could have done better,' said his trainer with pride.

In Ascot's Royal Lodge Stakes the previous season Lester was uncharacteristically left five lengths, but Royal Palace still won and set a new two-year-old second true for Ascot's Old Mile.

As for Bob Boucher's tall, active dark bay, Fleet: alert, bright of her eye and carrying a coat that shone like high summer, she looked a perfect racing machine, full of the joys of spring and ready to run for her life.

'She's as well as she looks,' said Noel, 'as you'd know if you rode her out in the morning. Her lads have to sit tight.'

An 11,000 guinea yearling, Fleet had a family reputation to maintain; Display, one of her sisters, had been narrowly beaten in the 1,000 Guineas. A second, Pourparler, had won the fillies' classic for Paddy Prendergast.

If these were the stars, the supporting cast looked every bit as promising in their own roles.

Five days after his arrival, in his first ride as Noel's stable jockey, George achieved a lifelong ambition. He won a race for the Queen at Newmarket. Although he claimed that he was not yet really fit, he had Hopeful Venture first out of the stalls in the Wood Ditton Stakes, pulled his whip through so smoothly when the colt started to sprawl, and won comfortably.

'It's too good to be true,' he said. But it was true and the following day in his second ride of the season he galvanised the grey Cranberry Sauce to sprint away with the Nell Gwyn Stakes.

Bold Lad for Ireland and Taj Dewan for France looked formidable obstacles to Royal Palace's success in the Two Thousand. Moreover, unlike the Murless colt, who was being aimed specially at the Derby, these two had both been laid out for the mile classic.

It might have been a different story if young Des Lake had obeyed Fred Darling's old principle and allowed Bold Lad to run in his hands. As it was, he pulled the big bay back and disappointed him with disastrous results.

At the Bushes Golden Horns went on followed by Taj Dewan. Running into the Dip the French colt took the lead, inadvertently squeezing Golden Horns on to Bold Lad, who had nevertheless already shot his bolt.

Meanwhile George had switched his mount and a hundred yards out he took the lead from his former pupil, nineteen-year-old Freddy Head. Taj Dewan fought back, but George kept his colt going to win by a short head.

'Freddy had first run,' he said, 'and my horse lost half a length down the hill, but then I just wore him down.'

The luck was changing at last for Royal Palace's owner Jim Joel. Although his father won the Derby with Sunstar in 1911 and Humorist ten years later, Jim had never been successful at Epsom. In fact, despite all the money he had lavished on breeding, he had won only one previous classic – the war-time version of the 1,000 Guineas with Picture Play in 1944. Now his colt was 2 to 1 favourite for the Derby.

'What's to beat him in the Derby?' asked Alec, who had accompained his son. 'He must be a good horse.'

The first-ever British classic to be started from stalls had proved a resounding success in every way. There was more to follow.

The next day Noel and George completed the Guineas double at Newmarket when Fleet defeated the best that Ireland and France could offer.

It was a great training achievement for Noel. His predecessor, Fred Darling, had won both classics with Big Game and Sun

Chariot, but these were war-time events and Noel himself had gone nearest to duplicating this with The Cobbler (second) and Queenpot in 1948.

Now Fleet was favourite at 6 to 1 for the Oaks. No jockey could have made a more sensational start than the ever-sensational Moore.

Unhappily, the following day Scobie, who was leading the jockeys' championship with seventeen winners, broke his collar bone in a three horse pile-up at Ascot. George however continued on his triumphant way, winning the White Rose Stakes stylishly on Good Society.

Of all the wonderful races I have seen him ride, one of the most memorable was his feat on Noel's Pink Gem in the Cheshire Oaks. It was his first visit to The Roodeye and, in a slow-run race, George had to keep Jim Joel's big, inexperienced chestnut filly in second place round that tight track until the final turn when she was left in front.

A furlong out, however, the Northern fans cheered 'Come on Lester!', as the British champion, riding locally-trained Ludham, swept past with a flourish.

Pink Gem sprawled, but her jockey, now half a length behind remained as cool as ice. Collecting and balancing his mount, he gentled her into her bridle again, so that she suddenly lengthened her stride and fought back in the last fifty yards to win by a head.

Noel's comment: 'That was a riding lesson,' he said. 'The filly has had only one previous race, is green and unsuited by this sharp track.'

As George unsaddled Pink Gem, he was paid the highest possible compliment by Lord Rosebery.

'He reminds me of Danny Maher,' said British racing's elder statesman, 'but rides like Frank Wooton.'

It was a fantastic bonanza for Australian jockeys in Europe. Apart from Scobie, George and Bill Williamson, Ron Hutchinson, Russ Maddock, Des Lake and Bill Pyers were all enjoying the fruits of that tough early training, which instilled judgement of paces and which was as intolerant of failure as the American stage.

But, despite all his success, George was not happy. 'All the travelling over here is terrible,' he complained. 'In Australia we ride only two days a week.'

When the Derby arrived, Royal Palace had to be the selection – not from wishful thinking, but simply on the formbook. So it proved.

Apart from the favourite, the field was not particularly impressive in the parade. None of the fancied runners gave any trouble in the first Derby to be started from the stalls. But several who had no right to be in the line-up caused an unnecessary delay.

The inevitable gimmick of this Derby was El Mighty, a Lambourn-trained colt, whose public form did not really justify his running in the classic, but who, on the strength of a much-publicised dream by a Peterborough store-keeper, had been backed from 200 to 1 down to 25 to 1 in a crazy betting spree. Running in blinkers and ridden by Paul Cook, the chestnut came from last to first after they had gone a furlong and had left the top of the hill. Here George began to make up ground on the favourite.

Moving smoothly down the hill, he was beautifully placed in fourth, or fifth, position at Tattenham Corner and took the lead much earlier than expected as they straightened out.

Lester Piggott, riding little Ribocco, now drew level on the wide outside but, as Royal Palace met the rising ground, George came right away to win by 2½ lengths, with Scobie on Dart Board two lengths away third.

It was Noel Murless's third Derby. He had produced Royal Palace trained to the minute and, with the first three classics already under his belt, had won £132,751 for his patrons – more than any other British trainer had achieved in a whole season.

George was thrilled. 'This is better than any Melbourne Cup,' he said. 'Our headman told me that Sir Gordon Richards always said you must be in the first four at Tattenham Corner. Royal Palace pulled hard for the first furlong, but then he settled beautifully, I nudged him up to them at the top of the hill.

'I was not going to let him flop down the hill, so I made him catch hold of his bit, and that was really why we went to the front so soon. I knew that as soon as he met the rising ground he would be all right. Piggott got right up to me on the outside, but I hadn't done much by then. I was just waiting for the hill. If it had been another half mile, I'd have come even more easily.'

There was no holding them. Fleet didn't stay the Oaks trip but she won the Coronation Stakes at Royal Ascot. In doing so, she earned a very special cheer for her great Australian jockey. She had realised the last of his ambitions – his 2,000th winner.

By a strange coincidence it was Ascot racecourse in Brisbane that he rode his first winner at the age of sixteen in 1940. At this stage of his career, the young prodigy looked so puny that he was sent back home as too small and weak when he appeared to ride the bottom weight in the Melbourne Cup.

This was Moore's fourth visit to Royal Ascot. He never failed to ride a winner at the meeting. In 1960 he had won the Coronation on French-trained Barbaresque before going on to take the Gold Cup on Sheshoon. Now he completed a double with Noel and Gwen Murless's splendid colt, St Chad, who is already making his mark as a stallion in Tipperary.

By the middle of July Noel had won twenty-nine races worth £171,905. He, himself, had held the previous all-time British record of £145,727 set in 1959. He had, and still has, no superior as a trainer. George's tender handling and understanding did the rest.

'I always wait until I have a horse truly balanced and racing under me,' said the Australian champion. 'I never ask him for an effort before he is ready and wanting to go himself.'

This is the secret of true horsemanship and race-riding, which we saw practised so successfully over the years by Scobie Breasley. Far too many young English jockeys have seemed anxious to get to the winning-post before their horses. The poor animals, particularly two-year-olds, sprawl unbalanced and never get galloping truly. They can't understand what is being asked of them. I like to think that the new resurgence of British jockeyship is due to the fact that our young riders benefited from watching Scobie and George. There is no doubt that both Willie Carson, Tony Murray, Philip Waldron and Pat Eddery keep their horses well balanced.

George went over to Paris to ride Petrone into second place in the Grand Prix. In the Irish Sweeps Derby he was runner-up to Ribocco on Noel's Sucaryl, underlining the worth of Royal Palace, who had beaten the little Ribot colt so easily in the Derby, and also of the entire Murless string.

So it seemed almost inevitable when the handsome big bay Crepello four-year-old Busted swept to victory in Ascot's King George VI and Queen Elizabeth Stakes.

After successes for the Murless-Moore partnership at Deauville, Ribocco, beautifully ridden by Lester, won the St Leger. But George was second, beaten only 1½ lengths, on Hopeful Venture, running instead of Royal Palace, who had been withdrawn at the eleventh hour.

'Royal Palace would certainly have won today,' declared George. 'No risk. As his best he's five or six lengths in front of Hopeful Venture.'

But now the horses, which had been ready so much earlier than usual, were going over the top. Moreover George, who had definitely decided to return and ride for Noel again in 1968, began to have doubts. He was subjected to some particularly nasty personal attacks. His house was broken into, his belongings mutilated, his car was daubed and he received threatening telephone calls from would-be race fixers.

'It's all true,' he told me. 'Now it's in the hands of Scotland Yard and I'm just relying on them to sort it out.'

He turned down big offers from the leading French stables.

'I stick to one man, Noel Murless,' he said, 'like I do to Tommy Smith back home. I believe in loyalty between trainer and jockey. That's just the way I'm made. I want very much to come back and ride here next year. But I've got my wife and our little daughter to consider. All I need is for someone to assure me that this is not a vendetta against us and that these attacks will not happen again.' It was a mystery which was to remain unsolved.

There were, however, still a few shots left in the Warren Place locker. It was National Cancer Day at Ascot on 29th September.

George had two chances – on Sucaryl in the David Robinson Stakes, and in the Michael Sobell Stakes on Fleet, who had suffered a terribly rough passage in the Eclipse, which would have soured oft many fillies for good. I saw her when she came in with heavy whip weals on her face and was dumbfounded when no disciplinary action was taken against the offenders. The classic filly's owner, Bob Boucher told me, 'Noel was so upset that he got a copy of the television film to show the Stewards Fleet being struck, but they did not act.' I have often wondered why.

Noel had achieved a great feat of training by keeping the filly going since the beginning of the season, when she won the One Thousand. Now George only had to remind her over the last few yards to win by a comfortable neck from Resilience II.

It was a different story on Sucaryl, who appeared badly placed lying last of the five runners in Swinley Bottom. Suddenly, before any other jockey knew what was happening, George had slipped past them all and taken the lead before entering the straight. This brilliant, surprise manoeuvre had gained Lady Sassoon's colt a decisive advantage and he held on well to win by 1½ lengths from Mariner. It was the versatility of the man which was so extraordinary. He could ride any sort of race.

The first sign that the luck was running out came in Paris on 1st October when the first horse entered by the Queen for a French race won comfortably. But then it was disqualified – after an objection by an English jockey!

Hopeful Venture, favourite at 7–4 and ridden, as usual by George, was first past the post in the Prix Henri Delamarre at Longchamp, an event worth £11,000 to the winner. The crowd went wild with excitement – how they love our Queen – as George rode Hopeful Venture past the winning post and kept on cheering until he had unsaddled and walked up the stairs into the glass-fronted weighing-room.

Then is was announced that Brian Taylor, rider of the runner-up, In Command, had objected. A French commentator, dismayed at this unprecedented action by a British jockey to one of the Royal horses, said 'The Stewards had no option but to hold an inquiry.'

After examining the film of the race the stewards found that Hopeful Venture had indeed crossed In Command's path. They awarded the race to Brian and placed the Queen's colt second. But the stewards demonstrated their feeling when they added that they absolved Moore from blame. They said he had 'done everything possible to avoid the incident'.

George said, 'I can't tell you how sorry I feel for the Queen. I think this must be the first time in the history of horse-racing that anyone has objected to the Monarch's horse. I cannot begin to tell you what I feel about the race. Just beyond words.'

And royal trainer, Sir Cecil Boyd-Rochfort said, 'I cannot remember an objection to a royal horse before.'

Of course the Escape affair at Newmarket was even before 'The Captain's' time! This was in 1791, when the stewards, led by Sir Charles Bunbury, inquired into the running and riding of Escape, who, ridden by Sam Chifney sen., had finished last of four and then proceeded to win the following day. They informed the owner, the Prince of Wales, that no gentleman would run his horse against him, if he continued to employ Chifney. The Prince stood up for his servant, shook the dust of Newmarket off his heels and never raced again. He promised to continue paying Chifney his 200 guinea retainer, but soon forgot, so that the jockey was tried and sentenced for debt and died in Fleet Prison.

In my opinion, unfortunate though it was that it should have happened in a foreign country under these circumstances, Brian Taylor was quite right. Moreover I think that this excellent, underrated rider showed great courage in objecting.

His trainer, Jack Leader, one of the finest, loyallest subjects the Queen could ever have, supported his jockey to the hilt. And I'm perfectly certain Her Majesty agrees that when a horse breaks the rules, it must pay the penalty whoever it belongs to.

God knows, races are hard enough to win these days and a trainer's first duty must be to his owners, who pay the bills. If I had been in Jack's shoes I would unhesitatingly have supported Brian. After all, although the French pay the most generous travelling allowances, it still costs a lot to send a horse and his entourage abroad. Moreover, travelling takes it out of an animal much more than people think. Five weeks later I watched In Command finish last at Laurel in the Washington International. She may have been starting to cough, but the Longchamp race had undoubtedly taken its toll. If she had been deprived of it through sentiment when victory was deserved, it would have been most unfair.

George was still wavering about his riding arrangements for the following year, when another George, the Paymaster-General Colonel George Wigg, joined the short list as successor to Lord Harding in the unenviable post of Chairman to the Levy Board. There was hope on the horizon if only the Establishment could learn to work with him.

George's last weekend on the eve of his departure for Australia was nothing short of disastrous. It was the same horse again, Hopeful Venture, on whom he had started this wonderful season, achieving a lifetime's ambition at Newmarket in April.

Now even the name, which had seemed so appropriate then, had acquired a sick, disillusioned ring. The party had been over just too long.

Possibly running the colt at all in Paris for a second time on 22nd October was one of Noel's few mistakes. The going was soft, and, when it's soft at Longchamp, where the watered summer ground is beautiful, believe me, it's soft. Moreover the Prix du Conseil Municipal is a notorious graveyard for good horses.

The Queen's colt started favourite at 6 to 5. Through travelling and his hard race lost on disqualification three weeks earlier, Hopeful Venture was much lighter and was never galloping strongly. He finished twelfth of twenty-two and was greeted with the most insulting boos, jeers and cat-calls on his return. This, of course, is part of the fun for the Parisian turfiste like old-time gallery audiences, but it often upsets many English visitors.

This was a sad, but, perhaps, inevitable sequel to Royal Palace's disappointing show in the Champion Stakes at Newmarket the previous day. The horses that had served the public so well since April just could not keep it up to the end of the season. Nor, for that matter, could many of the horses that ran on this soft ground. George had, in fact, less chance at Longchamp than with the Derby winner at Newmarket. He could never get within striking distance. Noel said simply, 'Hopeful Venture has gone over the top.' Which, of course, did not console punters on either side of the Channel or the twenty-eight out of thirty Parisian tipsters, who said the colt could not lose. But then the punter is an ungrateful animal, as fickle as the wind on a March day in Cornwall.

'I'm afraid he's just gone,' said George, still uncertain whether he would be severing his retainer with Noel Murless, which had helped him to a 32 per cent winning score. The punters had no cause to grumble!

The Murless winnings (only winning stakes, mind!) amounted to a fabulous new British record of £256,899, gleaned from sixty races. This figure was, of course, augmented by winnings abroad. It is high time that earnings were calculated as they are in other countries, so that place-money, frequently substantial these days, is included and the trainers' ten per cent is calculated on the total. This seems only fair to me. It's law in France.

How we needed George back again. But he didn't come, and on 29th November Noel announced that Sandy Barclay would be the Warren Place stable-jockey.

'I asked Moore to come back,' said the greatest trainer that Britain has ever known. 'At first he said he would, but then he started humming and hawing. I haven't heard a word from him since he left. So you can take it as definite that Sandy Barclay will be my stable-jockey in 1968.'

In Sydney, George stalled. 'I will contact Mr Murless as soon as possible, but I am confident that the situation will be the same as it was.'

The postcript came in December at the Gimcrack dinner in York, when the Jockey Club, through the retiring senior executive steward, Major-General Sir George Burns, took an unprecedented step in apologising to George for his treatment by the thugs, the threats and the damage to his car, his family's clothes and furniture.

'It was a deplorable and shameful affair,' he said. 'This kind of treatment by thugs and villains on those under the jurisdiction of the Turf will not be tolerated. Every effort will be made to bring them to justice.'

But they were never apprehended. It remains yet another of racing's unsolved mysteries. There are too many of them.

Back home in Scotland for his Christmas holidays, nineteen-year-old Sandy Barclay, who had learnt so much from George, said, 'I am delighted. It's a great honour. At present I am enjoying my mother's cooking, but I expect to ride at my strongest weight of between 7 stone 10 pounds and 7 stone 12 pounds.'

Poor lad, he was being thrown in at the deep end like an outstanding young swimmer suddenly asked to compete in Olympic class. One of the worst features of racing is the way people, usually talking through their pockets in one form or another, are constantly destroying the reputations of others. A journalist is said to be as good as his last story. It's even worse with a jockey. Let him ride one race which seems bad to the riders on the stands and all his fine performances are forgotten.

This was the case with Sandy, for whom 1968 was such a wonderful year, starting with victory in the One Thousand on Gwen Murless's Caergwrle.

Jim Joel paid him the compliment of putting him up on all his horses, including Royal Palace and Connaught. The latter finished second to Sir Ivor in the Derby and Royal Palace, returning to the scene of his 1967 triumph, won the Coronation Cup. Sandy followed up with five winners at Royal Ascot to make him champion of the meeting at the age of twenty.

Better was to come. There was that golden weekend in July when he won the Eclipse on Royal Palace and then flew over to Paris the following day to win the £51,000 Grand Prix de St Cloud for the Queen on Hopeful Venture.

Noel and Sandy so nearly arrived too late. The aircraft carrying them was held up for Customs clearance at Cambridge. An enormous crowd thronged the enclosures as the twenty runners paraded in the damp, thundery heat. Vaguely Noble, favourite at 2 to 1 on, seemed to have lost some weight and was sweating, as were Samos III, ridden by Lester Piggott, Taglietto and the previous year's French Derby runner-up Minamoto. The Arc de Triomphe winner Topyo and the French 1,000 Guineas heroine, Pola Bella, looked superb. Hopeful Venture was hard and fit in his bay coat, but was an outsider at more than 12 to 1 in spite of a large British gathering.

The going was perfect as Admiral's Boy, pacemaker to the favourite, set off in front, with Hopeful Venture close up and Vaguely Noble well in the rear.

When at halfway Admiral's Boy still led, Sandy was already

niggling at Hopeful Venture in sixth position and Jean Deforge, lying far out of his ground, was gradually moving up on Vaguely Noble.

Before the long final turn Freddy Head shot Minamoto into the lead, followed by Yves Saint-Martin on Pola Bella. A furlong from home these two were fighting out the finish, with Hopeful Venture four lengths behind and Vaguely Noble coming too late.

It looked all over until Sandy incredibly galvanised the royal colt and, forcing him up between the leaders, won by a neck from Minamoto, with Vaguely Noble two lengths away third and Pola Bella fourth.

Sensational scenes followed as the French cheered the Queen's first winner in their country, her jockey and trainer remembering the previous year the same horse had finished first at Longchamp, only to be disqualified.

Murless said, 'The race doesn't matter. It's so wonderful for the Queen.' And he asked an official for the patrol film to take home to the winning owner.

Nevertheless, among all his triumphs in that, his first year as stable-jockey to Noel, Sandy was probably proudest of his performance on gallant Royal Palace in the King George VI and Queen Elizabeth Stakes at Ascot.

Where most jockeys would have lost their heads, the young Scotsman, with his innate understanding of animals, remained cool when Royal Palace broke down 150 yards from the finish. Even when the French challengers came at him, he never went for his whip, but rode his mount out with hands and heels.

The Sandy story is still only starting. When at the end of 1970 he was replaced by Geoff Lewis, he went to France in the sympathetic care of Mr Edouard Pouret and Francois Boutin. Backed by his immense experience there, he will surely be one of the future Great Ones.

As it is, he must wait until the next instalment for inclusion in this hall of fame.

7: Joe Mercer and Jimmy Lindley

Throughout the Piggott-period these Newbury neighbours have provided steady opposition to 'the long fellow'. Now nearing forty, they are both first-class jockeys and a credit to the racing scene.

A year older than his friend, Bradford-born Joe was still a half-crown a week apprentice with Major Fred Sneyd at Sparsholt when he rode his first winner three years after he had signed on.

The son of a coach painter, he was born on 25th October, 1934. Although there is no racing blood in his family, Joe, while still at school, helped with the tack cleaning and mucking out at a local riding stable in return for the odd ride on a pony. In the meantime, his elder brother, Manny, later to be killed so tragically at Ascot, had joined George Colling at Newmarket and was doing as well as might be expected of one of the most brilliant natural young riders ever to grace the British Turf.

So well, in fact, that Major Fred Sneyd, who had trained the brothers, Eph and Doug Smith, wrote to Mr Mercer asking: 'Are there any more at home like him?'

Joe leapt at the chance and was sent to Sparsholt.

That was just before I went as assistant-trainer to Atty Persse. Sneyd, like my Guv'nor, kept his apprentices so short of pocket-money, that Joe was still earning only half-a-crown a week when he rode his first winner three years later.

Soon after this his wages rose to ten shillings a week and remained there until he finished his time in 1955 when he had ridden nearly two hundred winners, including the Oaks.

In the early stages he sometimes received even less money

at the end of the week than the pittance he was allowed. All through his time he was fined sixpence every time he fell off.

In those days there was no question of any Sunday off. 'I had one night off a week,' he said, 'and worked from 6 a.m. 'til 11 p.m. As well as riding out and working in the yard, I had to help in the house. I started off as kitchen boy and ended up waiting at table. I had to feed the dogs and cats too.'

He added: 'Towards the end of my time, I lived with the family and was even allowed a glass of sherry before dinner. Major Sneyd was a good master and taught me well. Even though I naturally wanted to follow in Manny's footsteps, I don't thing I ever tried to copy his style of riding. I always rode as I was taught by the Major.'

It was Ambiguity who gave Joe his big chance in the Oaks of 1953. He seized it with both hands. Tenth of the twenty-one runners entering the Epsom straight, the apprentice delivered a perfectly timed challenge to beat the Aga Khan's Kerkeb. Manny's mount, Happy Laughter, who had won the 1,000 Guineas, was fourth.

It is fair to say that Joe's whole career was made by this success. Ambiguity's trainer, Jack Colling, that most charming of men, who had just moved from Newmarket to West Ilsey, gave him a retainer.

The partnership prospered so well, that when Jack retired in 1962, Joe signed up again with his successor, Dick Hern. The continuing association of trainer, jockey and the stable's owners, notably Jakey Astor, is one of the best features of British racing today.

With his clear, concise brain, Joe, like most jockeys, prefers to ride a waiting race. But he is perfectly capable of waiting in front, if these tactics are forced on him.

Like Jimmy, he is a classical English stylist, riding with a long rein and a sensible length of stirrup leather, which allows him the use of his legs to correct tired horses and keep them perfectly balanced when they start to roll about in heavy going. Moreover in a tight finish he can really sit down into a horse and get behind him to drive him home.

Loyalty, as the keystone of Joe's life, has paid immense dividends.

When, in the summer of 1970, Sir Gordon Richards, finally forced to quit William Hill's Whitsbury stables, announced that he would have to give up training, his chief owner, Michael Sobell, bought the West Ilsey stables from Jakey Astor. He hoped that Gordon, who had just taken on Edward Hide as stable jockey as the successor to Scobie Breasley, would be able to continue training for him and Lady Beaverbrook in the famous yard.

Jakey, however, had other ideas. In what must have been one of the strangest deals he sold his training establishment only on condition that Dick Hern remained as trainer and Joe as jockey.

Since that Ambiguity year of 1953, when he finished with sixty-one winners, Joe has remained firmly, but always quietly among the leading riders.

In February 1959 he married Anne, daughter of the Royal Jockey, Harry Carr. She had already made a name for herself as a horsewoman. She had won more than fifty first prizes, collected more than two hundred rosettes in the show-ring and finished fourth in the hack class at the Royal International Show at the White City in 1956.

A year before his marriage, Joe broke his neck riding in Singapore. Another year, a broken arm prevented him from winning all five classic races in Bombay. When he was injured, he had already won the 2,000 and 1,000 Guineas. His father-in-law came out to substitute and win the Derby and the Leger on the horses he would have ridden. 'He'd have won the Oaks too, if he'd known his filly as well as I did,' says Joe.

Occasional injuries of varying severity are the lot of every professional horseman, but in June 1972 Joe emerged as a national hero after a truly horrible accident. The light aircraft, which was taking him to the races, crashed taking off from Newbury. Although badly shaken, Joe escaped injury and, with complete disregard for the imminent and almost inevitable explosion, pulled his fellow passengers, including leading trainer Bill Marshall out of danger. He had barely got them clear when the 'plane burst into flames. The pilot, unhappily, had died in the crash.

The next day Joe was a front page hero in every newspaper. But the racing world wondered whether he would be fit for

Brigadier Gerard in Royal Ascot's Prince of Wales' Stakes. This was one ride which he could not give up. He performed with such supreme confidence that John Hislop's great colt, inspired by the rider he knew so well, trounced his field and flew home to win like a true champion in record time.

Until 1970 Joe had always held firm to the belief that Hornbeam was the best horse he had ever ridden. That gallant little chestnut colt had won eleven races from a mile to two miles, including the Great Voltigeur Stakes. He failed by half a length to give 23 lbs. to Morcambe in the Ebor and was beaten a whisker by French Beige in the Doncaster Cup. Although he did not win a classic, Hornbeam finished only three-quarters of a length behind Cambremer in the 1956 St Leger.

I shall always remember that Doncaster. I was in training at the time and enjoying a most successful season with my small string at Upper Lambourn. I had always admired Jack Colling, who was particularly kind and helpful to young trainers like myself, and envied his beautifully run Yorkshire grouse moor. I asked him how the birds were and whether the prospects were good. He said: 'It's a splendid season, but it's properly messed up. For the first time for years I've got to go to Doncaster. I have this runner in the Leger and my owners think I ought to saddle him and see him run. Certainly he must have a bit of a chance, but I think it's most unreasonable!'

The Mercer's attractive house just outside Newbury, overlooking the River Kennet, is called *Hornbeam*.

But in 1970 another horse appeared – a handsome bay colt by Queen's Hussar, bred, owned and broken by leading racing journalist John Hislop, the best amateur-rider on the Flat I have ever seen or am ever likely to see, in partnership with his equally enthusiastic wife Jean.

Good horses deserve good names. You seldom find a decent animal with a bad one. Passifyoucan was always being passed and Jack Oldings Winagain never won at all.

The Hislop's colt was by Queen's Hussar out of La Paiva by Prince Chevalier. They gave him the superb name of Conan Doyle's hero, Brigadier Gerard. How delighted that happily conceited French cavalry officer would have been to find his name carried by one of the greatest horses of the time.

He would, of course, have considered it only right and proper!

Dick Hern and Joe handled the colt beautifully to win four races in his two-year-old season. But, partly because of his sire, who was not really expected to produce classic winners, he was generally believed to be out-classed by Mill Reef and David Robinson's unbeaten My Swallow, who disputed favouritism for the 2,000 Guineas.

Badly drawn in the Prix Robert Papin at Maisons-Laffitte the previous year, Mill Reef's only defeat had been by a whisker at the hands of My Swallow, who had gone on to become the first English horse to win all the French two-year-old 'classics' and our highest-ever juvenile stakes winner.

This pair were considered so outstanding, that the Guineas field was the smallest since mighty Ormonde won for the Duke of Westminster in 1886. Both the cracks had won their first races of the new season. Mill Reef was now made favourite at 6/4 with his rival, easier in the market, at 2/1. Brigadier Gerard was next in demand at 11/2. As the six runners paraded, John Hislop said: 'I have a first-class trainer and jockey. They assure me that my horse is supremely fit and did not want a preliminary outing. That's good enough for me.'

So it proved. Frank Durr made the running on My Swallow until the Bushes where Joe sent Brigadier Gerard smoothly into the lead. Geoff Lewis on Mill Reef tried desperately to get on terms down into the Dip and up the hill, but was still three lengths behind at the winning post with My Swallow three-quarters of a length away third.

As the year progressed and Mill Reef continued on his meteoric classic way embracing the Derby and culminating in the Arc de Triomphe, it was generally assumed that he had been defeated in the Guineas by a slightly inferior colt – a brilliant miler, trained specially for his only classic engagement, and that the Brigadier would never beat him again. This view was strengthened when the Hislop colt scraped home by a head from Sparkler in the St James's Palace Stakes on Royal Ascot's very soft going.

The going was soft at Goodwood, but the lovely old course drains better than Ascot and Joe won the Sussex Stakes with consummate ease, making all the running to beat the French challenge, Faraway Son, by five lengths.

At Ascot, in September, he beat another French horse, Dictus, by a contemptuous eight lengths in the Queen Elizabeth II Stakes as a curtain-raiser to his last race of the year, Newmarket's Champion Stakes, now boosted to £25,280. This was the Brigadier's first outing over a distance beyond a mile and those who doubted his stamina, felt fully justified when, after taking the lead before the Bushes, he only just held off the challenge of Paddy Prendergast's 20/1 four-year-old Rarity by a short head to retain his unbeaten record.

The doubters had ignored the fact that the Newmarket going was unusually soft on this last day of the Houghton meeting.

With typical courage the Hislops, who had turned down enormous offers for their horse, decided to keep him in training as a four-year-old, but at the same time did not intend to run him again on soft ground.

One of the stupidest trite sayings is 'A good horse acts in any going.' Many of the best horses have, like Brigadier Gerard, a lovely low sweeping action. How could you expect such a daisy-cutter to gallop through a ploughed field. Equally the horse with a high action, usually associated with stayers, brings his feet down hard and is totally unsuited to firm ground, although he revels in the soft. It is purely mathematical.

1972 was to be the great year. First the Brigadier won the one-mile Lockinge Stakes at his home course, Newbury. Then, reverting to one mile and a quarter, he won the Westbury Stakes at Sandown. At Royal Ascot, Joe was still very shaken by his aircraft crash, but was still determined to ride his wonder horse. Seldom have I seen more confidence. Travelling strongly on the bit from the start, he swept into the lead a quarter of a mile out and streaked home to win by five lengths from Steel Pulse, who was receiving 3 lbs. more than weight for age and was shortly to endorse the form by winning the Irish Sweeps Derby.

Joe could scarcely hear the tumultuous cheers. Delayed shock had set in and he collapsed as he was unsaddling.

So to Sandown and the Eclipse, which had been hailed as the 'Race of the Century', as it was expected to produce a clash with Mill Reef. Unhappily the little American champion had become a victim of the virus which crippled racing during this season.

Heavy rain had softened Sandown's famous Eclipse course, which is stiff enough at the best of times, and the Hislops were tempted to withdraw. But the opposition appeared so weak, that they decided to let their colt take his chance. He started at 11/4 on and beat Gold Rod by a length, obviously hating the going, but typically never giving in. John Hislop declared: 'We will never again run him on soft ground.'

In common with most great horses the Brigadier is lazy. Sometimes Joe had to ride like a demon to counteract the bone idleness of a colt who knew exactly how much was needed to win and wouldn't do a damn thing more. But never once was there the slightest sign of his being ready to quit near the finish. Always that handsome head was thrust out, battling on and on as if there were no limit.

His temperament was so wonderful that when, still unbeaten after fourteen starts, he was saddled for the £60,202 King George VI and Queen Elizabeth Stakes at Ascot, now sponsored by the diamond people, De Beers, his connections made no secret of their confidence in his ability to stay 1½ miles in top class company.

There was the Italian Derby winner, Gay Lussac, ridden by Lester Piggott, Steel Pulse, fresh from his Irish triumph with Bill Williamson in the saddle again; Riverman (Freddy Head), winner of the French Guineas, and Parnell (Willie Carson), who had won the 1971 Irish St Leger. Jim Joel's Selhurst (Geoff Lewis), the half-brother to Royal Palace, was probably the best of the other four starters.

John Hislop told my colleague on the *Sun*, Claude Duval: 'I'm certain that no horse in the world could beat mine from one mile to one mile and a quarter on firm going – and that includes Mill Reef. But to be judged the best of all time, he must win at 1½ miles.

'Ribot was a middle distance horse, and was bred with more stamina. But our horse has such a relaxed style that he does not take a lot out of himself, and I think he'll stay on. At four years old, he's at his peak.

'Owning him is a fairy tale come true. As a journalist I used to write about Ribot's wins. But I never dreamed that one day I'd breed and own a horse who could be mentioned in the same breath as Ribot.

'If he wins tomorrow I'm told that he will top £200,000 in prize money, but I honestly couldn't tell you how much he's won. I'm not interested in that aspect of racing. Last year we could have won a lot more money by hawking him around France. But he wouldn't be half the horse now.

'It's still difficult for me and my wife Jean to believe we actually own this colt. I used to win races on hunter chasers, a far cry from the Brigadier, for whom we turned down an offer of £250,000 as a two-year-old.

'Now in the form books he is rated higher than Nijinsky, who went to stud for two million. People approach me with blank cheques, and he's so valuable that I can't even insure him for anything like his true value.

'But I will never sell him and, at the end of the season, he'll go back to the Egerton Stud at Newmarket where he was foaled.

'The only thing he hates is rain. He has such fine skin, and I hope that the weather continues dry, and the going is like a brick at Ascot. His only gimmick is that he likes to go into the horse-box backwards. This was printed in an article recently but after the Eclipse, he walked straight into his box headfirst. So, he's obviously been reading the papers.

'I hope he's about fourth or fifth into the straight tomorrow, and that there is not a crawl, or a mad pace. Then, at the turn, if I was riding him, I'd make the best way home.

'Yves Saint-Martin says that Riverman is the best French horse for ten years, and I suppose the Italian, Gay Lussac, could be another Ribot.

'If the Brigadier does win it will only be two or three days afterwards that it occurs to us that we have picked up another £60,000.'

Sir Gordon Richards, too, talked to Claude before the race. Twenty-six times champion and winner of 4,870 races, he said:

'Brigadier Gerard is one of the finest horses of all time. His unbeaten record as a two-, three-, four-year-old proves this.

He's got such great guts that he just won't be beaten.

'For a horse to be called great, he must be unbeaten. That's why Ribot and Bahram were so outstanding. But, if Brigadier Gerard does win the King George, we must certainly put him in this bracket.

'Unbeaten horses fascinate me. We never really know just how great they are. I believe Brigadier will get 1½ miles for the first time. He's got such a wonderful temperament.

'Before Ribot won the same race in 1956 another horse bolted and delayed the start. But Ribot just stood there on three legs, and couldn't have cared less.

'Then the race started and he made mincemeat of his rivals. That was greatness. You can see the same qualities in the Brigadier.'

When they jumped out of the stalls, Geoff Lewis made the running on Selhurst. Before the six furlong marker, however, Willie Carson had sent Parnell into the lead and it was obvious that the Brigadier's stamina was going to be thoroughly tested.

Joe, who had once again been riding with supreme confidence, made a forward move in Swinley Bottom and was second entering the straight, where he soon ranged upsides with Parnell. 1½ furlongs from home he hit the front and the cheering started, only to diminish with fear as the favourite crossed over his rival towards the far rails.

Forced to switch to the outside, Parnell was starting to come again, but the winning post arrived too soon and he was beaten by 1½ lengths with Riverman 5 lengths away third and Steel Pulse fourth. The Italian challenge was fifth nearly ten lengths behind the Brigadier.

A steward's inquiry inevitably followed. After seeing the film they exonerated Brigadier Gerard and we were all delighted with the verdict as the Queen presented diamond trinkets to the Hislops, Dick Hern and Joe.

Nevertheless, the finish highlighted yet again the discrepancy in the interpretation of the rules between our amateur stewards on different racecourses in England and, particularly, their professional counterparts in other countries, which has frequently caused trouble for our jockeys abroad. There is no doubt that the Brigadier would have won in any case. But if this is to be taken into account when a rule is broken, it should be clearly stated. Otherwise the letter of the law must be obeyed and the winner might well have lost the race in France, Australia or the United States. Parnell's trainer Bernard van Cutsem, summed up: 'Brigadier Gerard was certainly the better horse on this going. But he definitely took our ground.'

However, it was a happy ending and a wonderful day for British breeding.

Richard Baerlein, as fine a turf writer as the Brigadier's owner – and that means the best of all time – wrote:

'Everything connected with the Brigadier is pleasing to every section of the racing community. It is the finest example ever known in history on how to handle a thoroughbred racehorse to the best of his advantage.

'Not until his fifteenth race was he first tested for stamina at 1½ miles. By then he was fully matured in every respect and had mastered the 1¼ mile races, which at one stage were even in doubt. After the Guineas he was considered a miler.

'Some horses stay a mile as a two-year-old and only seven furlongs later in life. Many people backed Stintino for the Derby two years ago because he won over 1¼ miles as a two-year-old. He only stayed about 100 yards further as a three-year-old. I believe the Brigadier stays 1¼ miles this year far better than he did last.'

Richard notes: 'Tom Watson, who compiles a private handicap for the benefit of *Raceform* subscribers and readers of *The Racehorse*, says his figures make the Brigadier the best horse he has ever rated. He has many years experience of handicapping horses and I find his figures more compelling than wordy arguments.

'Tom goes on: "If we allow Steel Pulse to have run to his Irish Sweeps Derby mark and Parnell to my rating of his win in the Rouge Dragon Handicap at Ascot in April, the mark the Brigadier returned on Saturday was just 4 lbs below the best mark I have for him over his ideal distance of 1¼ miles!"'

John Oaksey, that other Turf writer so eminently deserving to be bracketed with Hislop and Baerlein, wrote: 'No horse in the history of the Turf has been better, more openly or more boldly managed than this one and, as far as I am concerned, if the Brigadier retired tomorrow, he would still have done more – very much more – than enough.'

John noted: 'Before the race, knowing Brigadier Gerard's tendency to idle, Dick Hern had told Joe Mercer not to be afraid of giving him a slap if it was needed. But it never was and, striding powerfully home, the Brigadier showed not the slightest sign of weariness, fatigue or lack of stamina. The bogey of those two extra furlongs was well and truly laid.'

What a thrill for England to have such a horse to sire classic horses in future years. A great deal of the credit must go to Joe. In the lower echelons it is the trainer and his lads who make the horse. The flat-race jockey, riding like a monkey up a stick, has little or no influence on the production of the youngster as an effective racing machine, capable of earning money for its owner. Only those horsemen, who have ridden and trained jumpers, can appreciate the enormous help which an experienced jockey can give to a novice horse. Put Terry Biddlecombe up first time out, ride your horse again afterwards and see what I mean. It's a different animal. The same applies to the production of a top-class flat horse. And there is no doubt that despite all the skill and know-how of his owner and trainer, Brigadier Gerard's greatness must owe a lot to the expert, sympathetic handling of his devoted rider.

Let us leave Joe there – top of the world. A smart, well-dressed businessman with a controlling interest in two first-class garages already. Joe won't want to train. Why take on all that thankless worry when, after starting as a half-crown a week apprentice, you have deservedly 'got it made'? He has earned plenty of time to enjoy his favourite hobbies of shooting and fishing.

As for Dick Hern. No praise is high enough for his production and overall training of the Brigadier. But this book is about jockeys. Its sequel will be *Racehorse Trainers – The Great Ones*. (Pelham Books).

I believe that Joe has learnt and improved his riding more than any other jockey in recent years.

His friend, neighbour and business associate, Jimmy Lindley, did not have to have to learn so much. However, although a natural horseman, handsome Jimmy's life has not followed the steady upward trend of Joe's. Rather it has been a graph of switchbacks.

Four years before he won the 1960 King George VI and Queen Elizabeth Stakes on Aggressor, Jimmy was in the middle of the most disastrous season. From March to November he rode just one winner.

The son of an Eastbourne restaurateur, Jimmy, now one of the tallest members of his profession, became a jockey not only because he loved riding – he won innumerable prizes in shows and gymkhanas – but also because he was so small. When he went to Lewes trainer Tom Masson at the age of fourteen, he weighed just three stone!

He could not have had a better tutor than tall, debonair Tom with the Chevalier looks, the same naughty twinkle in his eye and a knowledge and understanding of the horse rivalled only by his friend Ryan Price.

As a young man, Tom had learnt a great deal about horses in the circus. In the last twenty years of his life he was universally recognised as the best man in the country with an awkward animal. In fact I believe there was nothing he couldn't do with them. This was how he came to train for the Queen.

It was a measure of the greatness as trainers of Sir Cecil Boyd-Rochfort and Noel Murless that they sent horses, which were virtually untrainable at Newmarket, to be corrected by Tom. Of course, with their enormous strings they really had no time to cope with such awkward customers. But still, most other trainers would have hung on without telling the owners until the animal could be sold abroad rather than admit defeat.

A typical case was Rousseau, who won the last race at a Brighton meeting in 1961.

Few of the large crowd – this was before the erection of that concrete monstrosity of a stand – realised that Rousseau, who appeared on the race-card with the maiden's weight of 6 st. 12 lbs., had in fact won two races at Milan and Turin. Moreover they were also ignorant of the colt's breeding. He was a half-brother to the mighty Ribot, unbeaten dual winner of the Arc de Triomphe.

With his weight corrected to 8 st. 6 lbs., Rousseau, obviously still far from straight in condition, won the 1½ mile Hove

Welter Stakes by a comfortable two lengths. If the dark chestnut three-year-old had not hung badly on the straight, tricky course, he would have won by a distance.

And, after paying a routine £5 fine for not correcting the weight beforehand, Tom Masson explained how this splendid Italian son of Owen Tudor came into his yard.

Brought over to Noel Murless by his breeders, the famous Razza Dormello, Rousseau's waywardness caused so much trouble that he was expelled from Newmarket and sent by Noel to horsemaster Masson for correction.

Tom said, 'He just had no steering at all!'

His new trainer's tall, slim sixteen-year-old-son Mick took the valuable colt in hand and taught him to behave like a normal well-schooled racehorse.

Meanwhile Australian Geoff Armstrong, who wanted a well-bred stallion to join his successful English importations, Squander Bug and Nullabor at his Victorian stud, had been offered and had refused the colt at a very large sum.

However, ten days before Brighton, at a reduced but still five-figure fee, Geoff bought Rousseau from the Anglo-Irish Agency acting for the Razza Dormella.

At about the same time, Bobby Elliot, who was Jimmy's successor in the Masson school, was given his first ride on the previously unrideable colt.

Tom explained: 'I had to make sure that the horseman had completed his task before the jockey got up. Rousseau knows his job at home, but it's a very different matter on a racecourse, particularly with a small field.'

He had no need to worry. As always he and his son had done their jobs well.

This was the school to which Jimmy was sent. The raw material was ideal for Tom, who made a horseman and a jockey out of the boy.

As a fashionable apprentice – he was always a very handsome lad – he rode many winners, including Damremont in the City and Surburban, and Orthopaedic in the Ayr Gold Cup. In his first year as a fully-fledged jockey he had thirty-seven successes.

Increasing weight, however, suddenly cut short his activities on the flat. It looked as though Jimmy was finished – a forgotten man at twenty-one.

So, to the rescue came that very clever trainer, Matt Feakes, the former jumping jockey, who had recently moved to Berkshire after being Tom Masson's neighbour at Lewes. He invited Jimmy to stay with him at Upper Lambourn in the yard which he had taken over from Reg Hobbs, and to take out a National Hunt rider's licence.

In Jimmy's first season over hurdles he rode fourteen winners and in his second, sixteen. He won several big races and rode Retour de Flamme, third in the Champion Hurdle. From a few rides on the flat in between he rode six winners.

The flat trainers began to get the message and to give him the rides as he managed to reduce his weight again. In 1958 he rode fifty-one winners on the flat. The following year he rode forty-seven and, with his favourite horse, Aggressor, he was our only representative in the Washington International at Laurel, Maryland.

To complete the happy ending to the story that year, in February he married Pat Feakes, daughter of the man who was chiefly responsible for his wonderful comeback. He celebrated in 1960 by winning the King George VI and Queen Elizabeth Stakes on Aggressor.

He had ridden a brilliant race to win and was now back again, recognised as a leading jockey.

During the lean years, Jimmy had ridden for my small Lambourn stable. I shall never forget his kind, generous help in 1957, when I broke my neck and was temporarily prevented from training my horses. He came round every day to ride out and lend his expert hand with the work.

One lovely summer day when I had recovered, Jimmy and I were discussing the morning's work on the Moss Hill side of the road at the right-angled corner on the top of the Faringdon Road gallop out of Lambourn, when a big sports car, which we recognised as Lester Piggott's, came hurtling up the hill from Wantage towards us, 'doing the ton' as it topped the brow.

Grinning all over his face, as he recognised us, twenty-two-year-old Lester drove at us for a joke – he has always handled a car superbly – whipping the steering wheel round to miss us with only a yard to spare.

Jimmy and I, laughing too, had stood our ground. But we and Lester had reckoned without some loose gravel on the road surface. He lost the tail of his car. As it broke away, we just managed to hurl ourselves backwards into the ditch with a split second to spare. We have laughed about it several times since. The racing world was so nearly deprived of a top-class jockey and a moderate trainer.

It was in 1961 that Jimmy and Scobie Breasley rode a cat-and-mouse six-furlong match at Salisbury, which delighted the crowd and was described by the Australian maestro as 'the funniest race I have ever ridden in.'

In the £390 Fleet Plate (look at that prize-money such a short time ago), Scobie's mount, Skymaster, one of the best sprinters in training from the Arundel stable, was opposed by John Baillie's Colour Blind, who had seemed only a shadow of himself that season and was receiving only 3 lbs.

But the Duchess of Norfolk told Scobie beforehand, 'Skymaster would never win more than a neck against a donkey.'

As Jimmy jumped Colour Blind off, Scobie tucked Skymaster in behind. Immediately Jimmy pulled Skymaster up almost to a walk. But Scobie had no difficulty in restraining Skymaster from taking the lead!

This performance was repeated three times. On each occasion Colour Blind was turned completely sideways like a crab with his white legs flashing. At half-way Jimmy suddenly set the gelding alight. But Scobie, the wily veteran, was ready. He shot Skymaster upsides; locked together, they raced for the line, where Skymaster got the verdict by a neck.

Jimmy got his revenge that day in the Champagne Stakes, when, riding Gustav for Jeremy Tree, he beat Scobie on Tamerlo.

1961 was Jimmy's first classic year, thanks to Ambergris, the charming Kildangan filly, who, trained by Harry Wragg, ran first in the colours of the late Sir Percy Loraine and then in the name of Roderic More O'Ferrall.

Unhappily for Jimmy, another good, genuine filly had been foaled in the same year.

Sweet Solera, a liver chestnut with a white clown face, by Solonaway, had been bought as a foal for only 900 guineas by Harold Clifton, owner of the Solario Stud, named after seventy-eighty-ear-old trainer Reg Day's only English classic winner to date in the 1925 St Leger.

So when Sweet Solera was resold as a yearling, it was one of Reg's owners, Mrs Renee Castello, who bought her for 1,850 guineas.

In the 1,000 Guineas of 1948 Ariostar, trained by Reg, had been narrowly beaten by another Kildangan filly, Queenpot. Now he was to get his revenge. Bill Rickaby, that popular jockey, who had ridden three runners-up in the 1,000 Guineas but had never won an English classic, had the mount on Sweet Solera. His father, Fred, had won the fillies' classic four times in five years, in 1913, '15, '16 and '17. Bill, who had risen to the rank of Major in the Royal Artillery during the Second World War, was forty-three-years-old.

It was the season of Pinturischio and of Opaline, the Aga Khan's brilliant French-trained chestnut filly, who had been hot favourite in all ante-post books from the moment that the market on the classic races opened. Neville Sellwood, the outstanding Australian jockey, was to have ridden her and she was regarded as a racing certainty. However, on the Sunday of Guineas Week Opaline was struck down with a *crise intestinale*, was running a temperature, very weak and unable to leave Alec Head's Chantilly stable.

So Sweet Solera was backed down to 4/1 with Ambergris at 10s.

Tudor Top made the running, but Sweet Solera was always leading the group on the stands side of the Rowley Mile. Ambergris challenged at the distance and actually got to within a head of her rival, but Sweet Solera battled stoutly up the hill to win by a length and a half with Indian Melody six lengths away third.

Said Jimmy: 'Ambergris didn't come down the hill too well, but she'll get the Oaks distance all right.'

Indeed we had little doubt about the chestnut daughter of Sicambre. It was Sweet Solera, by speedy Solonaway, whose stamina was suspect.

Nevertheless, over Epsom's $1\frac{1}{2}$ miles these two splendid classic fillies reproduced their Newmarket form to an ounce.

Soon after entering the Straight Bill Rickaby took the lead but was immediately challenged by Jimmy, who went half a length up and looked the winner. But, as they crossed the path at the foot of the hill, Bill rallied his filly, who came again to finish magnificently one and a half lengths to the good.

Bill said, 'When Jimmy came upsides, he looked sure to beat me. But when he was half a length in front, his mare started to hang a bit. I gave Sweet Solera one with the whip and she battled on splendidly.'

Jimmy discounted allegations that Ambergris had failed through lack of stamina. He said, 'They both stay, but Sweet Solera found a bit more than mine.'

At twenty-six, he was already a first-class judge, as he proved when Harry Wragg sent Ambergris over to contest the Irish Oaks on the stiffer Curragh circuit, although she had disappointed badly at Ascot.

Lester Piggott was now on Indian Melody and, when he hit the front in the straight, it looked for a few seconds as though the 'wonder boy' could inspire the Epsom filly to victory. But Jimmy, who had ridden hard for a place on the turn, was now full of confidence. He switched Ambergris to the outside and, a furlong from home, asked her to go on. Without a moment's hesitation she lengthened her stride and won comfortably by $2\frac{1}{2}$ lengths for Indian Melody.

Harry Wragg said, 'Ambergris was dead at Ascot. It just proved once again that you cannot run at Epsom and Ascot. They are too close together so that an animal cannot recover in time.'

It was Harry's seventh Irish classic success, but it was a first ever classic for Jimmy, who had proved beyond any doubt that he now possessed all the qualities that make up a top international jockey.

A quick word here about Bill Rickaby, one of the most charming and conscientious jockeys you could ever find. Bill was paid the greatest possible tribute when he became the first English jockey to be selected as a racing official. No-one doubted that, after a spell as stipendiary steward in Hong Kong, he would have returned to take over the same job in this country. Not long after his arrival in Hong Kong, however, he suffered dreadful injuries in a car crash, from which he is still recovering. He has been a great credit to his profession.

Significantly it was Jimmy who was to follow in Bill's footsteps in Hong Kong, where he also instructed apprentices. Both have done a great deal for their fellow riders at home and abroad.

Two years later, Jimmy was second in both the English fillies' classics again – this time on Spree, trained by Jeremy Tree for John Morrison, later to become Lord Margadale. This game good filly had the ill fortune to run up against two of the best of her sex of all time – Hula Dancer in the One Thousand and Noblesse in the Oaks.

In October 1962, Mrs Gertie Widener's grey filly, Hula Dancer, retired for the season with the 1,000 Guineas at her mercy after proving in Longchamp's Grand Criterium that she was one of the fastest two-year-olds of all time.

The unbeaten American-bred mare not only slammed the best of her age in France, but also smashed the all-age mile record for this classic course as she streaked home by four lengths to give Etienne Pollet his fourth Criterium triumph in four years. Relko was fourth.

She re-appeared at Maisons-Laffitte in the Prix Independence having done virtually no work and carrying a coat like a mountain goat. Nevertheless, as soon as Roger Poincelot shook her up, Hula Dancer defied the heavy ground and left her field standing to win by five lengths.

Before the One Thousand, Jimmy won his first English classic race on Only For Life in the 2,000 Guineas.

The hot favourite Crocket dropped out suddenly two furlongs from home to finish last. Once again thousands of punters had lost their money, but there was no official enquiry. The Jockey Club Secretary, the late Bill Weatherby, even went so far as to say: 'We can't have them testing every beaten favourite.'

Jimmy, on the 33/1 outsider Only For Life, bought by Jeremy Tree as a yearling for only 1,600 guineas, rode a particularly brilliant race. He came again with tremendous drive to beat the Irish challenger Ionian by a short head.

'I took the lead 1½ furlongs out,' he said, 'and went a length in front just before the Bushes. We knew at home that the colt would not come down the hill and, sure enough, Liam Ward went half a length up on me. But as soon as we met the rising ground, my chap stuck his head down and really battled. I must admit I thought it had gone just against me.'

Of course Jimmy had always been a gentleman and it was those very qualities which cost him the 1,000 Guineas and Spree's connections a £75,000 gamble.

For unbeaten Hula Dancer would not have won the One Thousand had Jimmy stuck rigidly to his rights. And Jeremy Tree would have taken the classic double back to Beckhampton for the first time since 1942.

'With three furlongs to go,' said Jim, 'I found Roger Poincelot on Hula Dancer, poking his nose where he had no right and trying to challenge between my mare and the rails. I checked him but realising that he would probably crash through the rails if I stuck to my rights, I let him through. If he had challenged on the other side, he would have won much more easily.'

As it was, the grey filly had to be ridden right out to beat Spree by a length.

A leading firm of Bond Street bookmakers said that if Spree had won, they would have had to pay out £75,000 to the connections who had backed Only For Life and the filly ante-post to win that sum in a £25 each way double.

Anyway, Hula Dancer won and Jimmy had great hopes for the Oaks with the Beckhampton runner-up. Unfortunately there was another international star trained at Rossmore Lodge on the Curragh by Paddy Prendergast and at Epsom on that last day of May in this vintage year when Relko had won the Derby and Exbury the Coronation Cup, neither they, nor anything else, could have beaten Noblesse.

Jimmy rode a copybook race on Spree, but even as he took the lead two furlongs out to make his best way home, so Noblesse glided – there is no other word – past her and flew on up the hill to win on a tight rein by ten lengths.

'It could have been twenty,' said forty-year-old Australian

Bill Williamson on Vaguely Noble. 'In a sport that is fraught with temptation, Bill has always been the personification of integrity'

George Moore is led in after another win on Hopeful Venture. 'I have written that he was the greatest, and I'll stick to that opinion'

Joe Mercer on John and Jean Hislop's Brigadier Gerard. 'Brigadier Gerard's greatness must owe a lot to the expert, sympathetic handling of his devoted rider'

Garnet Bougoure, who was winning his first English classic. 'This is the best horse I have ever ridden.'

Jimmy said simply: 'I thought I had a chance, but Noblesse went by like an express. It was a revelation.'

1964 looked like being a most frustrating year. His classic horse was Charles Englehard's tough, genuine Indiana. But it was the season of Santa Claus and Jimmy did very well to finish second only a length behind the favourite in the Derby.

The Epsom form was completely vindicated first in the Irish Sweeps Derby which English-bred Santa Claus won by four comfortable lengths and then the following day, in the Grand Prix de Paris, when Indiana ran a magnificent race to finish second only half a length behind White Label.

After considerable doubt and speculation, Mick Rogers decided that Santa Claus should miss the St Leger, with the result that Jimmy and Indiana finally came into their own at Doncaster.

Jean Deforge, the French star jockey, rode one of his less happy races on White Label.

The Rothschild colt, who had made nearly all the running to win over one mile seven furlongs at Longchamp, was now ridden inexplicably from behind. So far behind, in fact, that he was still two lengths last five-and-a-half furlongs from home. In the circumstances he did well to finish sixth.

Jimmy took the lead two furlongs out and looked like coming home alone until Bill Williamson brought Paddy Prendergast's Patti with a brilliantly timed run. Colt and filly fought out a memorable battle until right on the line Jimmy produced a final thrust so that Indiana stuck his nose out to win by a head.

Ten days later Mick Rogers announced that Santa Claus would run in the Arc de Triomphe and nominated England's leading stylist to partner the dual Derby winner in the great race at Longchamp. The choice demonstrated the heights to which Jimmy had risen. He has remained at this peak ever since – one of the few top class international riders in the world.

It was a strange Arc without two of this happy band. At Longchamp a week earlier Lester Piggott, riding Persian Garden in the Prix Henri Delamarre, had been brought down along with two other jockeys, Marcel Despalmas and former French champion Roger Poincelet. Lester was injured badly enough to put him out of action for three weeks. A few days later his French counterpart, Yves Saint-Martin, received a month's suspension for causing an accident.

The French stewards announced, 'We have established that Saint-Martin was responsible for the accident which brought down three horses, but we exclude any malicious manoeuvre on his part.'

This incident really marked the start of the tightening of discipline by the French authorities.

The big race field included Ragusa, concluding a triumphant four-year-old season as a great tribute to the courage of his owners, the Mullions, and the skill of their champion trainer, Paddy Prendergast, and the French Derby winner, Le Fabuleux.

In the glorious sunshine before the race Paddy declared, 'There will be no excuse for anyone on account of the going.' Nevertheless there were plenty of excuses for Santa Claus when he failed by three-quarters of a length to land the £79,500 prize, beating Ragusa into third place by a head.

The winner, a surprise to most of the big crowd, was the English-bred former Italian colt, Prince Royal II, a Ribot colt, bought by American cowboy, Rex Ellsworth, only three weeks earlier for £189,000 and now trained by George Bridgland at Chantilly.

For the first time the French stewards had ordered that all runners must keep their position in the draw for the first four hundred yards. What a pleasure it was for us, still deprived of stalls, to see a magnificent break as Nasram jumped off in front, soon to be followed by Mercure, the pacemaker for Le Fabuleux.

At halfway Mercure led from Belle Sicambre and Prince Royal, the mount of Roger Poincelot. Descending the hill, these three were in front of Nasram, surprise conqueror of Santa Claus in Ascot's King George VI and Queen Elizabeth Stakes, Le Fabuleux and Ragusa. Turning into the straight, the favourite, Le Fabuleux, ridden by Jean Massard, raced into the lead, followed by Santa Claus, on whom Jimmy had moved just at the right time.

But Le Fabuleux was tiring and, as Jimmy began his challenge, the 6/4 favourite bumped him heavily. Poincelet now sent Prince Royal on the front and made his best way home. Santa recovered and was in full cry after the winner, when he checked his stride crossing a path. In spite of all Jimmy's efforts, Roger kept Prince Royal going and held on to win his third Arc de Triomphe.

Jimmy, thrilled with Santa's performance, said, 'He's like a Rolls-Royce. If the race were run again, I'd still choose ro ride him rather than the winner. On the turn into the straight, I was lying fifth just behind Le Fabuleux. As he cracked, I moved up on his outside, but under pressure Le Fabuleux rolled into my horse, knocking him sideways, costing us one-and-a-half lengths. Then I went after Prince Royal only for my chap to change legs crossing the path.'

Immediately after the results had been announced, the objection siren sounded. It heralded a steward's inquiry into the fall of Mercure and resulted in a month's suspension for Garnet Boujoure because it was alleged that Ragusa had caused the French colt's fall. Scobie Breasley was grounded for four days for obstructing a horse in the Prix du Moulin on Arc Day.

Our jockeys were finding out the hard way the meaning of full patrol camera coverage. The French cameras are magnificent. Every inch of every race is seen in detail from three angles.

In the spring of 1966 we had an interesting situation. Noel Murless was still uneasily together with a jockey fretting at the ties of a retainer, which was now no more than a verbal agreement. Lester had ridden a lot the previous year for Paddy Prendergast, the first Irish-based man to hold the title, who had now completed three seasons as champion British trainer. With a stable full of promise 'P.J.' had signed on the young Sydney rider, Des Lake, as first jockey. In France, Lester had ridden Kashmir II in his three victories as a two-year-old. Yorkshireman, Peter Butler, the colt's owner, had always kept his sights on the 2,000 Guineas and would obviously have liked the assurance that Lester would ride his Tudor Melody colt.

Jimmy says: 'It was a bit of a muddle for Lester while he was waiting to see. But it was lucky for me.'

On 1st April, Kashmir ridden in his first start of the new

season by Mick Bartholomew's work-rider, twenty-four-year-old Max Brahinski, won the Prix Djebel at Maisons-Laffitte so smoothly. Although Young Emperor was Guineas favourite at 2/1, Kashmir was second in demand at 7/1.

Two days later, Jimmy flew over to Paris on a busman's holiday for the opening of the new stands at Longchamp.

This was a landmark in the world's racing history. The French on the whole are fair-weather sportsmen. But, as Hemingway and others have noted over the years, racing is part of the Parisian way of life. You have a good lunch on Sunday and then you go off to the races in or near the Bois de Boulogne to meet your friends, have a few bets, barrack the jockeys with Gallic ferocity and generally enjoy a good afternoon out. In every country there is a certain amount of loose money, which can be used for the benefit of the state and of those sports which generate the gambling.

In France, however, where there are no football pools and no bookmakers to make their own profits out of the sport, tote-monopolised racing with its attractive Tierce bet, which has caught the public imagination to such an extent, reaps an enormous harvest to the frustrated envy of other sports and, in particular, football! So, when it was decided to rebuild the famous Longchamp stands, we expected something good, but never dreamt of the superb functional palace which emerged. The Societé d'Encouragement, led by Marcel Boussac and his charming, talented Secretary-General, Jean Romanet, thought big from the start. Their architects and builders responded to their inspired enthusiasm and produced one of the most remarkable engineering feats to launch the new project.

Like the Windmill (not the old one on the course!) Longchamp never closed. They kept racing through 1965 while the sensational new stands were built at the side of the old ones on gigantic rollers. During the winter the whole edifice was rolled into place.

That was certainly a memorable April in Paris. I wrote at the time: 'Those responsible for English racecourses should be compulsorily transported to see the new Longchamp.'

The chairman of the Racecourse Association, Henry Hyde, said 'I have been all over the new stands. They are wonderful

– fabulous.' He added: 'I simply cannot find the words to express my admiration of the whole set-up.'

Instead of building for a contemporary social structure, the French had built a racecourse to last at least a hundred years. They rammed home the lesson, which most of the British Turf authorities still refused to accept, that racing must be highly competitive as entertainment.

With colour television at every point on every floor, innumerable bars, snack bars, telephones, interpreters, hostesses and even a travel agency, the public was sheltered in smooth white luxury to watch racing from a stand which, unlike Ascot's Queen Elizabeth II monstrosity, is perfectly angled.

30,000 people went racing on that cold spring Sunday afternoon. This remarkable attendance, which, with no discomfort, has seemed miniscule since, caused some serious rethinking among the world's turf rulers. Two American racing regulars, who had come over for the opening said, 'This is far better than any track in the United States.'

Only an hour away from London, in the world's most romantic capital, there has been ever since enough attraction in an afternoon's racing at Longchamp to tempt people from television and other rival entertainments.

At a time when English racing was still hide-bound by Victorian middle-class snobbery, there was no question there of having to be signed in by a member or applying months in advance for a voucher and subjecting yourself to a social screening. There were reserved seats available to all who could afford less than most London theatre seats. Those two Americans had paid about fifteen shillings for their entertainment and reserved seats.

During the succeeding years, thousands of English racegoers, as well as the natives, have grown to love this wonderful racecourse, whose superb amenities improve with familiarity. The size of the crowd on big race days has to be seen to be believed. Yet there is no discomfort, except at the tote windows. In this respect only, the French still have much to learn from the Americans and Australians.

Jimmy was offered the Guineas ride on Track Spare. But, after riding Kashmir in a gallop at Chantilly, he had no difficulty in deciding in favour of the French-trained colt.

So on 27th April, exile Mick Bartholomew returned to the land of his fathers to gain the greatest triumph of his career by winning the 2,000 Guineas. Appropriately the Irish-bred winner was English owned and ridden.

The sheen on handsome Kashmir's sleek ebony hide, contrasting strongly with the rougher coats of his English and Irish rivals, advertised the milder spring climate of the great French training centre, whither the Bartholomew family had emigrated a hundred years earlier.

It was probably just through that little extra fitness that the cold held on to win at 15/2 from England's only representative in the first six, the 66/1 outsider, Great Nephew, with Paddy Prendergast's pair, Celtic Song and Young Emperor, third and fourth.

After steady morning rain the winner's time, 1 min. 40.68 sec. was good – nearly 2½ sec. better than the average for the Rowley mile.

Just as Jimmy had won both his previous English classics – the Guineas on Only For Life and the Leger on Indiana – by the narrowest margins, so now he was to win again by a short head. And he still attributes his success to a lesson he learnt sixteen years before when he watched Charlie Smirke snatch the same race by the same distance on Palestine.

Best drawn at No. 1 on the stands rails, he settled Kashmir behind Lester on free-running Young Emperor and, approaching the Bushes, drifted towards the centre.

'As we came to the top of the hill,' he said, 'I thought of Smirke on Palestine, spurted down the hill into the lead and, having stolen that march, just managed to hold on, thanks to Kashmir's courage. It was a fair, truly run race, the best Guineas I have ever ridden in.'

Bill Rickaby, riding once more for Jack Jarvis, but this time on the stable's second string – Pretendre, ridden by Paul Cook, was 9/4 favourite – produced one of the finest efforts of a long career on Great Nephew.

Peter Butler, who commutes between York and Paris, bought Kashmir as a yearling at Newmarket for 8,600 guineas. 'Lindley could not have ridden him better,' he said, 'Piggott, who normally rides for me, had virtually promised to ride Young Emperor at the Gimcrack dinner. As he could not let me know his final decision in time, I had to engage another rider.'

Jimmy says now: 'Kashmir never really got a mile. He was a seven furlong horse. Great Nephew went on to prove in France that he was a top-class performer at a mile and even a mile and a quarter.

'But you can win the Guineas with a sprinter, Smirke showed how and I proved it again. As Gordon says, you musn't pull a horse back on the Rowley Mile. But you must jump him off and sit into him, quietly restraining him until the Bushes, just before the top of the hill. Then you must go like hell and hope that your speed and momentum down the hill carry you up the other side to the winning-post.'

So Jimmy has continued at the top of the tree, always troubled a bit by weight problems – he can't do less than 8 st. 7 lbs. – but an intelligent superb stylist, eminently fitted to be numbered among the great ones of all time.

The only trouble with him and Joe is that they happened to be contemporaries of Lester Piggott. Otherwise I am sure that each would have taken his turn as champion jockey.

8: Edward Hide, Willie Carson and Tony Murray

Edward Hide rode Forbear for me at Chester. He was only a boy, apprenticed to his father, Shropshire farmer Bill, one of the nicest men ever to hold a trainer's licence. She was a bonny, dark bay two-year-old filly, full of potential – the epitome of that old-time recipe, 'the head of an angel and the backside of a cook.' But she was still as buxom as a barmaid – she had been very well done at the Lambourn Stud – and I couldn't get the weight off at home. So she needed the race, but she must not be hurt.

I thought the sharp track would suit her and I gave Edward the only orders that it is fair to give to a boy, as I had been taught by Atty Persse: 'Get as close as you can, but don't knock her about.'

I didn't know my jockey, though he was already being hailed as a most promising young rider. I did know that, if he even touched my filly with the whip, I'd crucify him.

He rode her quite beautifully, kept her balanced throughout and gave her every chance. She finished close-up fifth and I was absolutely delighted. She had had a perfect education that would stand her in good stead for the rest of her days.

A week later Edward came up to me at another meeting. 'Did that filly eat up all right, sir?' he asked. In that moment I knew that any boy as dedicated to his horses as this, just had to be a great jockey.

Charlie Elsey, who will always remain my *beau ideal* of a trainer, thought so too and lost no time in signing him up. 'That lad knows everything that goes on in every race,' he told me. 'If I were a betting man I could make a fortune on the things he tells me. He's a fine jockey and, at the same time, a great help to his trainer.'

Edward rode 131 winners in 1957 and topped the century again in the following two seasons. He finished third on Brioche behind Ballymoss in the 1957 St Leger, and two years later won the Doncaster classic on bookmaker William Hill's good filly Cantelo.

He has ridden so many good races, that we are inclined to take him for granted. We have come to expect the highest standard of skill, competence and integrity and he never lets us down. In 1967 he rode a beautifully judged race to win the Oaks on Pia, the cosmopolitan filly nobody wanted, to notch up a first classic success for Bill Elsey, whose father had won the classic with Frieze and Musidora.

This was the year when Lord Harding left the Levy Board and British racing received the tonic it so desperately needed in the appointment of George Wigg. At the end of April 1968 the new Chairman was already making his presence felt. His new levy scheme was designed to raise £3,840,000 from the bookmakers in the year beginning 1st April, 1969. This scheme was £1,540,000 more than the current scheme. He announced then: 'We need about £5 million a year for British racing to become viable so as to take its rightful place in the world.'

He has achieved this aim, despite much opposition from some of those people, whom he has helped the most, the rich racehorse owners. The bookmakers fought him at first, but they learnt to trust him.

In 1969, the year when Edward came south as a successor to Scobie Breasley in the job of first jockey to Sir Gordon Richards, George had his first head-on clash with the old brigade.

It all started after the end of the season when David Robinson, self-made millionaire, former chief of Robinson Rentals and the admirable owner of Britain's largest racing stable, used the traditional Gimcrack speech for a slashing attack on the way racing was run in this country.

The fat was in the fire. Sir Randle Fielden, the Senior Steward, said, 'Mr Robinson's speech highlights the muddled thinking of what the responsibilities of the Jockey Club are. We are not responsible for the management of courses with the exception of Newmarket. I can assure Mr Robinson that I will certainly help him in any way I can as long as it comes within the responsibility of the Jockey Club.'

There was a different response from George Wigg. He declared, 'Racing's governing body must be formed by people of high competence drawn from all sections of society. Mr Robinson has brought the whole subject out into the open. It is now respectable to talk about it.' And he did so, in no uncertain fashion.

A few days later, speaking at the Bollinger Lunch, he said that racing's integrity and its fight to remove corruption at all levels is due to the stewards. On the other hand, he viewed the Jockey Club, an organisation of grandeur and majesty, with awe and astonishment.

'I have no hostility to it, no special love for it, and it would be irresponsible and even hypocritical, it I did not hold the view, held by many, that it is not a particularly appropriate machine to discharge the racing responsibilities which still fall upon it.'

During the two years that Lord Wigg had been in charge of the Levy Board his reforms included the doubling of prize money, the acquisition of Epsom and Sandown, and the benefit scheme for jockeys.

'When I took over,' he said, 'there was just a static income and rising expenditure.'

Matters came to a head at Ascot on the Saturday of that week three days before Christmas, when the Duke of Norfolk surprised the crowd by taking the public address microphone and making a vigorous speech in answer to those by David Robinson and Lord Wigg. This speech in turn provoked a strongly worded response from George Wigg. The sparks had begun to fly.

However, Major-General Sir Randle Feilden, senior steward of the Jockey Club, then said: 'The last two weeks have seen a fair quota of statements many of which have done racing little good.

'As far as I am concerned, the stewards of the Jockey Club and I have a job to do, and we will work with all those who are prepared to work with us for the future prosperity of racing.

From time to time, differences of opinion do arise, and my intention is to approach these problems without any consideration of personalities.

'The stewards, as always, wish to work harmoniously and in co-operation with every section of the racing industry.'

This confrontation cleared the air. Feilden emerged from the fracas with his position strengthened. He had shown considerable tact throughout and has been able to work with Wigg ever since to the benefit of the sport.

By October 1970 Edward Hide was thirty-three years old. His 1,350 successes included wins on every British race course. Since he had left his Malton home and stud to join Gordon at the start of the '69 season, he had already ridden nearly 150 winners and the call of the south was strong. Nevertheless he turned down a most tempting offer with Ryan Price's fast expanding stable and returned to a £4,000 a year retainer at Highfield, where he had spent most of his career.

But second claim on his services was taken by Bill Watts, who had taken over from Walter Wharton at Richmond. This was to prove the decisive factor. The high-class horses he now had to ride included Richard Stanley's lovely filly Waterloo.

After finishing third in her preliminary outing to the subsequent 2,000 Guineas winner High Top, Waterloo was allowed to start at 8 to 1 in the One Thousand. She looked superb. Edward sat into her until the Bushes, where he took the lead and had no difficulty in holding off Sandy Barclay on the French filly Marisela, to win by two lengths.

As I write, the virus-cursed Flat season of 1972 has just ended with Edward Hide third on the list. He rode 105 winners, which was two more than Lester Piggott, who was busy capturing the European Championship on the eve of Britain's entry into the Common Market. Eddie scored ninety seconds and eighty-nine thirds, so that he was unplaced in only 326 of his 610 races. The Hide fans know that they always get full value for their money.

I have always believed that, given, say, the Murless retainer when Warren Place was at its peak, Edward would have been champion jockey. He has the ability, intelligence and general outlook. Furthermore, his somewhat shy, self-effacing manner belies great determination and dash. He rides every type of course equally well and it is significant that Chester with its tight bends is, and always has been, one of his favourite tracks. Like Lester he shines on the Roodeye and, also like 'the long fellow', he rides that totally different, wonderful other northern course, Doncaster, brilliantly.

In 1967, however, a typically unselfish decision by Eddie won the £6,583 Lincoln Handicap for his father. He decided, entirely off his own bat, to forego the ride on Ben Novus in the year's first big flat-race.

Instead of putting up overweight, the course specialist watched from the stands as Peter Robinson took the lead a furlong out and drove the black five-year-old for a splendid victory.

Eddie, who had ridden the horse in nearly all his previous races, would have ridden him in the Lincoln if he had been able to do the weight of 7 st. 10 lbs.

'I ride at 7 st. 13 lbs.,' he said, 'and, while I might have risked one pound overweight, it would not have been fair to put up any more.'

So six weeks before the race Eddie and his father engaged Peter Robinson, who had previously won the Lincoln on Marshal Pil and Mighty Gurkha. And they were able to tell the owner, Irish veterinary surgeon John Peatt, who had just retired after twenty-six years practice at Leominster, that his 300 guinea bargain purchase had a great chance of winning.

'I have been backing my horse ever since then,' said Peatt. 'When I saw my green colours a furlong from home, I knew I was going to win. It is by far my biggest success. Robinson rode him just like Edward.'

There was a happy postscript five years later, which surprisingly escaped the Press at the time (possibly because I was still in limbo between leaving the *Daily Mail* and joining *The Sun*!).

When Peter Robinson, now a trainer, required a jockey for his strongly fancied Sovereign Bill in the Irish Sweeps Lincoln, he offered the ride to Eddie who had won the race on Double Cream, the previous year.

Sovereign Bill opened at 13/2, but was backed down to favourite at 9/2 in an infectious gamble. A quarter of a mile from home he was hanging badly to the left, but Eddie coolly straightened him, took the lead and rode him out strongly to win by three-quarters of a length from Dowdstown Charley. Peter had repaid the favour. There can have been few more satisfactory endings.

The only two jockeys above Eddie in the final 1972 list were Willie Carson and Tony Murray, who had for some months been running neck and neck rather as Scobie and Lester used to a few years earlier. Willie was backed by Bernard van Cutsem's powerful, superbly-run Newmarket stable. Tony was first jockey to Ryan Price, who, like Vincent O'Brien before him, was losing no time in proving that a great horsemaster is equally good on the Flat as over obstacles.

Both rode their first classic winners this year for their own stables; Willie took the 2,000 Guineas on High Top, Tony rode Ginevra to victory in the Oaks. Both are quiet, almost shy, level-headed intelligent young men imbued with the will to win. But there the resemblance ends.

Although the wee Scots champion is built in the ideal mould for an international jockey, he has taken time to mature and then has suddenly blossomed in the last three years. Consider the winning figures of the thirty-year-old champion. 1962 – 1; 1963 – 5; 1964 – 15; 1965 – 37; 1966 – 35; 1967 – 35; 1968 – 61; 1969 – 66; 1970 – 86; 1971 – 145 (runner-up to Lester), and 1972 – 132 (champion).

For Willie wasn't born into racing. He just became a jockey because he was so small. 'Everyone went on about how tiny I was,' he says, 'and joked about how I'd have to be a jockey, until I started to believe it myself.'

As a result his parents managed to afford riding lessons for him from the age of twelve with a Mrs Macfarlane of Dunblane in Perthshire, who finally got him into racing by writing round to suitable trainers who might have room for a likely apprentice.

Willie more or less tossed up between the three big trainers who replied favourably. He settled for Gerald Armstrong and is thankful that it turned out this way, because, on Gerald's retirement, his indentures were transferred to brother Sam, who had already established a great reputation as a trainer of boys as well as horses and owners.

This was a very lucky form of education for the young Scot,

because Gerald Armstrong, though nothing like as good a trainer as Sam, was an infinitely superior horseman – as outstanding an amateur as you will ever see.

So the half-a-crown a week apprentice learnt to jump his horses off, to sit into them until they were truly balanced before asking them for a special effort. Then driving with ever-increasing power-packed rhythm, inspiring them to produce all their reserves. It is this tremendous attack and this finishing style so reminiscent of Fred Winter that characterises Willie and will keep him at the top of his profession for many years to come.

In 1971, when his 145 winners made him runner-up to Lester, well clear of Geoff Lewis and Tony Murray, Willie was genuinely amazed. 'I can't believe it,' he told me at the December sales. 'I just have to pinch myself to make sure I'm still awake.'

And when a year later he was being congratulated on becoming champion, he kept repeating, 'I just can't describe how I feel. "The Big Fellow" must have been taking it easy this year.'

This is not false modesty. It is all part of the character of one of the nicest chaps I or you will ever meet. Moreover, his natural personality was helped by Sam Armstrong's treatment and by his wife Carole, whom he married before his twentieth birthday when he moved down from Yorkshire to Newmarket.

'Both the Armstrongs were tough masters, real pushers,' he says. 'In some ways Gerald was harder, but Sam had a fantastic record with apprentices – he knew enough to be hardest on the ones who were getting ahead. No fun at the time, but I know how it keeps a kid in line. No wonder I finished my apprenticeship without getting big-headed.'

Still you can't come without a horse and for all his skill, charm and integrity he might not have become champion without the van Cutsem retainer and the wisdom of that splendid trainer in sending him to winter in Hialeah. How well Willie responded. All the tribulations of Crowned Prince's abdication were forgotten and there was a tear in Bernard's eye as his jockey made all the running on the Rowley Mile and powered High Top home to hold off the subsequent Derby winner Roberto by half a length. Bernard, too, was winning his first classic.

Just as Willie, with his integrity, modesty and attack is a product of the famous Armstrong school, so his rival Tony Murray, who possesses the same qualities, was one of the star pupils of the current great schoolmaster, Frenchy Nicholson.

Tony was born into racing. I will remember his father, Paddy Murray, as one of the bravest of the second rank jumping jockeys. Paddy married a Wantage girl and it was only natural for him to entrust his son to his old friend, Frenchy. It was a wise move. Frenchy, who had already brought out Paul Cook and was soon to produce Jimmy Eddery's boy Pat as well as other rising stars, schooled this good little horseman to perfection as a top-class apprentice. In his first season, 1966, he rode fourteen winners. Subsequent years produced 37, 31, 44, 69, 112 and 122.

These figures would have been even more impressive, but for a horrible fall when he was put over the rails out in the country at a Windsor evening meeting. A fall, which nearly killed him, shattered his jaw and gave him a new tough, resolute look, older than his years, but in keeping with his character.

Incidentally, it is extraordinary to reflect that our Jockey Club refused to introduce skull-caps for flat-race jockeys until the late fifties after my good apprentice, Taffy Thomas, had been killed when his head struck one of the concrete uprights, when Tottenham, stumbling, hurled him into the Warwick rails. Apparently the objection had been that they 'didn't look nice.'

To his eternal credit John Rickman, referring to Taffy's death in the *Daily Mail,* reminded the Jockey Club, that in the opinion of most normal people, a live, plain jockey in a skull-cap looked considerably nicer than a dead pretty one without.

Like Lester Piggott, Jimmy Lindley, Martin Molony and many of the great ones of the past, including Fred Archer, Tony hopes to have a limited number of rides over obstacles.

His chief employer, Ryan Price, will always keep a few jumpers. 'We've got to have some fun and laughs during the winter,' says the Findon maestro.

British jockeyship is in safe hands. With the wealth of young talent about and strict, fair, brilliant instructors in the Armstrong-Nicholson mould, it is becoming again the envy of the world.

9: Lester Piggott

Genius – an extraordinary natural instinctive ability. That's what Lester has and what precious few jockeys have ever had before.

I saw it in action for the first time when I started training at Lambourn. One of the first yearlings I bought was a chestnut filly by Nasrullah, who had inherited some of her brilliant sire's temperament. The early days of a racehorse's training are vital. It is all too easy to ruin it by a stupid mistake. So, when I decided to send the newly broken youngsters upsides for the first time, I asked fourteen-year-old Lester to come and ride out for me.

He knew my little house in Upper Lambourn well. It had been his school. Originally he had gone to St Alfred's in Wantage but, once he had started race-riding at the age of twelve, in order to comply with the law, he used to bicycle up to have lessons with old Miss Westlake two or three times a week.

All the breaking period is fascinating, but nerve-racking – never more so than when, after they have been ridden away and taught to trot and canter in a string, you ask them to jump off and gallop two furlongs upsides for the first time. So, as Lester went down to jump the Nasrullah filly off with the others, I expected anything to happen. I needn't have worried.

While the others swerved, ducked and dived, the fourteen-year-old sitting quite still, completely unconcerned, brought her up the gallop towards me galloping into her bridle, going as straight as a gun-barrel. It was an education, which she was to appreciate for the rest of her life. She was my first winner on the flat.

You hear so much about hands, that God-given gift, which combines true horsemanship with a sympathetic understanding of the animal. Few people have good hands. Lester has always had perfect hands.

The essential quality of genius is, of course, that it is born in you and Lester Keith Piggott, who was born on Guy Fawkes Day in 1935, had all the right qualifications. His mother, Iris, was a Rickaby, sister of Bill and Fred. His father, Keith, was a magnificent, fearless jumping jockey and his grandfather, a champion jockey, rode three Grand National winners.

'I think it's harder to do that than to win the Derby three times,' says his grandson.

By 1948 when I arrived in Lambourn as assistant trainer to Atty Persse, Keith Piggott had been training for some time at his little yard on the Eastbury Road. This was the year, which saw his son, who had been riding in gymkhanas during the war years, having his first long-awaited ride in public.

He had been riding a racehorse in his father's string since he was ten, but it was not until his twelfth birthday that he was officially allowed to be apprenticed to Keith.

They lost no time. Only a fortnight after the opening of the new season Lester rode a three-year-old filly called Chase at Salisbury. But the first winner did not come until Chase had been downgraded to a Haydock seller with only 6 st. 9 lbs. on 18th August. Lester won by 1½ lengths.

By the end of the year he had had fourteen rides, yielding a winner and two seconds.

Helped particularly by the Cundell cousins, he had 120 rides in 1949, won six races and was placed eighteen times. To the delight of the Press the thirteen-year-old beat Gordon Richards in a close finish.

Now came the crunch. Look back at those form-books and study the names of the jockeys who were riding against this brilliant, gifted boy, who will be thirty-eight on the 5th November, 1973. Most of his rivals were at least that age already in 1950. There was Tommy Weston, Charlie Smirke, Charlie Elliott, Rae (Togo) Johnstone, Michael Beary, Eph and Doug Smith, Harry Carr, Ken Gethin, Billy Nevett, Cliff Richards, Tommy Lowrey, Edgar Britt, Sam and Arthur Wragg, Bill Rickaby and others of the same vintage. They were all old enough to be Lester's father. They had all made their names before the war. They all expected to carry on exactly the same as before, riding for the same trainers and owners just as though nothing had happened.

They, the local stewards and the members of the Jockey Club could not or would not understand that the ten years which included the holocaust had shattered the whole structure of British Society. As has been said on more than one occasion, when a major world crisis has been greeted by record prices at the sales, racing people only seem to read the *Sporting Life* and the back pages of the other papers. They only knew that they liked their little world as they had always known it and bitterly resented any interference.

The first sign of that interference took the form of a shy, deaf, slight lad with a jumping name, poker-face, the hands of an angel and an independence worthy of Nelson. It would have been all right if he had been moderate. As it was, he was brilliant and they couldn't forgive him.

Lester explains that surly, stubborn image, which has been at the root of so much of his trouble.

'I was deaf in one ear,' he says. 'Nobody knew how I got deaf and nobody could do anything about it. But it's much better now than it was when I was a boy. Being a bit deaf, you did live on your own a bit. It made you a bit shy. But it had its good points. You got on with things and did them your own way, and you didn't rely on praise or blame because half the time you never heard it.

'Not only am I not so deaf now, but I have learnt to lip-read and I watch people's faces. They're more expressive than horses' faces, but not so reliable. But even now if somebody says something when I'm not looking directly at them I may not hear. So sometimes people think I'm rude. Sometimes they think I'm disagreeing when I'm not. Sometimes they think I'm agreeing when I'm not, which is worse.'

He would arrive at the weighing room with his father, walk in, look neither to right nor to left – 'I've never been one of those Hello people' – get changed, go out and ride his race, intent on winning. The old jockeys were unhappy, jealous and frightened.

They had always been accustomed to the old type of apprentice, who was just a little boy doing what he was told by them, the senior jockeys. In their different ways they were prepared to help a boy of this type such as they had been themselves way back in those distant pre-war days. Their help, however, was sometimes not quite as philanthropic as it might have been.

On the gallops Michael Beary, as stable-jockey to Atty Persse, would order the boys about – 'come up a little. Don't hang back!' 'Pull him back to me now, you're riding work, not trying to win the gallop!' and so on.

Michael was riding in the Victoria Cup on one of the rare occasions when a Persse apprentice had a ride on a fancied horse. As the starter called them up, the lad brought his mount into line beside the great man, only to be told by Michael in that high-pitched Irish drawl: 'This is no place for you, little boy. It's very dangerous. Get back out of it. D'you hear what I say? Get back!' Accustomed as he was to obeying Michael's orders, the boy pulled back. At that moment the tapes went up and he was hopelessly left. That danger was out of the way.

Gordon, of course, was a law unto himself. As we have seen in his own chapter, he was a colossus among midgets, ever ready to help the boys, and, however old he might pretend to be, he was, and is, younger than any of them at heart.

The remainder bitterly resented the intrusion of L. Piggott into their cosy little world, where everyone was happy in a Walter Mitty way, even though the prize-money at Royal Ascot was, in many cases, lower than it had been in the twenties.

It is fascinating in a gruesome sort of way to look at the list of Jockey Club members in 1944, a year before the end of hostilities and four years before the advent of Lester.

Of the forty-three members, excluding honorary members (why, incidentally, did they have to insult the Aga Khan by making him an 'honorary' member? Did they think he couldn't afford the subscription?) twelve were elected before 1916 and twenty-seven before 1930. Most of them were far too old to fight and, therefore, they survived. Thirty-one of them, excluding members of the Royal blood, had hereditary titles. Few of them had any idea how to run a sport which was developing into a vast complex industry worth hundreds of millions of pounds in other countries.

The Duke of Portland had been elected in 1881, the Marquess of Crewe in 1895 and the Duke of Westminster in 1904. Even most of the members elected a little later were hardly more lively. More significant, apart from Lord Rosebery and Fred Withington, there was scarcely a real horseman amongst them.

The blame for the decline in British racing, which had led the world since the inauguration of the sport, must be placed squarely at the door of the Jockey Club. The most important lesson I learnt as a regular officer was that I must never blame anyone under my command. 'The fish stinks from the head sonny!' I was told. 'Nobody else is to blame but you!'

Talk about the generation gap. How could such men possibly understand the entirely new democratic thinking of the young Piggott – thinking, which, carried to extremes, has completely shattered the social structure of this country as those old men knew it. As well expect the M.C.C. rulers of those days to understand and sympathise with Mick Jagger. Look back to Newmarket in the nineteen-fifties. Visit the headquarters of racing with me as a young trainer with two runners at the meeting. Some time before, you have had to apply for car labels for your owners and for yourself. Nevertheless the car park was some way from the stands.

After a three-hour drive from Lambourn and a visit to the Links Stables to inspect your horses, you queue with the other trainers and jockeys for entrance by the little turnstile alongside the weighing-room. But, even so, it is only after an argument with two rude, surly elderly gatemen that you gain admission for your wife and are reluctantly supplied with a race-card.

Check at the weighing-room that your travelling headman's declarations were in order. Then, unless you're in the first race, look for some lunch. This is provided for 'owners, provincial trainers and their wives' on long trestle tables in a sort of boiler-room place, full of the large pipes that feed the stand with water and heat at the bottom of the back stand. It was not very good. I sympathised with one of my owner's wives, Olivia Feilden, sister-in-law of the present senior steward of the Jockey Club, when she burst out one day. 'It's just like having lunch in the servants' hall!'

Of course, although we were in fact paying to provide their

entertainment on their race-track, that was exactly how we were all then treated by the Jockey Club – as servants. Although Heaven forbid that one should ever be so ill-bred and bad-mannered as to treat servants as we were sometimes treated, including important foreign visitors. It was so shaming as to make one feel embarrassed for them. I always thought they must have had very bad nannies when they were children.

Membership of Newmarket was considered very exclusive and indeed it was recognised with VIP treatment everywhere. The whole of that enormous members' stand with all its viewing, eating, drinking and other facilities was occupied only by them and, of course, by members of the Jockey Club and of the Jockey Club Rooms, who enjoyed extra privileges in addition.

We were not allowed to cross the Members' lawn in front of their stand. If we wished to have a bet, we were forced to leave the paddock and go right round behind the stand into Tattersalls – a fair trek, particularly on a hot, big, crowded day.

Although the bottom tiers of the little stand looking straight down the Rowley Mile lead on to the Members' lawn, only they were allowed to use them. We ordinary trainers and jockeys were obliged to enter the stand from the back, i.e. out of the paddock, and were then confined in pens at the top.

The first time I used this stand as a trainer I was watching a race with my wife, when we were tapped on the shoulder by another of these surly little gatemen. 'No women allowed this side. This bit of the stands for men only. She'll have to move over to the women's section.' So we weren't even allowed to watch our own horses race together.

When Lester won the Linton Stakes for us on Forbear it was, of course, a great thrill to have our first success at Newmarket. But the gilt was somewhat taken off the gingerbread when we were eventually re-united with each other and with our owners in the winners' enclosure. There in one corner stood some Jockey Club members, either staring at us disdainfully or ignoring us completely; chewing the cud and occasionally muttering to each other; like a herd of old constipated cows with bowler hats and cigars. Although some must have recognised my owners, who had been the racecourse doctors in the Midlands for many years, not one of them said 'Well done!' They never even grunted. We felt we were lucky to be allowed on this course at all and that we had in fact sinned by taking one of their prizes. It was a horrible experience on what should have been such a very happy day.

Other racecourses, in varying degrees, possessed the same depressingly forbidding atmosphere of Newmarket. Looking back, it is obvious that the various degrees depended on the particular track's popularity or involvement with the Jockey Club members and their imitators among the local stewards.

So, while Ascot and Kempton were nearly as coldly controlled as Newmarket, Salisbury, Chepstow and nearly all the northern courses, influenced by racing's great impresario, Leslie Petch, remained fun.

There were no starting stalls and no camera patrol. The Stewards' decisions were final and binding. There was no legal representation and no appeal against their verdicts.

By the beginning of the fifties the immediate post-war bonanza was over. Certainly churchmen were complaining about the enormous fast-growing betting turnover, but none of it was finding its way back to the sport on which it depended. The prize-money was so abysmal, that we were speedily becoming the poor relations in a world where we had been the undisputed rulers. Races at Royal Ascot were worth less than they had been in the twenties even though the cost of everything had risen astronomically.

I won four races with a fast two-year-old, Cranford Cross, including the Cuddington Stakes at Epsom, but since they totalled less than a thousand pounds, the owner was actually out of pocket on the season.

The authorities didn't seem to care. In fact administration of racing was so slack, that the dopers began to move in, scenting the prospect of big money, with little risk of being caught and negligible penalties if they were.

This is one of the great disadvantages of the bookmaker system. As long as a criminal can make the equivalent of a bank robbery by preventing a hot favourite from winning, there will always be nobbling and attempts to bribe jockeys to stop horses.

This was the scene into which young Piggott was plunged.

The Jockey Club were his masters and judges, their old, sometimes scared, favoured jockeys his rivals on the course. It could hardly have been a more disastrous introduction. In retrospect, head-on collision was inevitable.

'The jockeys were always running off to tell the stewards not just what I did, but even what I said,' he told me.

In those days you lost the right to claim an apprentice allowance after riding forty winners instead of seventy-five, now that the rule has been changed. So, well before his fourteenth birthday, Lester was riding as a fully-fledged jockey on level terms with the old ones.

Four days after his fourteenth birthday he won a race for Atty Persse on Little Bonnet at Liverpool. The old man was pleased with his handling of the little bay two-year-old filly and the following season engaged him to ride June Ball in the Victoria Cup at Hurst Park. Unfancied at 25/1, Lester finished down the course.

When he came in to unsaddle, Atty, as granite-tough as ever at eighty, came hobbling up on his two sticks with the inevitable Churchillian cigar fixed firmly between his teeth. He glared at Lester with those wide china-blue eyes.

'Well boy?' he barked. In fifty years at the very top of his profession, he had had innumerable apprentices through his hands.

'Your filly needs a longer trip, Mr Persse,' said Lester. Atty couldn't believe his ears. 'What did you say?'

'I said she wants further. Just because she's by a sprinter, it doesn't mean she won't stay. And she gives me the feel of a stayer.'

The blue eyes twinkled.

'How old are you, boy?'

'Fourteen, sir.'

Atty turned to Lord Sefton. 'D'you hear that, Hugh? He's all of fourteen years old and he's teaching me how to train my horses!'

Looking back now, Lester says. 'I'd still do the same. If you can't help the trainer, who can? That's what you're there for, isn't it?'

He was being quite serious, dedicated to his life's task of riding winners, but they laughed at first and then regarded it as gross impertinence.

Lester's own explanation of the trouble that started now and was to follow him through his career is typically simple. 'Old jockeys, riding for old trainers and old stewards', he says.

In life there is always bitter resentment from moderate people who have enjoyed success against the upsurge of brilliant youth. Actors and actresses will use their experience to upstage young members of their profession, frequently with devastating effect.

By 1950, when Lester was fourteen, only Gordon Richards, now forty-six, was untouched by the success of 'the Golden Boy'. The great champion could still rely on his own immense skill to outride him. Gordon has denied that the powers that be 'had Lester in line', as they say in the Army when the authorities are determined to find fault with a soldier and bring him to book. I believe that the champion, who had always been brought up to respect authority and has always seen the best in everyone, was too good in every way to suspect it. He took things at their face value and I'm sure that, in this case, he was wrong.

First they changed the conduct of racing in this country, where limited suspensions were virtually unknown. An offender either lost his licence, was warned off or fined. The last was a ludicrous sentence on jockeys, earning thousands of pounds a year, expecting and usually getting their presents in hard untaxable cash. The fine, grandiosely imposed by the Stewards, was merely deducted from the jockey's taxed account at Weatherby's. He never noticed it.

A certain famous jockey riding a horse belonging to a member of the Jockey Club in a big sprint on a course where the draw was desperately important, was told. 'You've no chance from that draw.'

'Wot, me start from there in these colours?' he exclaimed.

Sure enough he started from the opposite side of the course, incurring a fine of £25. But when he duly won the race, the fine was not even a pin-prick on his thick skin.

On the other hand the 'Master', in this case Lester's father, is held responsible for his apprentice's conduct. And Keith, who was no longer riding, would have felt a fine and would have taken steps to ensure that his son did not repeat the offence. Why then were the Piggotts not fined for the alleged offences?

Lester had started 1950 still claiming the seven pounds allowance. By the Newbury meeting on 20th October he had ridden fifty winners in that one season. For minor infringements he had incurred two cautions and he had been suspended for the rest of the day at Kempton for 'injudicious riding'.

That was normal enough. It was the only form of suspension known in those days. A jockey could (though he rarely was) be suspended for the remainder of the meeting by the local stewards. Anything worse – and it had to be very bad indeed – was referred to the Stewards of the Jockey Club. Then it became a sensation.

So the Newbury incident will always remain to me the most extraordinary miscarriage of justice, particularly because it led to so many more, once a precedent had been set for young Piggott.

I remember it so well. Lester was riding Arthur Budgett's tough stayer, Barnacle, in the 2-mile Manton Handicap. With only 7 st. 7 lbs. he was well in and started joint-favourite at 9/2 with Gordon's mount Phalorain.

Third in demand at 5/1 was Royal Oak IV, ridden by the new Australian artist, Scobie Breasley, who was – let there be no mistake – a very great jockey by any standards.

Soon after entering that long Newbury straight Lester sent Barnacle into the lead. Scobie, like all Aussies, was hugging the rails as they have to on those tight circuits of the country meetings.

Now Keith Piggott had been a magnificent tutor for his son in every aspect of horsemanship and jockeyship except one. He had never taught him to pull his whip through or to use it in his left hand. Moreover Lester has always frustrated this manoeuvre by using an extra long whip – 'a man's whip, not a boy's whip,' he has said. When you remember the lightning speed with which Gordon, Steve Donoghue and George Moore pulled it through and how, as young amateurs, we were made to practise for hours with reins on the foot of a bed or the back of a chair, it is very surprising still to find this chink in the armour of a great champion.

Two and a half furlongs from home, Barnacle, racing on his own now, hung over towards the rails. Scobie, veteran of a thousand such incidents, stood up in his irons and made a great show of being crossed before riding like a demon to ensure that he finished second. It was legitimate gamesmanship, which we had seen so often from that great character, Charlie Smirke.

Nevertheless, Barnacle was running on so strongly (he was to win the Great Metropolitan and the Rosebery Memorial in the following year) that Royal Oak would never have caught him in any case and Lester had no difficulty in holding off his rival's challenge to win very comfortably by three-quarters of a length. The third horse was a further four lengths away.

Scobie hurried straight into the weighing-room and lodged an objection for interference and crossing. The patrol camera, already so widely used in other countries, was, of course, unknown to British racing. So the stewards had to rely entirely on the evidence of their own eyes and of the other jockeys. As the master of the apprentice, Keith Piggott had to be called to the inquiry as well as his son. But he has never been a smooth, easy talker and there was no sympathy from these flat stewards for the former jumping star and his slim, pale deaf boy, who shuffled in rather than marching and did not stand to attention in the approved military fashion.

They disqualified Barnacle and placed him last – a gross injustice because, although he must have won in any circumstances, he could not have been worse than second, come hell or high water. This, was, however, still the normal practice in this country. The fact that the owners, who had sacrificed a valuable run and exposed their horse to the handicapper and to the betting public, were, through no fault of their own or of their trainer, hopelessly out of pocket through not receiving even the paltry second prize money, apparently mattered not one whit.

This was bad enough. As long as I live I shall not understand what happened next. They informed Keith that the matter would be referred to the Stewards of the Jockey Club. It was an amazing decision. In those days only the most heinous crimes were so treated. It was like sending a little boy to be tried at the Old Bailey. For, remember, in the eyes of the law Lester was just that – a very little boy of fourteen. A caution, reprimand or even perhaps suspension for the remainder of the meeting would have been adequate punishment. This was as amazing as it was inexplicably unique.

Perplexed, worried but never dreaming that strange, powerful forces were working against him, Lester rode two more winners at the meeting on horses trained by the cousins Frank and Ken Cundell. One of these was Zina, his mount in the next week's Cambridgeshire.

The Newmarket Houghton meeting opened on Tuesday. Once again the Jockey Club broke with precedent and tried Lester's case as a matter of extreme urgency.

They were marched in front of the three Stewards of the Jockey Club. It was an awe-inspiring ceremony, but later Lester says: 'I wasn't afraid then and I've never been afraid since when I've been summoned before the stewards. Come to think of it, I don't think I've ever been afraid of anyone or anything.'

None the less, he felt that the atmosphere was all wrong. 'Everyone seemed against me,' he said. 'It was a nasty feeling.'

They heard the evidence and they then announced their verdict. Fourteen-year-old Lester would be suspended until the end of the season, which was still more than three weeks away. In my opinion it was a savage sentence, which branded him for the future. That was how it all started. The Establishment had shown what they thought of the most brilliant young jockey to come under their jurisdiction. No encouragement or guidance from the top – just hammer down with a feudal blunt instrument. All Jockey Club members, it has been said, are old by the time they are twenty-three. This particular vintage had, it appeared decided that the Piggotts must be put, and kept, firmly 'in their place.'

As the headlines screamed '£10,000-a-year boy suspended,' Lester had the consolation of knowing that the last laugh would surely be his. Out of 403 rides that season he had scored fifty-two wins, forty-five seconds and thirty-nine thirds. When the curtain fell at Manchester on 18th November, he was eleventh on the jockeys' list, just one behind Charlie Elliot, in front of men like Joe Sime, Ken Gethin and Charlie Smirke.

Now there appeared the first of those temperamental horses with which Lester has been associated and which have proved conclusively to me that he is one of the greatest 'naturals' of all time. Remember how he performed on my Nasrullah yearling? Zucchero was by Nasrullah, too, out of a mare by Bois Roussel – a combination which had imparted brilliance and stamina, but also a fair bit of temperament. As a two-year-old he won a race and gave an indication of his vast potential by finishing second in the New Stakes at Royal Ascot. Then he developed a dislike for the starting gate just as another Nasrullah colt, his speedy contemporary, Grey Sovereign, had done. At the end of that season he was transferred by his owner, George Rolls, from Michael Blackmore at Whatcombe to Ken Cundell, who was already helping young Piggott on his way. The big brown colt and the fifteen-year-old boy met for the first time on the Compton gallops and struck up an instant friendship.

After finishing fourth in the seven furlong Henry VIII Stakes at Hurst Park, the new partnership moved on to Epsom for the Blue Riband Trial Stakes, run over the last mile and 110 yards of the Derby course.

In Lester's hands, Zucchero did nothing wrong. Only slowly away, he took the lead a furlong out and won so impressively that he and his boy pilot were written up as having a possible chance in the Derby.

On the big day, however, it was not to be. The preliminaries proved too much for Zucchero. It was, however, a valuable experience for the lad, who was later to make the tricky Epsom track and the world's greatest race his own.

There is a photograph in Lester's cuttings book of the Derby field galloping off into the distance leaving Zucchero far behind at the starting gate. Here is actual evidence, rivalled only by that remarkable picture of The Tetrarch at the start of Sandown's five furlong National Breeders' Produce Stakes. 'The Spotted Wonder' is on his knees with the tapes caught in his teeth, as the rest of the field jumps off. At a conservative estimate he was left twenty lengths. You never realised how stiff that Sandown five is unless you go down and stand at the start. Only here on this sensational horse could Steve Donoghue have achieved the impossible. He sat still and waited until the field came back to him and got up in the last strides to win by a short head.

Although Zucchero did not win the Derby, he put up a remarkable performance once Lester finally persuaded him to start running through the field to finish thirteenth of thirty, three behind Arctic Prince.

'I have no doubt at all,' says his jockey, 'that, if Zucchero had got off with the others, he must have won.'

Zucchero won his next three races, including the Commonwealth Stakes at Sandown, where he beat the St James's Palace winner, Turco II, by six lengths. 'He was always left, but we sort of understood each other,' says Lester. 'I still say he was one of the best horses I've ever ridden.'

The King George VI and Queen Elizabeth Festival of Britain Stakes at Ascot on 21st July had attracted a worthy international field, the two Guineas winners, Ki Ming and Belle of All; the Derby winner, Arctic Prince; François Mathet's superb actioned Tantieme, who had just taken the Coronation Cup; the previous year's Leger winner, Marcel Boussac's Scratch II; Sir Winston Churchill's Colonist; Mossborough, Wilwyn, Supreme Court and four more Frenchmen. Nineteen runners in all.

Once again Zucchero was slowly away and Lester found himself at the back of the field with Supreme Court, ridden by that great international rider, Charlie Elliot. Manny Mercer set a strong gallop on Wilwyn, so that he and most of his rivals were nearly done with as they entered the straight. Here Jacko Doyasbere lost his chance by going too wide on Tantieme.

A furlong out Supreme Court took it up, but Lester still had a bit in hand. The two English colts battled it out and at the finish Elliot just held on to win by threequarters of a length. The third, Tantieme, was six lengths away.

On this showing Zucchero looked a good thing for the St Leger. It would have been sensational if Lester could have won a classic at the age of fifteen.

However, three weeks before the Doncaster race he broke his leg in a heavy fall at Lingfield and was out for the rest of that season.

Zucchero obviously resented his substitute jockey, Charlie

Spares, sulked and finished ninth of eighteen in the Leger behind the Boussac colt Talma II, who, ridden by Rae Johnstone, spreadeagled his field in the most extraordinary way.

Although he was grounded on 25th August with nearly three months of the season to go, Lester had already had 432 rides compared with 403 the previous year. They had produced fifty-one winners, including the Eclipse on that charming bay French colt Mystery IX.

Lester still reckons that he should have won the Derby in 1952. As it was, he came in for a certain amount of ridicule, which was totally unjustified and was mostly inspired by such quips as 'What did I Tulyar?' and so on.

Scobie Breasley, Neville Sellwood and Billy Cook had returned to Australia. So in Scobie's fortunately temporary absence, Lester rode for Druids Lodge and had the mount on Gay Time in the Derby.

Tulyar was a very good little horse, with that thrilling action possessed by the best. When they are fully extended, they seem to drop about a foot – actually 'getting down to it' and almost justifying the description *ventre à terre*. But the Aga Khan's colt, whose one two-year-old success had been in the Buggins Farm Nursery at Haydock, was, in Lester's opinion, still short of his best when the Derby came.

Gay Time was the sort of horse that I personally dislike – a large, light chestnut with a flaxen mane and tail, generally signs of softness. He was a grandson by Rockefella of Hyperion and had a distinct look of the great little stallion's son, the Queen's Aureole, who was now a two-year-old. Both these two were the exception to the rule. Although highly-strung, they were very game.

Unhappily everything conspired against Gay Time at Epsom. He pulled a plate off in the paddock before the race and, after being replated, had to go down to the start by himself. No picnic for a highly strung thoroughbred in the fairground atmosphere of Epsom Downs on Derby Day. By the time that he had made his way through the shouting, down that pathway past the blaring noise of the swings and roundabouts and up the other side to another mass of people thronging the starting gate, he was in a muck lather. He had virtually lost his race already.

Nevertheless he was made of sterner stuff than his appearance indicated. A slow beginner, he was unable to lay up in the early stages. He was drawn on the outside of a large field of thirty-three runners. As always, those with little chance determined to make a show, galloping as far and as fast as they could up that long pull to the top of Tattenham Hill. When, equally inevitably, they began to fall back beaten, Lester was forced to come wide, thereby losing a lot of valuable ground.

Rounding Tattenham Corner into the straight, Smirke sent Tulyar into the lead, but now Gay Time slipped into top gear and, galloping on resolutely, began to make up ground and overhaul the little bay. How close he would have got is anyone's guess. Lester is convinced he would have won if Tulyar had not come across him below the distance and checked him before going on to win by three lengths. Lester determined to object. Knowing the attitude of the hierarchy to their young star, it is most unlikely that his complaint would have been entertained and the Aga Khan's colt disqualified. In the event how happy they must have been.

The boy jockey was tired. Gay Time, a big heavy colt was tired and sprawling. The pull-up at Epsom was the worst in the world, except for a point-to-point course I remember near Taunton, where we had to pull up into a brick wall!

Lester says: 'As I tried to pull him up, Gay Time collided with the rails, fell over on his head, throwing me off, and then galloped away into the wood behind the paddock. When he was eventually found, and I arrived back at the weighing-in room to weigh in, lots of people said I had grounds for objection. So I told the Clerk of the Scales that I wanted to lodge an official objection to the winner for crossing and taking my ground.'

The Clerk of the Scales looked at him and said bluntly, 'You're too late to object!'

This was the Derby. Even in 1952 the difference to the owner of a potential stallion between winning and losing was several hundred thousand pounds. Even if he was late (which Lester still disputes) it was due to an unavoidable painful accident.

The relevant rule of racing has been slightly altered. In 1952 Rule 168 (iv) read: 'An objection to a horse on the ground of a cross, jostle or any act on the part of the jockey . . . must be made within five minutes after the winner has been weighed-in, unless, under special circumstances, the Stewards are satisfied that it could not have been made within that time.'

How could they possibly have signalled 'All right', when the runner-up in the world's most important race was still missing? Were these not special circumstances?

This was the year when John Schapiro, who, with his father, had taken over the Laurel Park race track in Maryland, made history by inaugurating the Washington International. The first two English horses to accept invitations were Wilwyn and his easy Ascot conqueror, Zucchero. Manny Mercer, the other young hopeful of British racing, was to ride Wilwyn. Lester, who, as we have seen, really understood the horse, was to have been on Zucchero.

Unfortunately George Rolls chose this moment to change trainers again and sent the colt from Ken Cundell, who had a claim on Lester's services, to Bill Payne, another friend of the Piggotts, who very much wanted to maintain the successful horse-jockey relationship. Ken and his owners would not let Lester go. They needed him in England. The seeds of that famous freelance decision were undoubtedly planted at a tender age. Charlie Smirke was substituted.

Now Lester, who knew the horse so well, had always accepted the fact that Zucchero would be slowly away from the start. Smirke determined to get him away on terms at all costs. He was a great horseman and he succeeded. But the tactics were mistaken. The colt, surprised, took a tremendous hold and fought for his head all the way, so that he had nearly had enough when he took the lead entering that short straight. He was run out of it by Wilwyn and the American entry, Rube.

'He would have won easily if I had ridden him,' says Lester, 'He was a different class.'

This is indisputable. He had proved it at Ascot. But in fairness to Charlie, the sharp American circuit may have been at least partly responsible for the hard pulling. Horses are apt to dislike our wide staring English course, whereas they love going round bends. This is always the time when they will try to run away and will do so if you let them. Bald Eagle, who won two

Lester Piggott on Sir Ivor. 'Lester now inclines to the view that Sir Ivor was the best horse he has ever ridden'

Sir Ivor, ridden by Lester, wins the 1968 Derby. 'Lester had brilliantly held his colt up, delivered his challenge with split-second timing and made it look easy'

Jimmy Lindley winning the 2,000 Guineas on Kashmir in 1966. 'An intelligent, superb stylist, eminently fitted to be numbered among the great ones of all time'

Waterloo, ridden by Edward Hide. 'We have come to expect the highest standard of skill, competence and integrity, and he never lets us down'

Washington Internationals, and Amerigo were perfect examples of this. They resented English tracks, but came into their own in the United States.

Now twenty years have passed. John Schapiro's dream has almost come true. When Lester and the English Derby winner, Sir Ivor, won the International, it was indeed a great moment. Unfortunately the risk of infection produced a ban on the importing of horses to Europe from America in 1971, which set the race back badly. John's tremendous enthusiasm and hard work deserve to succeed. As one who has helped him in recent years, I can vouch for the innumerable difficulties he has had to overcome. We will return to Washington later for Lester's two triumphs and his row with the American Press.

In 1953 the Piggott Derby partner was Prince Charlemagne, a handsome colt, who was not up to classic standard, but whom Lester rode to victory in the Triumph Hurdle during the Spring of the next momentous year in his career.

Old Joe Lawson, now training at Newmarket, had a backward American three-year-old for Robert Sterling Clark, called Never Say Die, a big liver chestnut son of Nasrullah. Ridden by Scobie Breasley, now happily returned from Australia, he had finished third in his last race of the season, the Dewhurst Stakes.

Lester rode Never Say Die in his first race as a three-year-old, the Union Jack Stakes at Liverpool. They finished second. Then Manny Mercer had the mount in the Newmarket Stakes and was third behind Elopement, the chestnut full-brother to Gay Time.

Suddenly out of the blue a telegram arrived at the Piggott's Lambourn home from Joe Lawson. It said simply, 'You ride Never Say Die in Derby.' One of the oldest trainers had selected the youngest jockey.

He had no cause to regret his choice. Eighteen-year-old Lester handled the colt with all the superb cool of a veteran, to win comfortably by two lengths from Arabian Night with Manny on Darius a neck away third.

If Joe Lawson had been younger, I don't think that he would have run his Derby winner again at Royal Ascot. He would have realised that the colt was so one-sided that he acted badly on a right-handed track. This too, was probably due to the trainer's age and lack of his supervision when the colt was broken.

From birth everything conspires to make a horse left-handed. As soon as he has his little head collar on, he is led on the near-side. So when you start to lunge him, he automatically goes round to his left. And, unless he has been particularly well-handled at the stud, will resent being sent round to the right when the trainer starts to break him as a yearling. If you don't persevere at this stage, someone is in for a lot of trouble later on. This is one of the advantages of driving on long reins. You can make the animal go just as easily to the right as to the left.

In the past the Irish have been great sinners in this respect. Many an expensive potential jumper has had to be remade before he can achieve the even balance required in a top class performer. I remember Fulke Walwyn and Bryan Marshall having awful trouble with Dorothy Paget's splendid young jumpers when they first arrived from Ireland. Inevitably it seemed, they were all left-handed.

So was Never Say Die to a marked degree. It did not matter in the Derby because the Epsom track is left-handed and Lester gave the horse a smooth, easy ride to win comfortably.

Ascot, on the other hand, is constantly turning to the right, and Lester knew that he would have his work cut out to keep his horse balanced in the King Edward VII Stakes, in which he was giving eight pounds to the Epsom runner-up. So, at the weights, Arabian Night was just favourite at 13/8 with the Derby winner at 7/4. Rashleigh, trained by Noel Murless and ridden by Sir Gordon Richards in his last season, was third in demand at 5/1. Gordon had just returned to the saddle after being laid off with injury following that nasty crash at Salisbury.

In fairness, I will give both jockeys' accounts of the controversial Ascot race, which sparked off one of the racing sensations of the decade.

Gordon: 'Coming into the straight, Blue Prince and Dragon Fly were making the running, with Rickaby on Garter third, Gosling on Arabian Night fourth, and I was fifth. Dragon Fly dropped out, and Rickaby and I began to move up to the leader.

All of a sudden, Lester Piggott on Never Say Die started to make a move. I was on the outside, and so I do not know whether Never Say Die was hanging or not. Lester claimed he was. At any rate, Never Say Die charged into Garter, and Garter hit my quarters and practically turned me round. Then Never Say Die charged Garter again, and Garter turned me broadside on. I suspect that it did look, from the Stand, as if my horse was doing the damage: but if another horse hits yours in the rump, it will throw you into him, and that is what happened.

'Rashleigh recovered marvellously, and he and Tarjoman – being ridden by that splendid French jockey Poincelet – went on to challenge Arabian Night who had taken up the running with Blue Prince. Arabian Night dived twice, first of all putting Blue Prince on to Tarjoman, and then Tarjoman on to me. But Rashleigh would not be beaten whatever happened to him, and he went on to win.

'Of course it was a most unsatisfactory race, and the stewards objected to me. But immediately they had heard the evidence, they withdrew their objection.

'They did, however, stand Lester Piggott down.'

Lester: 'It all happened soon after we entered the straight. I was lying handy on the rails. As there were three horses in front of me, who were beginning to weaken, I decided to switch to the outside to give my horse a chance of a long, unimpeded run with that great stride of his.

'As I started to move, however, one of the leaders dropped back and, at that moment, Gordon came from behind further outside and proceeded to ride in. First he lay on the other horse. Then, although looking across, he could see I hadn't much room, he pushed the other horse (I think it was Lord Rosebery's Garter, ridden by Bill Rickaby) right on top of me. Of course there was a big bump and the other horse was half turned. My horse was hanging too, towards his favourite left-hand side, which, of course, didn't help matters. Anyway Gordon went on and won by a length. I finished fourth.

'As soon as we got back, the stewards objected to Gordon – rightly, in my opinion – but, when they heard the evidence of the other jockeys they withdrew the objection and turned their attention to me, claiming that I had been trying to force my way out.'

Clive Graham (*Daily Express*) said: 'Piggott and Never Say Die began to move half-a-mile out when he saw an opening between Dragon Fly (Doug Smith) and Garter (Bill Rickaby). When he was half-way there, the horses came together and there was a collision.'

I saw the race and I'm not going to take sides. I think that a certain amount of blame for the incident could be attached to Gordon, Lester and Tommy Gosling. Certainly it was by no means an open-and-shut case.

But once again, the Ascot stewards, with no film to guide them, completely exonerated everyone but Lester. They listened to the evidence of the other jockeys and heard his stumbling version. Then they suspended him for the remainder of the meeting and reported him to the stewards of the Jockey Club.

The Duke of Norfolk headed the Cavendish Square inquiry. This seemed strange to me at the time, because of his connection with Ascot.

Once again there was no question of a caution or a fine, even though the issue was so controversial. They suspended Lester for six months and ordered his father to send him to another trainer.

He says: 'I was absolutely dumbfounded. I just couldn't believe it. Again I felt that everyone was against me and I still insist that this was an unnecessary savage sentence, which did no good at all.'

He was ordered to leave home and go to Newmarket to 'do his two' and rode out under the instruction of Lord Rosebery's trainer, Jack Jarvis. 'As the old man was sick in bed the whole time I was there,' says Lester, 'that was a fat lot of good!'

Few people realised what suspension meant to the dedicated boy. 'My life stopped,' he says, 'because racing is my whole life. It's my work and my pleasure at one and the same time. Apart from my family it provides me with all the fun I ever need. Which, of course, is why I never want a holiday.'

The blow was struck at the height of the season. Apart from all the other winners, he missed riding Never Say Die in the

Leger. Charlie Smirke substituted for him and won by twelve lengths.

That race alone was worth £13,372. Clark was a very generous owner and would have given his winning rider more than ten per cent of the stake.

So, from a purely financial point of view, the sentence must have cost the Piggotts thousands of pounds.

The same *Racing Calendar* that carried the official announcement of Lester's six-month sentence reported that Manny Mercer had been fined £50 for striking Davy Jones with his whip in a race.

How can you possibly reconcile the two sentences? It is hard to escape the thought that poor little Manny, one of the nicest and best jockeys ever to grace the Turf, was retained by a number of Jockey Club members.

After Doncaster perhaps the Jockey Club realised that they had overstepped the mark.

They lifted the ban a fortnight after the Leger, when Lester had served just over three months of his sentence. On 4th October he was appointed to succeed Gordon as first jockey to Noel Murless, who handled many horses for Jockey Club members. He could be pardoned for thinking that it was a strange world.

It was a highly successful, but always uneasy partnership. There was that day at Ascot when Lester had ridden a placed horse for the Queen, who was a little slow arriving in the unsaddling enclosure from the royal box. Her jockey, who was riding in the next, touched his black velvet cap, muttered 'Thank you Ma'am,' and hurried off into the weighing-room.

Noel came storming after him, 'The Queen wanted to talk to you,' he fumed. 'Oh, what did she want?' asked Lester, raising that blank, innocent face. 'She wanted to say that she doesn't like ill-mannered little b———s riding for her!'

Still, Noel headed the trainers' list four times with Lester. They won two Derbys with Crepello and St Paddy, and Lester won the jockeys' championship in 1960, '64, '65 and '66, the season when the sensational break-up occurred.

It was in 1962, when he was due to ride Noel's Young Lochinvar in the Derby that Lester had his next big brush with the authorities, who so often seem to have people up for the wrong offences.

It happened at an evening meeting at Lincoln on 30th May, a week before the Derby. Bob Ward was a likeable selling-plate specialist who had been training for sixteen years at Hednesford in Staffordshire. He was not the Establishment's favourite trainer.

Bob had two runners in the same race, Polly Macaw and Ione. Lester was booked for the latter, who opened at odds-on for this very reason.

Soon, however, she dropped in the betting, as money came for her stable-companion, who was justifiably installed as favourite in her stead.

'As soon as we jumped off I realised that the punters were right. My filly had no possible hope of beating Polly Macaw. So, rather than give the little thing a hiding, I did my best until I found that she had nothing more to give and then I dropped my hands.'

Major-General Sir Randle Feilden, who had not yet risen to his present state of eminence as Chairman of the Turf Board, thought it was a bad case, accused Ward and Piggott of stopping Ione and referred the matter to the stewards of the Jockey Club.

'I told them the truth,' says Lester, 'that Ione could never and would never beat Polly Macaw and that she was utterly useless as she later proved. But they obviously didn't believe me.'

He was suspended until the end of July and Bob's licence was taken away indefinitely. On this occasion Lester was very angry. Faced with the prospect of two months of nail-biting frustration and the loss of an immense sum of money, he had a right go at the reporters, who besieged his house when he returned home to Newmarket. He hit one hard on the jaw and then chased them off, throwing stones out of his garden at them.

Lester had married Susan Armstrong on 22nd February, 1960. He celebrated by being champion jockey for the first time.

When, on his twenty-fifth birthday, Lester found himself champion jockey, I talked to Sir Gordon, his predecessor at

Warren Place. It was a most revealing interview with the great champion, who had doubted whether Lester would top the list because of his weight.

'If only he were seven pounds lighter,' said the man who had filled that position for the first time ten years before Lester was born.

We talked about the will-power and determination of this young man, who, built on the tall mould of Fred Archer, had had to overcome more obstacles to success than any other rider since Archer, beaten in his battle against weight, killed himself in 1886.

Though he had had to see his own jockey, Scobie Breasley, take second place in the riders' table, Gordon was as delighted with Piggott's success as if he had won the championship again himself.

'By resisting the temptation to eat and by depriving himself of all the other good things of life that a young man wants, Lester has shown the most amazing strength of character,' he said.

'The secret of his success is confidence. Confidence in his own genius. For he is a genius as Steve Donoghue was before. From the very beginning he has always known instinctively exactly what to do and when to do it.

'Take Epsom, the trickiest course of them all. Lester never worries about the bends or the crowding or what the other jockeys are doing. Like Steve, he gets into exactly the right position – about fourth or fifth – and then at the psychological moment he goes. That was how he won the 1957 Oaks on Carrozza. This was one of the best races he has ever ridden.

'Just think of it! he was only twenty-one . . . riding for the Queen . . . and it was the Oaks. But it made no difference to Lester. He behaved just as if it had been a selling race and at precisely the right moment, before the other jockeys knew what was happening, he went. Believe me, he stole that race.'

Then I asked Gordon about the cheekiness and rough riding, which had threatened to ruin the young champion's career. He answered firmly: 'A lot of nonsense has been talked and written about Lester's behaviour on and off a horse.

'For example, that story about him calling me Grandpa was

quite untrue. Of course he would stand up for himself if necessary, but I always found him very respectful and well-mannered.

'None of the rough riding was deliberate. It was all part and parcel of his genius. He just knew that he had to be in a certain place at a certain time to win.'

I shall quote Gordon on Lester again. But this was the most important verdict from the champion of champions at a time when he had been out of the saddle for only six years.

When Lester had stopped growing, he started to pull his stirrup leathers up. I have a photograph of him winning the Linton Stakes at Newmarket for me on Forbear in 1954 and he is riding at a normal length. He could use those lovely long legs for the purpose for which they were designed – to drive and guide.

Many of to-day's top jockeys – Geoff Lewis, George Moore, Jimmy Lindley, Bill Williamson – ride at about the classic length like Steve Donoghue, Michael Beary or Charlie Elliot. Gordon used to ride almost the full length of his little legs.

I have aroused the wrath of certain fellow journalists through criticising Lester's ultra-short leathers. How dare I find fault with the master? Well, as a professional horseman, I stick to my guns. I think that's what journalism is all about. You are paid to be a critic, not a sycophant and, if you are convinced that you are right, you should always say so. Anyway, Lester only laughs about it when I tell him he just does it out of bloody-mindedness, pulling his leathers up so short that he is almost standing on the saddle.

'I've been pulling them up all the time,' he says, 'and I'm still pulling them up! Although I may not look very comfortable, I feel more comfortable. Everybody has to ride the way he feels most comfortable.'

He goes on: 'One of the disadvantages of being tall is style. Style is the way you look. If you're small, it doesn't matter so much how you look, because there isn't so much of you to be seen and your legs don't take up so much room. If you're big you can be seen better and there's less horse showing. I smile when people ask why I ride with my bottom in the air. I've got to put it somewhere, haven't I? Anyway it works and I'm comfortable.'

This is undeniable. But I have seen him lose races he ought to have won. When a horse starts hanging badly he has no legs to correct him and so he must use his whip. But, as we have seen, he still lacks dexterity in pulling this weapon through and using it with his left hand.

Furthermore, I think that he is always at the risk of losing a race on an objection. Although horses go so uncannily straight for him, there is the odd one that swerves under pressure, which could mean the sacrifice of a major prize. Lastly, great horseman that he is, he is more likely to be unseated than if he had been riding with longer leathers, as we have seen on several occasions like the day when Ribero dropped him and galloped off to eat rhododendrons before the King George VI and Queen Elizabeth Stakes at Ascot.

'Horses have always run straight for me,' he says. 'Ever since I first started riding work as a kid. I suppose I'm especially lucky. To me it's just instinct. I'm so used to a horse going straight, that, if he gets on the wrong leg, I can just put him right. I don't even think about it.'

So while still insisting that this beautiful natural horseman would be better advised to ride longer than he does, I freely admit that his unorthodox style is wonderfully successful – for him.

This is one of the major troubles. Other jockeys and, in particular, apprentices, inevitably imitate the champion. See how Stan Mellor modelled himself on Fred Winter, while Geoff Lewis deliberately copied Gordon.

Lester's father-in-law, Sam Armstrong, says; 'It's becoming increasingly difficult as stable lads and apprentices, copying Lester, pull their knees up to their chins. He can ride like that, but they can't. It's bad for them and for the horses, whose mouths are bound to suffer.'

Sam, one of our finest horsemasters, says: 'The style seems to suit Lester. Horses appear to run for him with his weight just forward of the point of balance. But it doesn't work for anyone else.'

Arthur Budgett, now in the happy position of having his own former apprentice, Geoff Baxter, as stable jockey, agrees wholeheartedly.

'All the boys try to copy Lester,' says the Whatcombe trainer.

'I'm always having to make them let their leathers down. It's disastrous. They're so insecure, that, if they don't fall off, they're hanging on to their horse's mouth.'

Even as Lester passed the Epsom winning post on St Paddy in the 1960 Derby the favourite, Angers, was shot by the course vet, James Garrett, who had been following the field in the official car. The French were furious. They believed that the Strassburger colt, for whom bookmaker William Hill had offered £200,000 a week earlier, could have been saved for stud. But Garrett, finding the colt on three legs two furlongs down Tattenhim Hill, like that other French favourite, Holocaust, in 1899, had no hesitation.

'There was nothing else I could do,' said the vet. 'The horse's near foreleg was smashed to smithereens. The fetlock and cannonbone were broken and the horse had a split pastern.'

He was probably right. So much depends on the horse's individual constitution and temperament and Angers was a highly-strung colt. You need a very sensible sort of thoroughbred to endure months in plaster as well as all the intricate surgery required.

However, Ryan Price and his vet did achieve it around this time with a far humbler French colt called York, who recovered from multiple fractures to win two hurdle races and was subsequently given to me.

And Europe's top vet, Dr Edouard Pouret, had a remarkable, much publicised similar success when a very valuable potential stallion smashed his leg at Longchamp in 1971.

One thing is certain. If an animal's genital organs are undamaged, it is crazy not to make an effort to save a well-bred colt or filly for stud. For years, frightened of charges of cruelty, our racecourse vets have been somewhat trigger happy. One of the major faults with English horsemastership, horsemanagement and, indeed, horsemanship, is that too many people in this country credit animals with the same feelings and minds as human beings.

In fact, since a horse has no imagination and a very small brain, it does not suffer pain to the same extent as a human. Watch a horse being fired or castrated by a good vet and you will know what I mean. So I believe that public opinion should be re-educated to recognise the humanity in curing an animal which can enjoy a happy and productive life at stud rather than 'putting it out of its misery.' It is terrifying how a bullet can convert half a million pounds to fifty pounds in a split second.

But, of course, this is the other side of the coin. Insurance companies only pay out on death. They give nothing, despite their large premiums, to compensate owners of horses that can never race again, but which will cost a fortune in keep and vet's bills while attempts are being made to save them. Many owners would prefer to recoup their outlay from the insurance with that quick humane race-course vet's bullet than risk the alternative.

The following day at Epsom, Lester broke another record. He became the fastest man on four legs in the world.

The world speed record by a horse had been set up way back in 1933 – two years before our hero was born. A three-year-old filly Devineress, carrying 7 st. 5 lbs., clocked 54.6 secs. for the sharp Epsom five furlongs.

In the Tadworth Handicap Stakes with the big weight of 9 st. 5 lbs., but with the invaluable aid of Lester, four-year-old Indigenous smashed the record by one whole second, recording an incredible 53.6 secs.

This was the year when the British camera patrol was introduced on 30th June at Newmarket. Now twelve years later we still have the most limited camera coverage of any major racing country – not only in the number of meetings, but also in the actual amount of each race that is covered when the cameras are operating.

In view of the date, 25th May 1972, I feel that the letter from Brighton's Clerk of the Course, Derek Hubbard, in reply to a *Sun* reader's letter is almost a historical document!

25th May 1972.

Dear Tim,

Brighton Races

Thank you for your letter of May 23rd.

At Brighton we have particularly asked each year for the fullest Camera Patrol coverage, but not all meetings are yet so covered.

I understand that of the Camera Patrol Film Units, one was at Ayr on the 15th moving to Catterick on the 17th. It was impossible for this unit to cover Brighton on the 16th. The other unit was being serviced. Needless to say the Stewards of the meeting and the Race Ground Lessees would welcome full camera patrol coverage. Perhaps there may be a third Camera Patrol Film Unit next year.

On television at Brighton, the Brighton Race Ground Lessees have had meetings with representatives of the B.B.C. and Commercial Television to see if they could prevail on them to cover Brighton Races. In this way we might be able to get the Sponsors we so badly want. We have no Saturday meetings and midweek racing television coverage is pretty limited and we have had no joy as yet.

Closed Circuit television is at present inordinately expensive to install and run.

Incidentally we do now have Starting Stalls at all meetings.

I hope this answers your correspondent's comment on Brighton. I return the letter.

Yours sincerely,

Derek

The rulers of the Turf in 1960 took little trouble, it seemed, to present good, entertaining sport to the public. Nobody bothered about watering the racecourses, for example. One day during that summer, Nottingham provided one of the most ludicrously bad afternoon's racing in the history of the sport. Eighteen runners turned out for six races. There were TWO walkovers, two fields of THREE, and two of FIVE. Although there was (and is) a certain amount of validity in the executive's excuse that there was too much racing at this time of year, the main reason unquestionably was the unnecessarily hard going.

Always we seemed to be given the same answer. 'It's nothing to do with us. It's up to the courses concerned.'

I suggest that it was everything to do with them. Obviously in the Brigade of Guards you could always pass the buck. As Cavalry officers, we were brought up to believe that 'the fish stinks from the head.' And, if the head happened to be you, that was just too bad!

The Jockey Club and local stewards were still keeping the public in the dark in 1960. Inquiries were held in private and objections were either sustained or overruled with no explanation to the punters who lost their money.

By then doping was rife. Doping to stop. The kind of doping which is so profitable – only in a country where bookmakers still hold sway. Under a Tote monopoly, such as is enjoyed throughout the rest of the civilised world, you can't lay against a hot favourite, knowing that it is 'dead meat'. You can here. What's more you can make as much as a big bank robbery with very little risk of detection. And, if you are caught, you'll probably get no more than a year for 'conspiracy to defraud.'

A famous American millionaire said at the time, 'Nothing would induce me to leave a horse in training in England. We put our own house in order some years ago when we abolished bookmakers and I do not want to get involved in a dirty sport again. Your racing stinks!'

Still retained in 1960, was that outrageous rule of racing, which was habitually feared by every trainer – Rule 176(II) which read:

'If in any case, in which the stewards have ordered a horse to be examined it shall be found that any drug or stimulant has been administered to a horse for the purpose of affecting its speed in a race, the licence of the trainer shall be withdrawn and he shall be declared a disqualified person.'

I shall never understand how such a grotesquely unfair rule could have been countenanced only thirteen years ago. A casual word misinterpreted could have caused a test to be taken, and a trainer's entire livelihood could easily depend upon the whim of another person.

But the rule was kept and acted on until the Arundel horses, Red Letter and Skymaster, were found to have been doped.

It was not, of course, a Jockey Club inquiry. The Duke of Norfolk revealed the dope findings, but his trainer was not tried under Rule 176 (II).

More controversy was to follow. On 15th August I wrote from Newbury:—'Newbury's stewards, led by former Rhine Army commander General Sir Miles Dempsey, on Saturday missed a heaven-sent opportunity of restoring public faith in the impartial rules of the Jockey Club and of retrieving the badly damaged, tumbling, prestige of British racing. They should have ordered an official examination of Kipling.

'Consider the facts. In the 1m. 5f. 600yd Oxfordshire Stakes, watched by thousands of punters on the course and on T.V., the even-money favourite, Lord Sefton's St Leger colt, Kipling, who had won his last three races and beaten St Paddy, the Derby winner, at Goodwood, finished tailed off last. He was more than 20 lengths behind the winner High Hat and 15 lengths behind his own pacemaker, Tobago (second).

'Jockey Geoff Lewis agreed that Kipling ran a long way below form. Said Geoff: 'It was no gallop. Kipling's poor showing was due to nothing that I could account for.'

'Trainer Peter Hastings-Bass said he was not satisfied with the colt's running.

'But although Peter, acting on the friendly advice of a vet, had a saliva test taken at his Kingsclere stables, no official test was taken on the course.

'If the stewards had ordered such a test, and if Mrs Munday, the Jockey Club analyst, had returned a positive result, Peter's training licence would have had to be withdrawn and Kipling would have been barred from racing again.

'On the other hand, such a test would have exposed once and for all the injustice of the present rule, for the outstanding integrity of owner and trainer in this case is well known.

'Even if it were not, it is obvious that Kipling's connections could only lose by defeat of their favourite.

'Peter does not bet, and Lord Sefton, an owner-breeder, stood to lose thousands in the depreciated value of a potential stallion.

'Thus, as in the recent case of the Duke of Norfolk's Skymaster, another potential stallion, only a criminal bookmaker, or someone else in a position to lay the favourite, could benefit from Kipling's defeat and from the subsequent loss of punter's money.

'An official test on Kipling might well have proved negative but, in the interests of Lord Sefton, of Peter Hastings-Bass, of the little owners and trainers, and of British sport itself, it should have been taken – if only to prove that in racing, there is not one law for the rich and one for the poor.'

Eleven days later I reported again:—

'With the new jumping season already under way in the West Country, a terrifying fresh slant on this doping business was put to me at Brighton by Ryan Price, king of National Hunt trainers and employer of Fred Winter, greatest jumping jockey of our time.

'Said Ryan: "This nobbling of favourites is bad enough on the Flat. But unless it is stopped before jumping starts in earnest jockeys could easily be killed. Just think if anything should happen to Fred?'

'Ryan is right. If the police fail to find the culprits before November when the flat ends and N.H. racing becomes the medium of the nations gambling, manslaughter could well be done.

'For the drug which merely makes a favourite drowsy and incapable of exerting himself fully has no disastrous consequences on the Flat.

'But imagine if you can the shattering fall when a dopey horse tries to negotiate an obstacle at speed.'

And, again on 27th August, when it was becoming obvious that in order to get at horses, the dopers must be employing lads or ex-lads, who were so hopelessly underpaid despite a five-year apprenticeship, that they would be desperate to earn some easy money:—

'August, normally the dullest month, this year finds British racing simmering with frustration and discontent.

'Among post-war industries, racing is unique in that it is the only one not to recognise the old service axiom that the interests of the worker – the chap who actually tends the production line – must be studied before those of anyone else.

'For example: despite the pathetic little stable lads' strike, when the Betting Bill was in committee stage early this year, nobody – so far as we have been told – produced the one argument likely to influence modern politicians and top businessmen: that is, that the only reasons for owners needing more prize money is to enable them to pay more to their trainers and lads.

'After all, no one is compelled to own a racehorse any more than he is forced to buy a Rolls-Royce.

'It is important to remember that, despite remuneration which makes our sport the laughing stock of the world, the English form book works out to a remarkable degree. Thus the integrity of our working trainers and lads is still the envy of all – yet these men are never consulted on any of the major matters of policy which affect their lives and their livelihoods.

'Furthermore, neither they nor the public, are kept 'in the picture' about the operational, disciplinary or administrative side of racing – with the result that, instead of narrowing, in keeping with the times, the gulf between rulers and ruled widens terrifyingly.

'As the trainer shamefacedly pays out all that he can afford – about £9 each a week – to lads working a seven day week, he hears that the average wage for dockers, asking for more money and a forty-one hour week, is already £15.

'What is the Jockey Club doing about it? No information or friendly guidance is given.

'It may not be generally known that the ruling body, through their secretaries, force a trainer to pay a jockey's retainer (which has to be recovered from the owners), but refuse to help the trainer in any way to recover money owed to him by defaulting owners. Fines are imposed with monotonous regularity, but no one knows where the money goes.

'It is proposed to popularise racing at Newmarket – surely a big-business venture requiring the know-how of a Jack Hylton – but a committee of well-meaning amateurs is formed to deal with an issue which affects the livings of all the professionals. At least, that is what we are told – and with no further information we can only assume the worst.

'So the feeling of grievance and sense of injustice among the professionals about, for instance, the application of the dope policy (if indeed one exists) is very real.

'I have gone into this in some detail because the popular Press is being called sensation-seeking and irresponsible, whereas it is, in fact, speaking very responsibly for the men who are the backbone of racing.

'Only repeated official explanations and assurances can dispel this horrible feeling of uneasiness and distrust, which haunts our race-courses.'

It is a horrible season for all but Lester, who won the Leger so easily on St Paddy and finished up as the new champion jockey. Even he was to suffer from the dopers the following year.

During the winter we managed a few steps forward. The Duke of Norfolk led a three-man dope investigation and the Jockey Club finally surrendered to tremendous pressure and introduced overnight declarations from the start of the new Flat season.

Immediately I demanded the commonsense reform of overnight blinkers. But I was constantly told this would be 'interferring with the rights of owners' and we had to wait another eleven years before they were introduced. We are still waiting for overnight jockeys.

While on the subject of reforms, it is worth noting that on New Year's Day, 1961, Ryan Price came out strongly in favour of women riders, who had just been introduced in France. He was on his own. Noel Murless said: 'A damn silly idea. Women are bad enough in point-to-points. There are two things that would drive me out of racing. Races for women is one. '

Now in 1972 we have women's races and, I'm happy to say, we still have our finest trainer.

What an uncivilised little world it was. Not only was Vincent O'Brien wrongly accused and convicted, but he was not even allowed to live in his own home, lovely Ballydoyle, until the end of a season, in which his horses took his stand-in brother, Phonsie, to the top of the trainer's list. His owner, Frank Burmann, was leading owner. The horse which put them there was none other than the alleged dope victim, Chamour, who later won the Irish Derby.

Second in the owner's table was the Turf Club Senior Steward, Joe McGrath, who presided over the inquiry which resulted in Vincent's suspension. It could only happen in Ireland. It looked as though they would have to call on the 'little people' to sort out the comic opera situation, which the Irish Stewards had created for themselves.

In the end, Vincent started training again in May 1961, twelve months after his suspension. He was completely vindicated in court and, graciously accepting an unconditional apology, took no further action. It was the first major body blow to the traditional Turf authorities in these islands.

To show how far removed the racing industry was from today, the £336,000, at which the Aga Khan syndicated his French Derby and Grand Prix winner, Charlottesville, was a record prize for a syndicated horse.

Already in 1961, Lester had his sights set on the big money in Tote-monopolised France. But the new champion had great hopes at home. That sleek grey greyhound, Petite Etoile (I'll bet she would never have passed a pre-Olympic sex test for male hormones if she'd been a human) was still in training, superbly handled as ever by Lester's retaining trainer Noel Murless.

Also in the Warren Place Stables that spring was a big unraced bay colt by the 1953 Derby winner Pinza, called Pinturischio.

Noel had no doubt about his ability. 'He is definitely a good horse,' he told me. The public had no doubt either. Before he ever saw a racecourse he was quoted at 3/1 for the Guineas and 5/1 for the Derby – odds which shortened still further after a smooth victory with Lester in the Wood Ditton Stakes. Once again the combination of Murless, Piggott and a good colt was irresistible.

Public opinion and support for 'Pint o' Sherry' forced Noel to go for the gloves in the Guineas though the colt was still too backward and the distance too short.

When Lester drew his whip in the Dip, the big bay favourite found no more and finished fourth behind the 66/1 Rockavon, a 420 guineas bargain, the longest-priced Guineas winner in the century and Scotland's first classic hero in living memory.

Despite support for the French colt, Moutiers, a half-brother to ill-fated Angers, Pinto was still a warm order for the Derby. Looking back now, Lester says: 'He'd have won it all right.'

It was not to be. The nobblers got at him, not once but twice, and on the second occasion they made such a good job of it that they nearly killed him.

Was I so wrong when I wrote at about this time just after the death of my old guv'nor, Atty Persse?

'Racing needs more money far more urgently than is generally realised. And this money must come from betting.

'The first racing levy on bookmakers, likely to be made towards the end of next year, is expected to produce an annual £1,250,000. It is an attempt to restore a sick industry to health.

'For racing is sick. Most trainers lose money on 95 per cent of their horses. They have to make good their losses by other means.

'Many bookmakers feel that this is the thin edge of the wedge because a large section of the racing industry is openly saying that only a Tote monopoly can save racing.

'These people point out that although the increased popularity of National Hunt racing has swelled the estimated total of £350,000,000 gambled every year, our prize money is ridiculously low and our admission charges fantastically high compared with countries where the Tote reigns supreme.

'One disastrous result is that the English owner seeking our own best bloodstock at Newmarket or Dublin is outbid by foreign rivals.

'When the subject was debated in Parliament the only politician to put his finger on the real problem was Mr Eric Johnson, member for Manchester (Blackley) and nephew of the late and great Atty Persse.

'Persse wrote shortly before he died last year: "I was very proud of my profession twenty-five years ago and I would have been happy to see my son following in his father's footsteps. Today I would do everything in my power to stop him training horses in England."

'In 1939 training fees were five guineas a week. Today owners cannot or will not pay more than ten guineas, although the cost of living has risen four times.

'In the House of Commons, Mr Johnson cited the case of Bruce Hobbs, who, after a successful career as a steeplechase jockey and later as assistant trainer to Cecil Boyd-Rochfort, has decided to join a firm of saddlers rather than set up on his own because: ". . . with stakes so small and costs so high, a man cannot be sure of a living unless he bets and wins."

'Mr Johnson commented: "For Bruce Hobbs that was not good enough, and he was quite right."

'So the very foundations of racing are shaky. Tax evasion, betting and dealing are no substitute for a decent living wage.

'To restore the sick industry to health it is essential that owners should get free travel and sufficient prize money to enable them to reasonable training fees.

'Until it is worth every trainer's while to run horses on their merits the ordinary punter will suffer.

'Moreover the new post-war public attracted to the sport by television has been largely repelled by the antiquated, run-down condition of most racecourses.

'And where courses are in this condition it is in spite of the help of increasing Tote grants, course bookmakers' payments and the abolition of entertainment tax.'

Poor Noel had a terrible time trying vainly to overcome the nobblers and prepare his colt for the Derby. The Press didn't help. They knew that there was something wrong that might prevent the favourite from running at Epsom. But, although they were dope-happy at the time, they never suspected the true cause of his mysterious illness.

Under orders from the office, I spent days down at Newmarket with a photographer. Noel was as courteous as he always is at Warren Place, but pictures were not allowed. I remember hiding behind bushes on the Heath as the horse was being exercised while my photographer wielded an enormous weapon like a Vickers machine-gun. This was one of two £6,000 cameras then in the possession of the *Daily Mail,* which had been designed for tracking satellities. It was child's play to capture a horse galloping a mile or so away.

Lester says: 'Pinturischio would certainly have won that Derby.'

Noel was one of the first to welcome the Norfolk Committee's report when it finally appeared on 4th May.

'An excellent report – a big advance,' he said.

The most important recommendation was that trainers should no longer be warned off automatically if stopping dope were found in their horses unless it could be proved that they had been involved. It hardly needed great intelligence to work this one out. The rule should never have existed. After all, an elementary knowledge of horses and racing would show that no trainer would ever use drugs to prevent his own horse from winning. There are so many other ways of giving an animal 'an easy' without risking its health or his licence.

Routine tests on at least two winners a day and other horses ordered by the stewards. Each sample to be split into three parts, one for a new Jockey Club laboratory, the second for the owner's chosen analyst, and the third to be kept in case of disagreement. The analysts' reports to be evaluated by an advisory committee of experts before the stewards took any action. These were the main recommendations of this historic document, which at least made a start in righting a grievous wrong.

There were to be no more secret tests. That was very important except for the fact that all stewards' inquiries were still held in secret with no Press and no legal representation for years to come.

The Royal Institute of Chemistry and the Society for Analytical Chemistry had come out strongly against secret tests such as those conducted hitherto by Jockey Club analysts. In a memorandum the chemists said: 'We are strongly opposed to the suggestion that those analysts who make the tests in this country must be members of the American Association of Racehorse Chemists and thereby presumably precluded from stating the methods they use or discussing them with other analysts. We cannot stress sufficiently strongly that nobody should be condemned on secret tests, which cannot be challenged.'

This sort of expert statement, coming on top of the O'Brien case and the apparent injustice of the case of the Irish chaser, Zonda, shattered all the previous ideas of the Jockey Club and their private analysts.

Compelled to take action, no doubt by the Zonda case, the Norfolk Committee insisted that more discretion should be exercised with regard to the disqualification of horses which had been found to be doped. They suggested that the rules should be altered to permit such animals to race again after a maximum suspension of six months.

A cynic might be excused for reflecting that, if the previous June's test on Skymaster after that Ascot race had been official instead of private, the tough Norfolk colt would have been banned for life. He would never have won the Middle Park

Stakes and fetched a handsome price before carrying Scobie Breasley and the second highest weight ever for a three-year-old to victory in the Steward's Cup.

Trainers were to be warned on their licences that a horse should receive nothing but normal nutrient within a period of seventy-two hours before noon on the day of its race.

Coinciding with the Norfolk report, Vincent O'Brien's suspension ended after twelve instead of eighteen months. His litigation against the Irish Turf Club Stewards was still pending.

Meanwhile in France, Elizabeth Couturié's magnificent brown colt, Right Royal V, ridden by Roger Poincelot, was going from strength to strength and, after he had spreadeagled his field in the £35,000 Prix du Jockey Club (French Derby), we looked forward to his clash with four-year-old St Paddy in the Ascot's King George VI and Queen Elizabeth Stakes.

Lester, who was, of course, to ride the 1960 Derby winner in the big race, had been seen at his very cheekiest when steering the splendid grey, Petite Etoile, to her second Coronation Cup victory at Epsom. Not only his cheekiest, but his best, because, at five, the 1959 Oaks winner was becoming a little temperamental. She needed kidding too and so did the other jockeys. Lester made it look so easy, but he had very little in hand at the end of a mile and a half.

It was one of those starts, which were – and still unhappily are at some meetings – a disgrace to the sport. This was the Epsom Derby meeting and the race in question was one of the world's classics for older horses. But England had no starting stalls.

Moreover, Epsom was still in an atrocious state. The ground was not only hard, but appallingly rough so that the tough French challenge of Javelot, winner of the previous year's Eclipse never materialised.

Percy Carter said, 'My horse will never act on such going. If I'd known it was going to be like this, I'd never have brought him.'

This from one of the loyalest ex-patriate Englishmen, whose jockey, Freddy Palmer, soon discovering the truth of his trainer's words, kept Javelot last all the way round and sensibly made no serious attempt to get on terms.

When the five runners came under orders, Sir Winston Churchill's Vienna charged the starting gate. His jockey, Tommy Gosling, was saved from a crash by the alertness of the starter, Alec Marsh, who released the tapes with a split second to spare, at the same time shouting, 'No start' to the other four runners. Vienna went about three hundred yards before returning to the gate.

When they were eventually dispatched, Vienna led from Proud Chieftain. The pace, slow at first, was gradually increased but Lester lying third, made no move until a furlong from the post. He hardly moved even then, but let the filly glide up to the leaders. As she passed Vienna to win by a neck, he still had her on a tight rein.

'It's damn silly,' said a very successful trainer, who once had been a famous jockey. 'If the filly had stumbled slightly she would have lost the race.'

But Noel Murless said happily, 'Knowing her as I do, I was never worried.'

Petite Etoile was running for the first time in the presence of her new owner, the Aga Khan, who had inherited her from his father, Prince Aly Khan, that outstanding judge of racing and racehorses. She had won £65,061, a record for a filly in Britain.

By the time Ascot's July meeting arrived, I had watched all Right Royal's races, including that farcical misjudgement of Roger Poincelot in the Prix de Fontainebleau, when he allowed his pacemaker too much scope and suffered ignominious and unnecessary defeat. Fortunately, of course, the two Couturié runners were coupled for betting purposes, so that the French punters did not lose their francs.

So, alone of the so-called experts, I sided firmly with the French champion to beat St Paddy.

In the paddock the big Murless bay, who had dwarfed his rivals before Lester's record-breaking, front-running Eclipse ride the previous Saturday, was now, in his turn, outclassed by Right Royal, who had grown to a powerful 16 hands 3 inches.

The cheer for St Paddy, which started two furlongs out, died to nothing as soon as Roger asked Right Royal for effort.

Then the British crowd witnessed what we had seen at Longchamp and Chantilly. The great colt immediately lengthened his stride and swept majestically past St Paddy to win as he liked by three lengths.

His trainer, Etienne Pollet, who was later to handle Sea Bird, declared: 'Nearco is the only horse I have seen in my life as good as Right Royal.'

And Noel said: 'It was no disgrace for St Paddy to be beaten by a horse like that.'

The one consolation for British breeders was that Right Royal was a son of our own Hyperion-bred Derby winner, Owen Tudor.

In the same month we saw at Kempton just how brilliant Lester had been throughout Petite Etoile's sensational career. The race was almost designed for her. It was the Aly Khan Memorial Gold Cup and I think that Noel, as one of Aly's oldest friends and greatest admirers, would have given anything to win with the grey mare. But the distance was 1½ miles. This was the flat Kempton circuit and Lester's bluff was called at last. With a superb display of courage and stamina worthy of his great owner, Sir Winston Churchill's High Hat beat the mare fair and square at that evening meeting.

The Aga Khan was perplexed and bewildered at the defeat of his champion, whom he had believed to be the best in the world.

'What happened?' he asked Lester. 'Why didn't you come away and win?'

His head slightly tilted to one side, Lester looked steadily at this dark handsome young man about his own age. He answered simply 'He ran me into the ground.'

Walter Nightingall won many races by teaching his horses to make all the running if necessary. Riding to a plan, his jockey, Duncan Keith, jumped off in front and set a fast, true gallop throughout. Lester was sitting as still as ever on the grey wonder filly two lengths behind. Was his bottom not quite as high in the air as usual?

Two and a half furlongs from home Petite Etoile started to make her move and it looked as though once again she was to sweep by to a, this time, memorably appropriate victory. But it was not to be. Lester urged her on, she got to within a length of High Hat – but could produce no more. Lester gave her a back hander. In vain. She shot her bolt and High Hat drew further away to win by two lengths.

I have often thought it would be interesting to take a sex test on these brilliant race-mares. In many cases their head and general bone structure have few feminine characteristics and I wonder whether they possess a preponderance of male hormones. If it's fair and necessary to test women-athletes before the Olympic Games, then why not before the Oaks or the Prix Vermeille. We might well find that certain fillies were not entitled to that vital three pounds allowance in big races like the Arc de Triomphe and the King George VI and Queen Elizabeth Stakes. That allowance, which must be worth about two lengths over a stiff 1½ miles.

The trouble is that our veterinary profession has been falling steadily behind the other leading racing countries. Whereas in America, a vet has the status of a doctor and in France the leading vet, Dr Edouard Pouret, was qualified as a doctor before deciding to take up veterinary studies, the English have tended to treat vets as people lower in the social scale.

This is grossly unfair to as fine a bunch of men as you could wish to find anywhere and has had a serious effect on recruitment for the profession. It is only now gradually being overcome. In an industry as important and full of valuable delicate products the best brains are essential. Veterinary Science should be as advanced as medicine instead of lagging behind.

Ironically, of all the great horses that he has ridden, the three which stand out are those on whom Lester has suffered defeat in his bogey race, the Arc de Triomphe: Sir Ivor, Park Top and Nijinsky.

Lester now inclines to the view that Sir Ivor was the best horse he has ever ridden. 'Crepello was a very good horse,' he says. 'I don't think we ever saw the best of him because of his legs. I think he was better than he showed.' Crepello, who won the Guineas and Derby in 1957, is as bold and brave with his mares at the Eve Stud as he was on the racecourse.

That was the year when Lester and Noel also won the Oaks for the Queen with Carrozza by a short head from Silken Glider, ridden by Jimmy Eddery, whose son Pat is one of our fine young riders today. 'Carozza was only a pony,' says Lester, 'but as game as a pebble. I was a bit lucky. I got up on the inside. The second would have beaten me in another stride. My filly had done everything.' This was, in fact, on of the most brilliant feats of Jockeymanship I have ever seen, as Gordon commented earlier in this chapter.

From the moment that he arrived at Ballydoyle as a yearling in the autumn of 1966 Sir Ivor was looked on as something special by that genius of trainers Vincent O'Brien. The handsome bay son of Sir Gaylord had everything you look for in a really high-class horse, combining power and grace of body and action with a lovely intelligent all-male head and the boldest outlook, which gave him the most tremendous personality and presence.

He had already won his only two races, including the National Stakes at the Curragh when Vincent took him to Longchamp for Lester to ride in Europe's most valuable two-year-old race, the £32,000 Grand Criterium. In this traditionally all-French contest, which, like Phil Bull's brainchild, the *Trueform* (now *Observer*) Gold Cup, seldom tells a lie, Sir Ivor fairly spreadeagled the best two-year-olds in France.

Next Spring Vincent revealed that the colt had actually grown two inches during the winter and now stood 16 hands 2 inches. As we watched him work, his trainer said proudly, 'Whatever he does, he is a truly magnificent specimen of the thoroughbred. He's on his toes, too. Last year he was like an old sheep. Now he can really jump and kick.'

Watching Sir Ivor's smooth, daisy-cutting action as he cantered up the sawdust gallop behind his lead-horse Missile, third in the 1967 Guineas I marvelled at his superb development. I had never seen such an impressive classic prospect.

Lester was in an enviable position. He could choose between Sir Ivor and the top English colt, Petingo, on whom he had won the Gimcrack for his father-in-law, Sam Armstrong. This brilliantly fast, rich bay son of Petition with the distinctive white face and hind socks, now stood 15 hands 3½ inches. He had lengthened into a shape which might not please the purist, but which epitomised power and produced the action of a perfectly-oiled machine. Clearly on his breeding he would not stay the Derby distance. Nor would he be asked to do so.

His rival, on the other hand, had always been earmarked for Epsom. There was never any real doubt, therefore, about Lester's decision and, on 17th March when he announced that he would ride Sir Ivor, the American colt was already 5 to 2 for the Guineas and 5 to 1 for the Derby.

He was 6 to 4 for the first classic after he had won Ascot's 2,000 Guineas Trial comfortably by half a length in a time nearly half a second faster than the average for the track, despite the earliness in the season. It was only 5th April.

As in the Grand Criterium, Sir Ivor showed that he possessed three essential qualities – he could settle, accelerate and had the killer instinct.

The massive colt, drawn on the outside of seven runners, cut his tongue as he hit his mouth on the stalls – he had done the same at The Curragh – and was last away. Inside the last two furlongs Lester let the 15 to 8 on favourite sweep smoothly past his field. But he had to shake him up to resist Bill Williamson's typical opportunist late dash on Dalry.

Vincent said, 'When he heard the other horse coming, my fellow quickened instinctively to win. I was very pleased with him.'

Lester was genuinely enthusiastic, 'I wish we had ten more like him,' he said. To which Vincent quietly replied, 'If I had one as good, I'd be more than satisfied.'

Nevertheless the Newmarket horses were so forward in condition that season, that they were sweeping the board and a few days later the American colt drifted to 2 to 1, while Petingo shortened to 11 to 4. And when, ridden by Joe Mercer, the latter made all his own running to win the Craven Stakes over the Guineas course and distance, the positions in the market were reversed. Petingo became favourite at 7 to 4, while Sir Ivor went out to 5 to 2.

It's strange to look back. Sir Cecil Boyd-Rochfort, watching Petingo being unsaddled, said, 'That's the one I'd want to be on. I wish he were mine.'

Greek shipowner Marcos Lemos, whose colt he was, revealed that he had turned down a million dollars for his unbeaten star during the winter. 'I'll sell ships,' he said, 'but I won't sell Petingo. Socrates believed fame was more important than money.' Clearly, as one of the last and best of Petition's stock, the colt was already worth more than this figure as a stallion.

The initial phase of the Newmarket face-lift was well under way. The expenditure of £600,000 had been severely criticised, but racing must have a suitable headquarters and this excellent compromise, involving the complete modernisation of the solid old stands, a change in layout behind them and the democratisation of the whole, has proved an outstanding success.

When May Day arrived, Sir Ivor had returned to favouritism at 11 to 8 and Petingo had retreated to 9 to 4. The market was fully justified when Lester's mount won in the style of a true cchampion. His rival, however, ran an excellent race to finish second 1½ lengths away and 2½ lengths in front of Jimmy Reppin. Time was to show that this was a very good Guineas indeed.

Now Sir Ivor was naturally a strong favourite for the Derby and, in spite of an excellent gallop by Connaught with the previous year's winner Royal Palace, he started at 5 to 4 on to become the shortest priced winner since Cicero, 11 to 4 on, in 1905.

Revelling in brilliant sunshine, an enormous crowd saw the perfect judgment of Britain's champion jockey and the supreme skill of a great Irish trainer win the Derby for the United States. Class characterised the whole performance.

In the parade the favourite stood out as a superb, sleek, perfectly-trained thoroughbred, towering above his rivals as he jumped and kicked with well-being. Burly, temperamental Connaught, though sweating a little, went straight into the stalls and the remainder followed quickly.

Blinkered Benroy, ridden by Duncan Keith, jumped off in front and led at the top of the hill, followed by Connaught, Laureate, Society, Atopolis, Remand and Sir Ivor. Halfway down the hill Sandy Barclay sent Connaught into the lead in front of Laureate with Society close up third. At this stage Lester had Sir Ivor on the rails inside Mount Athos.

Now Sandy, handling his big mount with outstanding horsemanship, adopted the only possible tactics. He made his best way home. Lester, however, had faith in Sir Ivor. He did not move until a furlong and a half out. Then we saw the big horse's fantastic acceleration. He flew up the hill to overhaul the leader close home and win, apparently still barely extended by a length and a half.

Sandy said, 'I thought Sir Ivor wouldn't stay, but when I saw him there half a furlong out, although my chap was running on, I knew that we'd had it. He's the most brilliant horse I have ever seen – in all my nineteen years!'

This opinion was – and still is – shared by the winner's thirty-one-year-old jockey, who was winning his fourth Derby. 'It was over in a few strides,' said Lester. 'I didn't ask him to do anything until one and a half furlongs out. He was always going well and never gave me a moment's anxiety. Sir Ivor is the best horse I have ever ridden.' Again this was to prove him right, as the form unfolded to demonstrate the true worth of this Derby.

Lester says, 'He was a really great horse and a wonderful character. But he didn't get more than $1\frac{1}{4}$ miles.'

Only he really knew this. As with Petite Etoile and so many other non-stayers, Lester had brilliantly held his colt up, delivered his challenge with split-second timing and made it look easy on the track where, despite its vaunted tradition for being the most testing course in the world, a short-runner can triumph.

So he was far from worried when Vincent's Irish stable-jockey, that magnificent horseman and delightful character Liam Ward took over the colt at Curragh for the Irish Sweeps Derby. Liam was under contract to ride the O'Brien horses in Ireland, although the Ballydoyle trainer was free to engage any other rider, such as Lester, for his runners abroad.

So Lester, knowing that Sir Ivor's stamina would be much more severely tested on the stiff galloping circuit of the Curragh with its long, hard pull up to the finish, was happy to accept the ride on Charles Engelhard's tough, plain bay Ribot colt, Ribero, trained by young Fulke Johnson-Houghton at Blewbury.

A few days before this wonderfully organised race, which has now become one of the world's great classics, half of Vincent's horses were stricken with a mild infection, but Sir Ivor, who had been isolated, escaped and was in great form to justify the faith of his many supporters. I wrote from Dublin:

'Sir Ivor will bring his earnings to £173,557 if winning the Irish Sweeps Derby for the United States on rain-softened turf at The Curragh this afternoon.

'Many visitors, including your correspondent, were prevented from landing at Dublin yesterday owning to heavy rain and mist, and were redirected to Belfast, but the going is expected to be just the soft side of good.

'There is never a certainty in racing. But, barring a stroke of cruel fate such as crippled Relko before this race, or the sudden infection of his stablemates' virus, the big, handsome bay is the nearest thing since Arkle in his Cheltenham Gold Cups.

'Moreover the favourite was heavily backed yesterday with inspired money at the prohibitive odds of 2 to 1 on and is likely to start still shorter.

'You can back his rivals three ways with Ladbrokes – at starting price, or without the favourite, or to be second to Sir Ivor. But if you back an outsider each way with the favourite at odds-on you will get no better than 3–1 a place.

'I understand that bookmakers have helped to balance their books by investigating in sweep tickets, but William Hill says, 'Sir Ivor has ruined the Sweeps Derby as a betting proposition. Our field money on the race is 66 per cent down on 1967.

'There were some doubts about Sir Ivor's stamina before his brilliant speed for a final dramatic burst.

'But Vincent O'Brien says, "Now that we know he gets the trip, its so much easier. We won't need to hold him up like that". And thirty-eight year-old Liam Ward, one of the world's most accomplished jockeys, knows this stiff Curragh track even better than Piggott knows Epsom.

'Although La Lagune won the Oaks, there were no French challengers for the Epsom Derby, so that this afternoon's clash will provide the year's first guide to the classic form of the colts in the three countries.

'While there are three English runners, the French should surely win the battle for second place with the only other genuine classic colt in the event, Val d'Aoste, who ran a great race to finish third in the French Derby.'

How wrong you can be. Poor Liam. Sir Ivor, done with after

$1\frac{1}{4}$ miles, struggled on unhappily and scrambled into second place behind Ribero, on whose stable-companion Ribocco Lester had won the previous year. He finished so distressed, that Vincent thought he must have caught the virus, which had threatened his preparation. 'His galloping companion Ballygoran, who was isolated with him, caught it two days ago,' he said. But the day after the race he reported, 'Sir Ivor appears to be very well and none the worse for his race.'

Lester had been widely criticised for his riding of the colt at Epsom and for leaving his effort so late that he did not take the lead until fifty yards from the post. He was now completely vindicated, although many of the critics still insisted that Sir Ivor got the trip all right and directed their barbs at Liam. 'Change the jockeys and you'd change the result,' they said.

Now Raymond Guest, the giant former international polo star, who was currently American ambassador to Ireland, decided to aim Sir Ivor for the Eclipse, taking on not only Royal Palace, who had won the Coronation Cup most impressively, but also the French colt Taj Dewan, so narrowly defeated by Royal Palace in the previous year's 2,000 Guineas.

American owners believe that racehorses are for racing and that one defeat entails no disgrace for a champion. 'You can't win them all,' Raymond repeated constantly, with genuine conviction, if not originality, after the Sweeps Derby.

But, although the $1\frac{1}{4}$ miles of the Sandown event was his ideal distance, the going was firm and Sir Ivor probably had a touch of virus. Running on at the finish, he could finish only third in a thrilling race won by Royal Palace from Taj Dewan.

Lester says, 'He was wrong in himself and he was never striding out. Royal Palace was a good, but lucky horse. Everything went right for him. Even when he broke down at Ascot it was right on the line!'

Owner and trainer decided to rest Sir Ivor now for an autumn campaign with the Arc de Triomphe as their objective.

So Lester resumed his partnership with Ribero in the St Leger. I have always believed that he rode the race of his life to win his fourth victory in the Doncaster classic run over 1 mile 6 furlongs 132 yards on a colt, who just did not get the trip. He displayed superb artistry, sitting and suffering when Bill Williamson challenged on Canterbury in the final furlong, for Ribero was out on his feet. Yet somehow they held on to win by a short head.

David McCall, Charles Engelhard's racing manager, whose charm is matched only by his skill and knowledge of every phase of racing and breeding, said, 'It's fantastic how any jockey could stay so cool. Ribero died in Lester's hand after $1\frac{3}{4}$ miles, but somehow he kept him going for the extra 132 yards.'

Neither the slow time of 3 minutes $19\frac{4}{5}$ seconds – it was the worst of the century – nor the closeness of the finish detracted in any way from the triumph of the late Charles Engelhard, the platinum king, who was Ian Fleming's friend and model for Goldfinger, and of his twenty-eight year-old trainer, Fulke Johnson-Houghton. They had won both the Irish Sweeps Derby and the Leger with two full-brothers by Ribot out of the British mare Libra in successive years.

Now all attention was focused on the Arc de Triomphe, already worth £83,400 to the winner. Sir Ivor, rested, came back to the track at Longchamp after two months absence and, giving the winner 9 lbs., was beaten half a length by Prince Sao in the 11 furlong Prix Henri Delamarre. He went out to 10 to 1 for the Arc, although on several lines of form the result was fairly predictable after his lay-off. Vaguely Noble was, of course, hot favourite at 3 to 1.

That splendid colt duly won, as I have described in Bill Williamson's chapter. Lester commented, 'I was always with the winner, but he was pulling over me all the time. That's the best race Sir Ivor has ever run.'

The answer was, of course, that, whereas Vaguely Noble stayed every inch of $1\frac{1}{2}$ miles, Sir Ivor did not.

Two days later that brilliant, indefatigable story-hunter Peter O'Sullevan, who had spoken to Vincent, wrote in the *Daily Express* that Sir Ivor would never race again, but would be retired to stud.

Every racing journalist in England seems to find his way to the Arc de Triomphe, which is always a huge bun-fight and, of course, a one-day wonder. Very few, however, find their way back to Longchamp the following Sunday when the Grand Criterium is run. To me there is no comparison. The Criterium is far more exciting because it is the future. Here are the classic contenders for next year doing battle for a wonderful prize.

So, as usual, I flew out after racing in England on Saturday. At Longchamp on Sunday I met Sir Ivor's owner, whom I have known well for some years. 'What's the matter, Raymond?' I asked. 'Is your horse sick?'

'No, Vincent tells me, he's as fit as a fiddle.'

'Then why on earth are you of all people backing down from the Champion and the Washington International? I'll never believe that Raymond Guest is too scared to accept a challenge. You've got them at your mercy.'

It had the desired effect on the grand silver-haired sportsman.

That evening I hurried back to my hotel to file an exclusive story for the *Daily Mail.*

'The Derby winner, Sir Ivor, is not to retire after all.

'He will run in the Champion Stakes at Newmarket on Saturday, and is quite likely to go for the Washington International on 11th November.

'On the eve of his departure for the United States, the colt's owner Raymond Guest, said at Longchamp today; "He definitely runs at Newmarket and we are thinking about taking on Damascus at Laurel. I'm not going to say *No* to anything."

'Lester Piggott will ride Sir Ivor, who returned to his best form when second in the Prix de l'Arc de Triomphe, and who will be ideally suited by both the stiff Newmarket 1¼ miles, and the easy 1½ miles of the International.

'A unique confrontation between the Derby and Oaks winners may now occur at Laurel Park. François Boutin said that La Lagune is definitely running. "I would like to have run her in the Champion," he says, "but her owner particularly wants to go for the International." '

The Champion Stakes fell like a ripe plum into Vincent's lap. Sir Ivor, appreciating the return to his best distance of a mile and a quarter, won with impressive ease. The Washington International must surely be his, if only he could stay the 1½ miles as he had done in the Derby.

For those of us who visit the United States just once a year, and that only if we are lucky, the trip to Laurel is an adventure. John Schapiro is not only a wonderful organiser, but a most fabulous host. At last he was seeing the realisation of a dream, which had started in 1952 when, always an idealist, he inaugurated this United Nations of racing on the famous Maryland circuit which his father and he had acquired. The winner of the English Derby, still recognised as the most famous traditional race in the world, was included in the field for the Washington International.

Tired, as always, from the long flight and the unaccustomed change in time, Vincent and I, friends of long standing before I dreamt of becoming a journalist, dined together in the restaurant of the motel, where we were staying, waited on by girls in black leather mini-skirts, who looked sexy enough in dark, pink-lighted, smoke-laden atmosphere, but whom the daylight might not have treated so kindly. It was ten o'clock. We were trying to forget that at home we would by now have been in bed asleep for at least four hours. Vincent was very worried about his horse's lack of work since the Champion, but he remained his cool, charming self, even when an apparently drunk, burly man in a loud check jacket lurched into our table.

Our sozzled newcomer did not bother to introduce himself. He glared at Vincent. 'I know you,' he said, 'You're a trainer from England. Let's see. Murless, isn't it?'

I opened my mouth to correct the error, but Vincent, saying nothing, shook his head slightly in discouragement. Europe's most famous trainer, who had already brought the favourite to Laurel, was not to be drawn.

'I got it. You're Prendergast, aren't you?'

Vincent smiled, 'I often wish I was,' he said. 'He's a wonderful trainer.'

'Well, well, then, you've got to be O'Brien. Vincent O'Brien, isn't it? You came here with Ballymoss and got beat.'

A slight nod and the Tipperary trainer carried on with his meal.

'Now tell me about this horse of yours. He's a big colt. Bigger than Ballymoss, huh? And Ballymoss was beaten by the sharp track.'

Silence.

'Wouldn't you say this track is a damned sight too sharp for a fine leg colt like Sir Ivor?'

'No,' said Vincent, 'I wouldn't. I think the course is in wonderful shape. And I never said that it was too sharp for Ballymoss. You said that.'

Our new 'friend', disgruntled, left without another word.

Vincent said, 'That chap knows me very well. He's a leading racing columnist called ——————————. All he was trying to do was to get me to criticise the course in any way. Then you'd see the headlines tomorrow – 'O'Brien slams Laurel!' And that wouldn't be fair on anyone, least of all John Schapiro.'

The little Cork man, who had already produced three successive Grand National winners and won two Derbys, told me that Sir Ivor had been unable to leave his box from the time of the Champion Stakes at Newmarket until he flew over to Laurel.

'A little gravel worked its way up into his hoof and he was as lame as a cat,' he said. 'I poulticed him myself night and morning to get him sound, but he had done nothing at all when he left for Laurel.'

As a result Sir Ivor had to be worked on successive days in order to clear his wind. The American turf-writers all wrote that O'Brien was giving his horse too much galloping.

Unlike the previous year, when Ribocco was beaten out of sight in a typical Maryland Indian summer, the weather was more cold and wintry than in the England we had left behind.

Vincent did, in fact, confide: 'The course was too sharp for Ballymoss and I'm afraid it may be the same for Sir Ivor. However, not only is he smaller than both Kelso and Mungo, who each won the International, but, like them, he is bred for American circuits.'

Moreover since Ballymoss's years the course had been considerably improved. It had been banked very skilfully, so that it no longer resembled a flat Newton Abbott and it had a good, solid covering of grass, which in the previous year's dry spell had had to be sprayed green!

It is all so different from English racing that I am reprinting the articles that I filed from Laurel in this, our greatest year with the best horse we have ever sent from these islands to compete for the Washington International.

* * *

Laurel, (Maryland), Thursday

'A bare-back rider galloping a big-race candidate enlivened this morning's scene at Laurel Park, where a night of steady rain has just removed the last obstacle to Sir Ivor's triumph on Monday.

'Vincent O'Brien, who had said on arrival: "The Laurel course is excellent – you won't find a better grass track anywhere," was even more enthusiastic as we watched Sir Ivor at work. 'That rain is just what the doctor ordered for my horse,' he said. 'The ground should be perfect.'

'The 11–10 favourite for the £42,000 Washington International is eating well and has even put on weight, despite, the 3,500 mile journey from Tipperary. "He slept most of the way," said travelling head-man Maurice O'Callaghan, who brought sufficient plastic containers of Tipperary water for Sir Ivor and his lead horse, Ballygoran.

'Local pundits enthused about the Derby winner's condition as he walked on to the track, ridden by newly-wed jockey Vincent Rossiter.

'Led eight lengths by Ballygoran, Sir Ivor galloped five furlongs down the back stretch, round the bend and up past the finish. Unbalanced coming into the turn, he changed legs happily and, when Rossiter asked him, simply flew past the leader.

'Even O'Brien gasped. "He just eats him," he said. Then, as the big bay came back, his trainer noticed that he was blowing a little. "That was just what he wanted. He'll probably do the same tomorrow."

'Starter Eddie Blind is satisfied with Sir Ivor, and will not test him through the barrier. "Lester Piggott and the horse know enough about it for me," he said.

'Monday's field has now been whittled down to eight probables, all of whom have now arrived. Last year's winner Fort Marcy, came in from New York, today.

'Absentees are the Brazilian Derby winner, Sabinus, who refused to return to his aircraft after a stop in Rio, and the Peruvian Trastevere whose papers were held up by a local revolution.

'Tiny British-bred Czar Alexander – barely 15 hands 3 inches

– worked five furlongs in fractionally faster time than Sir Ivor.

' "I'm pleased," said his trainer, Angel Penna. "He did it easily and we didn't push him too hard."

'Oaks winner La Lagune looked and moved really well on the dirt track, so familiar to a Chantilly-trained animal, but was not given serious work.

'Her countryman, Carmarthen, however, the tall, leggy French chestnut who finished third to Vaguely Noble and Sir Ivor in the Arc, comes from the Strassburger stable which won the 1953 International with Worden.

'His trainer, Lucien Baldisseri, said, "Another furlong and I'd have beaten Sir Ivor at Longchamp." This big horse may find this track too sharp.

'Petrone, last of the French trio, has just arrived and was given walking exercise, but Japan's Takeshiba-O, sired by the Blagrave horse China Rock, went through the starting gate before working, his tail plaited against the mud.

'The most unusual sight of all, however, was the saddle-less Argentine Azincourt, who galloped twice round with work jockey Nicholas Pisano.'

Laurel (Maryland) Friday

'Lester Piggott's decision to challenge the English weather by riding at Haydock tomorrow before flying to Baltimore has flabbergasted the Americans.

'They say: "With millions of pounds depending on the result how can he possibly risk it all for a £5,000 race?"

'The British champion, however, is so confident of getting here by Saturday evening that Vincent O'Brient has no jockey standing by.

' "I am expecting Lester to be riding Sir Ivor out on the track on Sunday morning," he said.

'The Derby winner was allotted No. 6 in the eight-horse field, to the satisfaction of his trainer, when for the second year I was one of the guests invited to make the draw at a lavish breakfast ceremony.

'Czar Alexander is drawn 4, Fort Marcy 8, and the Oaks winner, La Lagune 7.

'Sir Ivor showed his appreciation of the Laurel turf when the skies cleared at last this morning. He breezed five furlongs in 1 minute 23.5 seconds, on a tight rein and then lashing out with sheer high spirits, missed a British journalist's head by an inch.

'The big bay colt stormed past Ballygoran and pulled up in two strides. With O'Brien I ran to listen to his breathing. He would not have blown a candle out. "I don't believe he could be any fitter," the trainer said.

'Local horses are ridden round the track by coloured stable-lads, whose short stirrup leathers make Piggott look like a policeman.

'No races will be run on the grass circuit before the International which will start at about 10.15 p.m. British time on Monday.

'François Boutin, trainer of La Lagune, has arrived on his first visit to America accompanied by his jockey, Gerard Thiboeuf. Once again according to the eminently successful French tradition, the Oaks winner only cantered, freshening-up for the big day.

'It is becoming increasingly clear that, provided the ground dries up, the bay filly is the one real danger to the favourite. She showed in the Arc that she is coming to her best, and she is the only other true classic animal in the field. She will start at a long price.

'Fort Marcy, last year's winner, galloped a circuit of the track on the dirt, and will work five furlongs on the grass tomorrow.

'British-bred Czar Alexander was "ponied"! That is to say he was led round riderless at a slow canter by an exercise boy, colourfully dressed and riding one of the many ponies on the track.

'American experts believe that Sir Ivor will not start favourite. It is expected that Czar Alexander, who won the Man o' War so impressively, will be made favourite, and that his victim on that occasion, Fort Marcy, will perhaps be preferred to Sir Ivor.

'The Argentine Azincourt, once again ridden bare-back, galloped at half speed twice round the circuit. The Japanese candidate, Takeshiba-O worked again. From the amount of galloping he has done, there will be precious little left of him by Monday.'

Laurel (Maryland) Sunday

'Snow and slush greeted Lester Piggott as he arrived at the track this morning to ride Sir Ivor in the final race-winning blow-out for tomorrow's Washington International.

'Local rumours about his well-being were quickly dispelled, and the big bay nostrils never quivered when he pulled up. As we paddled through the mud Vincent O'Brien said: "He's as fit as he can be. I am very happy about everything. The going will not be as heavy as it was at Longchamp last month."

'And since travelling head man Maurice O'Callaghan reports the horse as "just perfect" Raymond Guest's courageous gamble will surely pay off in a triumphant boost for British racing by the even-money favourite.

'Oaks winner La Lagune, who slaughtered the Arc de Triomphe third, Carmarthen, over five furlongs on Saturday, should finish second in this historic clash of an Epsom classic pair. At 12–1 she looks fair value.

'But her trainer, François Boutin, says, 'I think the ground is too heavy for her.' After the race she is off to stud in Florida.

'British-bred Czar Alexander has a good record on soft-going, and at 4–1 is probably the chief danger to Sir Ivor.

'The little bay impressed shivering watchers in the rain, including the British contingent, with a fast three-furlong spin, clocking 37⅖ sec. on a tight rein.

'Last year's winner, Fort Marcy, the Argentina's Azincourt, who has been backed from 100–1 down to 20–1, were given walking exercise.

'Elliott Burch, trainer of Fort Marcy, said: "Racing is like show business. You are as good as your last performance." Emphasising that the recent form of Paul Mellon's four-year-old has not been that of a big race-winner. He was beaten four lengths by Czar Alexander in the Man o' War Stakes.

'Connections claim that Takeshiba-O is the best three-year-old in Japan and, indeed, the best horse that country has sent over for the race, but the hard-working bay does not look good enough.

'Azincourt, now owned by American Bert Firestone, is clearly a good strong five-year-old just below classic form.

'Australian Bill Pyers, wearing a pale blue and brown check Balmoral bonnet complete with pompom, rode Petrone in a three-furlong spin.

'While agreeing with his trainer, Maurice Zilber, that the brown four-year-old, a tough improving sort, will run well, I fancy that the going will be too soft for him. And Carmarthen, the tall French chestnut, does not appreciate the turf.

'Prize money of £62,500 is distributed right down for the first six places. It will be the seventeenth running of this ambitious promotion.

Further rain to disperse the snow is forecast for today, and drier weather tomorrow, but with a temperature of only 40 degrees. What a good thing that the entire stand is covered in with glass and centrally heated!

It is a very different world, but one which Sir Ivor, the best horse ever sent over from England and Ireland, and British champion jockey Lester Piggott, are all set to conquer tomorrow.'

Laurel (Maryland) Monday.

'Lester Piggott rode the race of his life to win the Washington International on the English Derby winner, Sir Ivor, and realise John Schapiro's dream of international racing.

'The British champion jockey, showing the cool cheek of a great horseman, overcame all difficulties and pounced in the last 50 yards to win by three-quarters of a length from the American favourite, Czar Alexander, at the remarkable odds of nearly 2/1.

'Master trainer Vincent O'Brien said to his American rival, Angel Penna: "Sorry you had to come second."

' "Sir Ivor is a super horse. He was in difficulties all the way round. Once he got the opening, then, ping! This is the best horse I've ever trained."

'Takeshiba-O led for the first half-mile in front of Czar Alexander, with Fort Marcy third, Petrone fourth, and Sir Ivor sixth on the rails.

'At the mile post the Japanese colt fell back, yielding to Czar Alexander who then disputed the lead with his countryman,

Fort Marcy, last year's winner, ridden by Manuel Ycza, winner of his only three internationals.

'At this stage Sir Ivor had actually dropped back to last place, but in two furlongs, while the leading pair remained the same, with Carmarthen now third, the favourite had moved into fourth position.

'But he still appeared to be hopelessly shut in.

'As they turned into the short straight, Piggott got his mount balanced and slipped through in the last 50 yards to win decisively by three-quarters of a length from Czar Alexander with Fort Marcy a head away third.

'Carmarthen was 1¼ lengths away fourth, La Lagune fifth, Petrone sixth, Azincourt seventh and Takeshiba-O last.

'Piggott said, "If the ground had not been so soft I could have won by 100 yards. When I shook him into action I knew I would win."

' "I had a little trouble getting through."

'The winning owner, Raymond Guest, lost one of his contact lenses on his way to the unsaddling enclosure.

' "This is my lucky day though", he said. "I am so delighted. I was a bit scared all the way. It was very close."

'Sir Ivor will not return to Ireland to stand at stud for one season available to British breeders as a special gesture from Guest, the former international polo player, who has just completed four years as American Ambassador to Ireland. The horse will then return to the United States.

'None of Sir Ivor's opponents had any valid excuses. British Derby form has now been boosted sky-high.

'O'Brien said, "I must pay tribute to the efforts of John Schapiro to bring together these horses for this race." '

On the same day that my piece appeared in London the American papers published the most vitriolic reports, criticising Lester's riding of the winner in the most vicious way, even referring to him as a 'bum'. Of course they were unfamiliar with his style, so different from any that they are accustomed to, and wrote in complete ignorance of the difficulties with which he was faced. Trying to hold up a brilliant, unfit, big non-stayer, who would stop when he hit the front, in a moderate field, so that he would get a mile and a half was the problem which only Lester could solve.

Looking back now and thinking of this wonderful horse, whom he grew to love, Lester says, 'I have never known a horse so tired as Sir Ivor after that American race. They go flat out for the last mile. That is why their horses are so hard to beat.'

Horse and rider had given their all and he resented the venomous critics bitterly. Quite apart from the fact that he had won, it was, after all, an invitation race and he was a guest in their country.

In the words of the old saying, however, 'there's always another day in racing.' It came for Lester next year when he won again on Lord Iveagh's grand colt, Karabas, trained by Bernard van Cutsem.

A columnist in the *Washington Post* described the British champion's post-race treatment of him and his colleagues: 'On entering the jockey's room, Piggott shouted; "I'm not saying anything to you guys after what you wrote about me last year. Just clear the hell out!"'

In fact the words used were quite a bit stronger!

But the chief writer in the same paper, under the headline, 'Piggott silences the critics with Karabas,' said his performance was 'a masterful ride'.

Under the expert guidance of Richard Baerlein they made a glorious film entitled *The Year of Sir Ivor.* It is the best film ever produced about racing, in keeping with its subject, the greatest horse of the post-war era.

Raymond announced that his horse would begin stud duties in Ireland for the benefit of breeders in these islands, as a measure of his gratitude for the kindness he had received over here. There was, however, consternation and some bitterness, when he decided on an American-size stud fee of £8,000 – nearly three times the highest European figure. On the usual ration of forty mares a year this represented an income of £320,000. Nevertheless within a week the list was full, and the bluest-blooded mares on this side of the Atlantic were being booked for Sir Ivor's services at Raymond's Ballygoran Stud in Co. Dublin. As his own contribution to the harem the owner paid a European record price to acquire the brilliant Hula Dancer at Deauville.

Then the tug-of-war started. American interests, headed, by Bull Hancock, applied the strongest pressure to persuade Raymond to transfer Sir Ivor to Kentucky. The result was inevitable.

A spokesman for Ballygoran told me in March 1970: 'Mr Guest is in a very difficult position as the man in the middle of this tug-of-war, and he can't make up his mind. He promised to send Sir Ivor to Bull Hancock some time ago, and Bull is anxious to have the horse right away. But all the people over here in Ireland and England are trying to persuade him to stay. We need him badly. He will just be one of twenty-six stallions at Hancock's Claiborne Farm. If we could only keep him here for another five years, it wouldn't be too bad. His foals are so lovely.' They were indeed and from the moment that they first appeared on the open market it was clear that Sir Ivor was going to dominate the sales as he had the race-track. His departure at the end of 1970 covering season was a tragedy for British breeding.

Of Nijinsky, the superb Engelhard Triple Crown winner, Lester says, 'He was a brilliant racehorse, of course, but he was highly strung. He never really talked to you. He always seemed to be looking at birds. He hadn't Sir Ivor's character.'

He enthuses over the Duke of Devonshire's 500 guinea bargain mare, Park Top, who was so splendidly handled by Bernard van Cutsem.

'She was a marvellous mare,' says Lester. 'Undoubtedly she was far better if she didn't have to lie up and could be held up for a late run. You can't do that in a race like the Arc. Even if I hadn't left it too late, Levmoss might well have found more.'

He doesn't like riding on the dirt tracks of America. 'It's terrible to ride on. It's like someone hurling sand at you. You come back with red marks all over your body. The first time I wondered what on earth had happened. English horses won't face it the first two or three times they run over there. I don't blame them!'

One of the most momentous and far-reaching events in Lester's life – and in racing generally – was his break with Noel

Murless in May 1966 after a ten years' partnership which produced two Derbys, two Oaks and two St Legers. Since Lester had taken over from Gordon as first jockey to Warren Place, Noel had headed the trainers' list four times, and Lester had won three jockey championships.

The retainer system had become so much a traditional part of the English racing scene that the very idea of a break was a tremendous shock to everyone. Lester came in for such a lot of harsh criticism that it is only fair to let him tell his own version of the events which the public first heard of in my *Daily Mail* story of 18th May, just nine days before the Oaks, for which Charles Clore's Irish 1,000 Guineas winner, Valoris, a half sister to the French Derby winner Val de Loir, trained by Vincent O'Brien, was favourite.

Long before 1966 Lester had been toying with the idea of giving up his £2,000 a year retainer – 'It wasn't much, was it?' – and going freelance. He makes no bones of his admiration for Noel – 'a wonderful trainer, equally good with colts and fillies. A great man at his job.' But he found him a difficult character to deal with sometimes.

For a long time Lester kept quiet in face of all the criticism. 'Loyalty,' said Gordon Richards, 'is the essence of racing. When Steve Donoghue was offered all those Derby rides, gave up his retainer and turned freelance, I took over as first jockey to Fred Darling and I also took over the jockeys' championship for him.'

Now nine times champion Lester defends himself.

'This is the true story,' he says, 'of what happened in that break-up.'

'I told Noel towards the end of 1965 that I had decided to go free-lance next season. He tried to dissuade me, but I was determined, and, when I refused to accept the retainer for the first time, he must have realised that I was serious.

'Certainly we carried on as though nothing had happened, but I knew things were bound to come to a head sooner or later.

'This was Charlottown's year, the year when French visitors were banned owing to swamp fever, a year when Noel had some moderate horses at Warren Place.

'Since he had no classic colt worthy of the name, I had been booked for Charles Engelhard's big black Right Noble in the

Derby. A soft, disappointing animal, who was often likened to a Life Guards' charger, he was trained by Vincent O'Brien.

'Vincent is a brilliant trainer. Anyone, who can saddle three consecutive Grand National winners and three Derby winners, quite apart from all the others, must be quite outstanding.

'He had won the Oaks the previous year, with Long Look. This time in the fillies' classic he had a half-sister to the French Derby winner Val de Loir, called Valoris, Vincent's brother Dermot and Alan Clore had bought her at Deauville Sales as a yearling for £11,000 on behalf of the latter's father, Sir Charles Clore.

'Since she had a late-maturing pedigree, Vincent didn't train her seriously before she won the Irish 1,000 Guineas. He had given her all the time she wanted. After that race at the Curragh we decided that she was probably a very good filly indeed, who would be worth a great deal of money if she won the Oaks at Epsom.

'And what was to beat her? Noel had a filly called Varinia, who was a fair performer, but just not in the same class. And Vincent really knew the time of day with fillies that year. He had won the 1,000 Guineas at Newmarket, too, with Glad Rags.

'I had won the Chester Cup on that splendid tough stayer Aegean Blue and wanted to ride him again in the big race at Ayr on Saturday 14th May.'

'This was the day, however, when Varinia was due to run in the Oaks Trial at Lingfield. Noel let me off and put Stan Clayton up on his filly, who duly won. Incidentally I broke the course record on Aegean Blue at Ayr. I hinted to the Press that weekend that I might not be on Varinia in the Oaks.

'Noel unhappily seemed to take it for granted that I was still stable-jockey even though he was not paying me a retainer, and I would automatically ride his filly at Epsom on 27th May. He announced: " I told Piggott on Sunday that Varinia would run in the Oaks and that I would require him to ride her. As far as I am concerned, he will be on my filly."

'In fact when he said that to me, I replied: "Stan won on her yesterday. He can ride her again." He had no claim on me at all.

'But he decided to bring matters to a head. So I told him that I had accepted the ride on Valoris. I was very sorry he took it as he did. It could have been a perfectly friendly agreement.

'But habit dies hard and big English trainers like Noel had always been accustomed to having their stable-jockeys riding the horses both in their home-work and on the racecourse. The whole thing was a shock to him. It upset all his arrangements and disturbed his way of life. The papers made a sensation of it.

'Vincent broke the news officially when he announced that I would ride for him in all three big Epsom races, the Derby, the Coronation Cup and the Oaks.

'The first two were disappointing. Right Noble, great gangling thing that he was – a caricature of his sire Right Royal – sprawled badly down the hill, while in the Coronation Cup Donato failed to reach the first four.

'My judgement proved right, however, when I won my third Oaks on Valoris, who had been installed favourite at 11/10.

'It would have been ironical indeed and would have delighted my many critics if I had been parted from Valoris before the race. I wonder how many officials would have bothered to catch her! It so nearly happened.

'Trained to the minute and looking superb, she was shying so badly that I took her back to the paddock and dismounted. Then, accompanied by Vincent's head-man, I led Valoris all the way through the crowds down the hill and up the other side to the start.

'Stan Clayton jumped Varinia off in front and made the running while I lay handy in about sixth place.

'Down Tattenham Hill I moved up fourth. When I let Valoris go to the front 1½ furlongs from home, it was all over. We won on a tight rein by 2½ lengths from Berkeley Springs with Varinia three lengths away.

'When the dust of that row with Noel settled, I was so glad that I had turned freelance and, apart from Noel's reaction, I have never regretted it since. Of course I would have ridden Royal Palace and some other good ones, but I would never have been associated with horses like Sir Ivor and Nijinsky.

'Noel and I patched up our differences and I rode a winner for him at Newmarket on 13th July. I saw him through till the end of that season, when he engaged George Moore for the following year.

'Some jockeys prefer the retainer system. They know exactly where they are.

'Geoff Lewis, whom I rate the hardest man in the world to beat today, is like that. It just doesn't suit his temperament to be a free-lance, which entails a great deal more work and travelling to ensure right rides in the right races.

'But I love it. It's the breath of life to me. Which is why suspension is probably worse for me than for anyone else.'

Incidentally, after the race Varinia's owner, Marcus Wickham-Boynton said, 'My filly ran much better than we expected.' So it would surely have been most unfair to have made Lester ride her.

It has taken a long time for Gordon's prophecy to come true. Now however, in 1972 it was the retainer system which seemed to have deprived Lester of his title at last. Will Carson and Tony Murray owe their success to their respective employers, Bernard van Cutsem and Ryan Price, for both of whom Lester has ridden regularly in the past.

Nijinsky, of course, went back to the United States as soon as he had finished racing. It is a pity that we should be used in this manner. The Americans enjoy the benefit of having their horses trained by the best men in the world on our wonderful turf gallops and raced in our European prestige races for our top prize-money. Then, having acquired the status of a top international stallion worth upwards of two million pounds, they take the horse back to the United States. If it had stayed at home in the first place, it would probably have been broken down on the concrete-based dirt tracks. Thank heaven for the few men like Jim Joel and now John Hislop, who breed on the best lines and keep their great horses in the country.

I feel that any horse which is trained and raced in Europe for more than a year, should be made to stand here as a stallion for at least three seasons and that this should be a condition of entry. Otherwise our classics lose all their value as the supreme racecourse tests, which establish the stallions of the future.

Lester has matured amazingly in the last few years. He is still a danger-man, always *sur un coup,* and I've no doubt that he will remain so. This is his magnetism. This is what makes him box-office so that sooner or later racecourses will surely be paying him appearance money, as they do with the stars of motor-racing.

But when he and Susan are at home in Newmarket with their two daughters, Maureen and Tracy, he will talk about racing's difficulties.

'Suspension is specially frustrating to me,' he says, 'It's a real punishment. Mind, I believe it's the only one that has any real effect on jockeys and, as such, I'm all for it. Fines mean very little. They are deducted from your account at Weatherby's and you don't notice them at all.

'Now suspensions are the accepted thing. A good thing too. The boys are all riding much better. I'm very glad that the Jockey Club are trying to have the same rules as other countries. But they must be enforced in the same way as in France and the United States. You can't have one set of rules or interpretation of the rules in one country and another somewhere else.'

He adds: 'The stewards must be consistent. This is one argument in favour of professional stewards. Otherwise we're all right as we are.'

He was, of course, born to jumping and had ridden schooling all his life. So, when he took out a National Hunt Licence it all came naturally.

'I enjoyed riding over hurdles very much. It was easy for me. You've got more time to think in a race.'

On trainers. 'Vincent O'Brien is a great trainer. So are Noel Murless, Paddy Prendergast and Bernard van Cutsem. Bernard's so tough – a great man.'

Lester has already planned his training establishment in Newmarket, and building is going ahead to counteract rising costs. 'There are far too many horses in Lambourn now for the gallops. I wouldn't go back,' he says.

On non-triers. 'A lot of rubbish is talked about non-triers. Racing's straighter now than it's ever been. Most trainers today have to run a horse to get him fit. Many's the time I've ridden a two-year-old for Noel Murless and it hasn't known anything. You do your damndest and get as close as you can, but you're well beaten. Then next time it goes and wins in a good race at Ascot and everyone says it wasn't trying the time before. Nowadays Paddy Prendergast, Staff Ingham and only a very few others can get a horse ready to win first time out. Paddy's two-year-olds all know their jobs.'

I was always brought up by Atty Persse to believe that that was the meaning of the word 'Trainer' – a man who could train his horses at home so that they absolutely knew their jobs when they appeared in public.

Lester is tall for a jockey – 5 ft. 7½ inches. 'There's an advantage in being tall. A horse responds to a good weight on its back – live weight – not the dead weight of lead under the saddle to make up the right scale. On the whole I think the horse feels the authority of a big jockey. If you have a good length of leg, you can communicate more with the horse, squeeze him with your knees, control him generally – show him you are there.'

He admits, of course, that there are notable exceptions like the great American jockey Shoemaker, a genuine lightweight at little more than seven stone, and Sir Gordon Richards at eight stone.

Then there are the disadvantages of earning your living in a strenuous sport working about 1½ stone below your natural weight.

'Some people exaggerate how I live,' he says. 'I don't starve and I don't live on cigars and the *Financial Times*. And I don't drive to every race meeting in a rubber suit.'

But obviously he can't eat and drink what comes naturally to him.

'If I'm riding at eight stone six, I have a boiled egg for breakfast. If I have to do eight stone five that day, I'll give up the egg. I have a sandwich in the jockeys' room after I've finished riding and I always have a meal at night. You lose the habit of eating. The less you have, the less you want.'

On his family. 'Susan's a great influence on me. She's almost like my manager. She's a trainer's daughter, of course. And the two girls influence me, my daughters, Maureen and Tracy. If

I'm getting too serious about something, they come in and one of them's bound to say something to make me laugh.'

As when we were talking, gathering material for this book. In came the two girls 'Can we have Mars Bars, please?' Lester said, 'No. You've had an enormous breakfast, elevenses, a dirty great lunch, a vast tea and now you want Mars Bars. No!'

'Oh, please, we do want them. We've got two friends with us.'

'God, how they eat! All right, you can have one.'

'But there are four of us.'

'So, you'll have to cut it up, won't you?'

Lester thinks of other jockeys and the small trainers.

'I think more money ought to go back into racing. A lot of money is involved in the sport – especially in betting. The prize-money here is nothing like it is in France. Over there it can be four or five times as much. It's the small trainer that's affected. It's harder than ever for him to stay in this game in this country. And he's the backbone of racing. Perhaps I'm prejudiced because I'm the small trainer's son.'

Completely dedicated as he is, Lester will surely make a great trainer, particularly since he will have Susan at his side to help him. He understands horses and, just as he has always had the will to win, so he will inevitably have the almost fanatical will to be as great a trainer as he was a jockey.

It's like the wasting business, which has taken its toll of so many other jockeys; Lester's absolute devotion to racing makes it easier for him to give up things and, of course, the steadier he keeps it up, the easier it is for him to live with it.

'It's the wanting to win that matters,' he says. 'The competition. It's competing more than winning. In keeping your weight down you're competing with yourself. After a time it becomes a habit and you're in a long competition with yourself, and you only keep winning if you're trying to win all the time.

'If I got on the scales one morning intending to be 8 st. 4 lbs. and found that I was 8 st. 6 lbs., even if I wasn't being asked to ride at 8 st. 4 lbs. I'd want to get those two pounds off. You've got to get what you started out to do. Otherwise you start getting beaten. The others start to beat you when you start being beaten by yourself.'

Lester is not only one of the greatest jockeys the world has ever seen he is also a remarkable man. Without a doubt he is the greatest figure in British sport today and, with George Wigg, he is one of the few real characters left in racing. Like the motto on the horse-boxes from his old home, Lambourn, Lester will always remain 'A distance in front of the others.'

General Index

Index of Horses